Teacher Resource Book
Introductory

VISIONS

Literacy ◆ Language ◆ Literature ◆ Content

Jill Korey O'Sullivan

Christy M. Newman

Australia ◆ Canada ◆ Mexico ◆ Singapore ◆ United Kingdom ◆ United States

INTRODUCTORY VISIONS
TEACHER RESOURCE BOOK
Jill Korey O'Sullivan and Christy M. Newman

Publisher: *Phyllis Dobbins*
Director of Product Development: *Anita Raducanu*
Director, ELL Training and Development: *Evelyn Nelson*
Director of Product Marketing: *Amy Mabley*
Field Marketing Manager: *Robert Walters*
Development Editor: *Kasia McNabb*
Associate Development Editor: *Yeny Kim*
Associate Development Editor: *John Hicks*
Associate Development Editor: *Katherine Carroll*
Technology Manager: *Andrew Christensen*
Editorial Assistant: *Lindsey Musen*
Production Editor: *Chrystie Hopkins*
Manufacturing Manager: *Marcia Locke*
Development: *Brown Publishing Network, Inc.*
Design and Production Services: *Pre-Press Company, Inc.*
Printer: *Globus Printing and Packaging*

Copyright © 2006 by Thomson Heinle, a part of The Thomson Corporation.
Thomson, the Star logo, and Heinle are trademarks used herein under license.

All rights reserved. Instructors using *Introductory Visions* may reproduce all pages of this *Teacher Resource Book* for classroom use only. Otherwise, no part of this work covered by the copyright hereon may be reproduced or used in any form or by any means—graphic, electronic, or mechanical, including photocopying, recording, taping, Web distribution or information storage and retrieval systems—without the written permission of the publisher.

Printed in the United States.
    4 5 6 7 8 9 10 — 09 08 07 06

For more information contact Thomson Heinle, 25 Thomson Place, Boston, MA 02210 USA, or you can visit our Internet site at http://elt.thomson.com

> For permission to use material from this text or product, submit a request online at http://www.thomsonrights.com
>
> Any additional questions about permissions can be submitted by email to thomsonrights@thomson.com

ISBN 10: 1-4130-1494-1
ISBN 13: 978-1-4130-1494-5

Contents

SUGGESTIONS AND TECHNIQUES FOR TEACHING WITH *VISIONS*
Suggestions for Classroom Management 1
Lesson Plan Checklist 3
Suggestions for Managing Cooperative Learning 5
Suggestions for Meeting the Needs of Diverse Learners 8
12 Principles of Modifications for Special Needs in *Visions* 9
Accommodating Hearing Impaired or Deaf Students and
   Visually Impaired or Blind Students 10
Suggestions for Teaching with *Visions* 11
   I. Teaching Listening and Speaking 11
   II. Teaching Phonemic Awareness, Phonics, and Pronunciation 12
   III. Teaching Vocabulary 13
   IV. Teaching Grammar 16
   V. Teaching Reading 16
   VI. Teaching Writing 19
   VII. Teaching Viewing 20
   VIII. Teaching Technology 20

LANGUAGE TRANSFER AND INTERFERENCE CHARTS
Cambodian 21
Chinese 22
Haitian Creole 23
Hmong 24
Spanish 25
Vietnamese 26
Sound-Symbol (Phonology) Transfer and Interference Chart 27
Sound-Symbol (Phonics) Transfer and Interference Chart 28
Word Study 30

LESSON PLANNING GUIDE
Unit A 31
Unit B 34
Unit C 37
Unit D 40
Unit 1 43
Unit 2 47
Unit 3 51
Unit 4 55
Unit 5 59
Unit 6 63
Unit 7 67
Unit 8 71

BLACKLINE MASTERS
Bingo (3 x 3 card) 75   (Also Transparency #17)
Bingo (5 x 5 card) 76   (Also Transparency #18)
Business Letter 77   (Also Transparency #86)
Cluster Map 78   (Also Transparency #71)
Cursive Alphabet A–I 79   (Also Transparency #14)
Cursive Alphabet J–R 80   (Also Transparency #15)
Cursive Alphabet S–Z 81   (Also Transparency #16)
Frequently-Used Sight Words 1 82   (Also Transparency #54)
Frequently-Used Sight Words 2 83   (Also Transparency #64)
Frequently-Used Sight Words 3 84   (Also Transparency #70)
Frequently-Used Sight Words 4 85   (Also Transparency #79)
Frequently-Used Sight Words 5 86   (Also Transparency #83)
Friendly Letter 87   (Also Transparency #53)
How-to (Step-by-Step) Instructions 88   (Also Transparency #96)

Interview	89	(Also Transparency #85)
Know/Want to Know/Learned Chart (KWL)	90	(Also Transparency #94)
Letter Tiles a–m	91	(Also Transparency #10)
Letter Tiles n–z	92	(Also Transparency #11)
Letter Tiles A–M	93	(Also Transparency #12)
Letter Tiles N–Z	94	(Also Transparency #13)
Narrative Brainstorming	95	(Also Transparency #73)
Narrative Draft	96	(Also Transparency #75)
Note-Taking	97	
Numerals 1–10	98	(Also Transparency #21)
Numerals 11–20	99	(Also Transparency #22)
Outline: Expository Compositions, Narratives, and Information Reports	100	(Also Transparency #89)
Paragraph	101	(Also Transparency #65)
Personal Dictionary	102	(Also Transparency #52)
Print Alphabet A–I	103	(Also Transparency #6)
Print Alphabet J–R	104	(Also Transparency #7)
Print Alphabet S–Z	105	(Also Transparency #8)
Reading Log	106	(Also Transparency #56)
Sense Chart	107	(Also Transparency #67)
Sentence Builders: Unit A	108	(Also Transparency #19)
Sentence Builders: Unit B	109	(Also Transparency #27)
Sentence Builders: Unit C	110	(Also Transparency #35)
Sentence Builders: Unit D	111	(Also Transparency #49)
Storyboard	112	(Also Transparency #95)
Story Map	113	(Also Transparency #74)
Sunshine Organizer	114	(Also Transparency #76)
Syllabication Spelling Pattern: Closed Syllables	115	(Also Transparency #43)
Syllabication Spelling Pattern: Open Syllables	116	(Also Transparency #44)
Syllabication Spelling Pattern: Final -e (Vce)	117	(Also Transparency #45)
Syllabication Spelling Pattern: Vowel Digraphs (Vowel Teams)	118	(Also Transparency #46)
Syllabication Spelling Pattern: r-Controlled Vowels	119	(Also Transparency #47)
Syllabication Spelling Pattern: Consonant + -le	120	(Also Transparency #48)
Test-Taking Tips	121	
Three-Column Chart	122	(Also Transparency #60)
Three-Paragraph Composition	123	(Also Transparency #84)
Two-Column Chart	124	(Also Transparency #66)
Venn Diagram	125	(Also Transparency #57)
Web	126	(Also Transparency #55)
Word Squares	127	(Also Transparency #58)
Writing Lines	128	(Also Transparency #9)

SCHOOL-HOME CONNECTION NEWSLETTERS (ENGLISH, CAMBODIAN, CHINESE, HAITIAN CREOLE, HMONG, SPANISH, VIETNAMESE)

Unit A	129
Unit B	136
Unit C	143
Unit D	150
Unit 1	157
Unit 2	164
Unit 3	171
Unit 4	178
Unit 5	185
Unit 6	192
Unit 7	199
Unit 8	206

ACTIVITY BOOK ANSWER KEY ... 213

Suggestions and Techniques for Teaching with Visions

Suggestions for Classroom Management

This section presents a practical, step-by-step guide for implementing effective strategies for classroom management. The following suggestions encourage teaching strategies that will facilitate English language learning.

1. **Provide for numerous speaking opportunities.**
   Students need opportunities to practice speaking English. Anytime students are speaking English, they are practicing what they have learned. Use pair/group work to increase the amount of time students spend talking. Many times students will monitor each other. This is an opportunity for students to practice without the pressure of speaking in front of the entire class.

2. **Incorporate real events.**
   Incorporate current events, things that happen in class, and students' interests into activities as a way to increase interest and to link classroom learning to their lives outside the classroom.

3. **Use different ways to read texts.**
   Use a variety of reading techniques to develop different skills and keep students interested. Reading techniques in *Visions* include echo reading, audio reading, choral reading, paired reading, and repeated reading.

4. **Be concise when giving instructions.**
   Students want to understand everything the teacher says. Avoid commentating when giving instructions, because students may have difficulty separating instruction from nonessential comments.

5. **Be explicit when giving instructions.**
   Make sure students know what they need to do to complete an activity. They need to know who should do what, when they should do it, and how long it should take. Whenever possible, break down the task into discrete, numbered steps. Additionally, learners should also know why they are doing a particular activity, as this can help to engage them in the learning process.

6. **Follow up instructions with a model.**
   Research shows that people understand directions best when the instructor includes a demonstration. Explanations often require more sophisticated language. When setting up a classroom activity, provide concise and explicit instructions. Then model the expected answer/action for the students, and/or ask a student to demonstrate what you want the rest of the class to do.

7. **Use gestures and body language to encourage and direct students.**
   Gestures can be used to clarify instructions (for example, by signaling the person who should answer a question) without increasing the linguistic demand on students. Be aware that some American gestures may be offensive in other cultures.

8. **Vary your voice.**
   Stress, pitch, speed, and pauses can be used to call attention to vocabulary items, grammatical structures, or new information. Pauses also help students understand because they group related pieces of information together.

9. **Try to understand students' silence.**
   Silence does not mean that students are not engaged. It is important to understand the reason behind silence. Students might be struggling to understand the task or be preparing their answers. Silence could also be the students' way of taking a break from the strenuous task of making sense of a new language.

10. **Give students enough time to answer questions.**
    It takes students time to answer questions when learning a new language. If necessary, silently and slowly count to ten before giving another student a chance to answer a question. One way to encourage students to speak is to pass a talking stick, such as a ruler, from one student to another. This avoids putting one student on the spot, and everyone gets a turn to speak.

11. **Keep your language to a minimum when students are working on a task.**
    Talking while students are working on an activity can disrupt or confuse them. Allow students to have a quiet period of time so they can complete their tasks without distraction. This will increase student concentration and productivity.

12. **Correct errors when appropriate.**
    Timely, specific, constructive, and sensitive feedback is recommended, appropriate to the students' proficiency level. Students need to know exactly what they said/wrote incorrectly, but accuracy is a growth issue. As students gain skill, different levels of correction are called for. If you are seeking oral fluency in an activity, you may want to let errors pass if they do not interfere with meaning. If you are teaching a specific grammar point, you will want to correct in more detail, to be certain that correct forms are reinforced. Be sure to give students a chance to self-correct. One strategy is to repeat the student's statement as a question with emphasis on the correct form and allow time to correct the error.

13. **Change the seating plan for different activities.**
    Change seating often to increase the number of different people students interact with on a regular basis. Varying the classroom setup also allows people to see the room (especially the board or word walls) from different angles. Some activities are best done in pairs; others are great small-group activities. Make sure the seating arrangement is appropriate for the activity. Use different ways of assigning pairs or groups, such as grouping by color of clothing.

14. **Consult your students.**
    On occasion and when appropriate, give students an opportunity to express preferences for types of activities, pacing, and grouping. Rather than speculate about what students understand, are able to do, or want to do, ask them.

15. **Allow L1 use when appropriate.**
    Sometimes a quick explanation in L1 is better than a long, complicated explanation in English. At teacher discretion, allow students to consult with a speaker of their native language when appropriate. Students may be on task even though they are not speaking English. To encourage students to think in English, have them write, speak, and share, rather than just speak and share. Writing helps pre-teens and teenagers focus on thinking in English.

16. **Prepare, use, and revise lesson plans.**
    To maintain student interest and maximize student learning, prepare and use well-planned lessons. Use the Lesson Plan Checklist (pp. 3–4) to ensure your lesson plans are complete and comprehensive. After teaching, evaluate the success of the lesson and revise the lesson plan accordingly for future use.

Lesson Plan Checklist

for *The Sheltered Instruction Observation Protocol*

I. PREPARATION

_____ Write content objectives clearly for students.

_____ Write language objectives clearly for students.

_____ Choose content concepts appropriate for age and educational background level of students.

_____ Identify supplementary materials to use (graphs, models, visuals).

_____ Adapt content (e.g., text, assignment) to all levels of student proficiency.

_____ Plan meaningful activities that integrate lesson concepts (e.g., surveys, letter writing, simulations, construction models) with language practice opportunities for reading, writing, listening, and/or speaking.

II. INSTRUCTION

Building Background

_____ Explicitly link concepts to students' backgrounds and experiences.

_____ Explicitly link past learning and new concepts.

_____ Emphasize key vocabulary (e.g., introduce, write, repeat, and highlight for students to see).

Comprehensible Input

_____ Use speech appropriate for students' proficiency level (e.g., slower rate, enunciation, and simple sentence structure for beginners).

_____ Explain academic tasks clearly.

_____ Use a variety of techniques to make content concepts clear (e.g., modeling, visuals, hands-on activities, demonstrations, gestures, body language).

Strategies

_____ Provide ample opportunities for students to use strategies (e.g., problem solving, predicting, organizing, summarizing, categorizing, evaluating, self-monitoring).

_____ Use scaffolding techniques consistently (providing the right amount of support to move students from one level of understanding to a higher level) throughout the lesson.

_____ Use a variety of question types throughout the lesson, including those that promote higher-order thinking skills (e.g., literal, analytical, and interpretive questions).

Short, D., and Ecchevaria, J. (1999). *The Sheltered Instruction Observation Protocol: A Tool for Teacher-Researcher Collaboration and Professional Development.* Center for Research on Education, Diversity & Excellence, University of California, Santa Cruz.

Lesson Plan Checklist (cont.)

for *The Sheltered Instruction Observation Protocol*

Interaction

_____ Provide frequent opportunities for interaction and discussion between teacher/student and among students about lessons and concepts, and encourage elaborated responses.

_____ Use group configurations that support language and content objectives of the lesson.

_____ Consistently provide sufficient wait time for student responses.

_____ Give ample opportunities for students to clarify key concepts in L1 as needed with aide, peer, or L1 text.

Practice/Application

_____ Provide hands-on materials and/or manipulatives for students to practice using new content knowledge.

_____ Provide activities for students to apply content and language knowledge in the classroom.

_____ Use activities that integrate all language skills (reading, writing, listening, and speaking).

Lesson Delivery

_____ Support content objectives clearly.

_____ Support language objectives clearly.

_____ Engage students approximately 90–100% of the period (with most students taking part in and working on task throughout the lesson).

_____ Pace the lesson appropriately to the students' ability level.

Review/Assessment

_____ Give a comprehensive review of key vocabulary.

_____ Give a comprehensive review of key content concepts.

_____ Provide feedback to students regularly on their output (e.g., language, content, work).

_____ Conduct assessments of student comprehension and learning throughout lesson on all objectives (e.g., spot checking, group response) throughout the lesson.

Short, D., and Ecchevaria, J. (1999). *The Sheltered Observation Protocol: A Tool for Teacher-Researcher Collaboration and Professional Development*. Center for Research on Education, Diversity & Excellence, University of California, Santa Cruz.

Suggestions for Managing Cooperative Learning

Using Pair and Group Work in the Classroom

Visions places an emphasis on and provides numerous opportunities for students to work together, either in pairs or groups. Pair and group work have the following advantages: learners speak more frequently and for longer periods of time; they produce more interactional modifications; and they use a wider range of language, according to Crookes and Chaudron (in Celce-Muria, 2001). Working in pairs and groups offers other benefits, such as:

- Provides more opportunity for personal relevance and individual and group achievement.
- Gives practice speaking with just one or a few individuals instead of the entire class.
- Allows for full class participation, giving students more speaking practice time.
- Reinforces language acquisition and fluency through eliciting and repeating answers.
- Provides structure and accountability for student responses.
- Allows for peer modeling.
- Allows for teacher assessment of individual progress.
- Encourages higher-order thinking, such as synthesizing information, summarizing, paraphrasing, defending opinions.

It is important to establish pair and group work as a convention in your classroom. If students are accustomed to working with others, they will learn to quickly arrange themselves in pairs or groups. Such work should be well organized, however. Students should understand that they will be responsible for a final product, and each student within the group should be responsible for one aspect of the product. Make pair and group work a consistent and considerable feature in your classroom.

Tips for Pair and Group Work

1. In general, it is best to choose pairs and groups yourself, especially early in the year. When appropriate, occasionally allow students to pair or group themselves.
2. Use a variety of grouping techniques: same level or mixed levels, same L1 or mixed L1s.
3. Make sure everyone knows with whom he or she is paired/grouped.
4. Make sure everyone understands what he or she will be doing.
5. Assign students roles: leader, researcher, recorder, reporter, for example.
6. Walk around the room to monitor that students are engaged in the activity and to assess student progress.
7. Time the activity. Give a warning when 1 to 5 minutes remain. Stop the activity when most of the pairs or groups are finished. It is important that students learn to work efficiently and to not waste practice time.
8. Always follow up the activity with a presentation by some or all of the pairs or groups.

Cooperative Learning Group Structures

The following structures support group activities. Such activities can be used to vary learning strategies and are especially valuable in a block schedule, as they help with pacing. They stimulate a lesson, help students process information during a lesson, and serve as culminating activities where students apply what they learn. Use the simplest ones first and move to more complex activities as appropriate.

Numbered Heads Together

1. In small groups, students count off. (Make sure students know their numbers.)
2. Teacher presents a question or a problem or a task for the group to resolve.
3. Group discusses and decides on an answer. Full participation is critical because any student may be called to report.
4. Teacher calls a number and the student from each group with that number reports for the group.

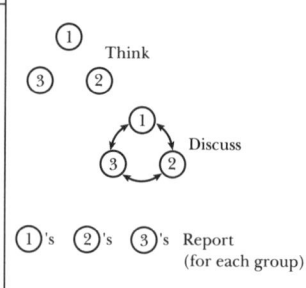

Benefits
- Group discussion provides students with language and concept understanding.
- Random recitation provides an opportunity for evaluation of both individual and group progress.

Think, Pair, Share

1. **Think:** Students think individually about a topic or task assigned by the teacher or from the textbook. They may take notes.
2. **Pair:** After one or two minutes (depending on the complexity of the task), students share their topic with a partner. Teacher serves as timekeeper.
3. **Share:** Finally, students present their pair's information, thoughts, and activity with a another group or with the entire class.

   Note: This structure may be used with the Listen, Speak, Interact activities in the *Visions* Student Book.

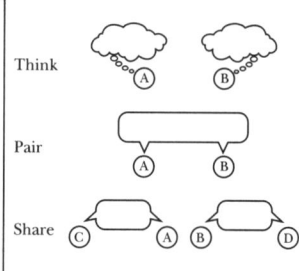

Benefits
- Provides opportunities to begin processing thoughts in English as students organize their ideas for speaking.
- May enhance understanding and performance of students who are more comfortable sharing with a partner by eliminating the stress of sharing with the entire class.

Guided Small Groups

Each student is given a "job" in the group:
- The *leader* is responsible for organizing the activity and for keeping the group on task.
- The *researcher* may be asked to find out information.
- The *recorder* takes notes and/or outlines the presentation.
- The *reporter* presents the group's work to another group or the class.

Note: Jobs can be assigned based on language abilities.

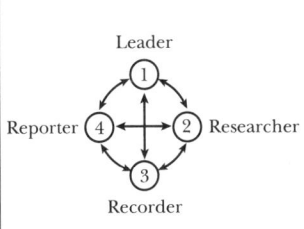

Benefits
- Provides the option of assigning jobs either according to skills/strengths of individual students, or areas of student weakness (to build students' skills and abilities).
- Assigning jobs teaches cooperation and coordination skills.
- Assigning jobs enhances organizational skills of the group toward task completion.

Roundtable

1. Seat four or more students in a circle or around a table.
2. Ask an open-ended question or a question with multiple possible answers.
3. Each student writes an answer on one piece of paper that travels around the table. The list is a collaborative effort.
4. Teacher chooses a student to report for the group.

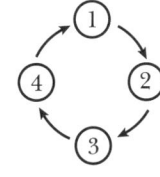

Benefits
- Encourages collaboration.
- Gives an opportunity for writing because every student must answer.
- Requires quick thinking and writing.

Compass Points or Four Corners

1. Designate each corner of the classroom for a focused discussion of an opinion on a topic, situation, or dilemma.
2. Students form groups, numbered 1-4, or named for the points of the compass, based on possible opinions.
3. Groups discuss the matter in the designated corner.
4. Groups prepare their topic for presentation.

Benefits
- Encourages students to form an opinion or formulate possible solutions.
- Allows students a chance to consider a topic carefully and thoughtfully.
- Provides students opportunities to hear many points of view about a topic.

Suggestions for Meeting the Needs of Diverse Learners

Multi-Level Students

The 1997 TESOL publication *ESL Standards for Pre-K-12 Students* (Teachers of English to Speakers of Other Languages. ESL Standards for Pre-K-12 Students. Alexandria, VA: TESOL, 1997) defines four different proficiency levels of students learning English: Newcomer Students with Limited Formal Schooling, Beginning, Intermediate, and Advanced. Below is a summary of the characteristics of these proficiency levels.

Newcomer Students with Limited Formal Schooling have usually been in the United States for only a short period of time. Their educational background is most likely nontraditional and they have little or no understanding of the culture and organization of school. These students may be pre- or semi-literate in their native language, or entirely unfamiliar with the concept and practices of literacy. These students perform below grade level.

Beginning students understand very little English and almost never use it for communication. Gradually, as their awareness of the language increases, they begin to comprehend some oral language. Their language use is very unconventional.

Intermediate students are much more likely to use English spontaneously because their comprehension is greater. Because of their limited vocabulary, they often struggle to express themselves. Their language use is somewhat unconventional because of their limited knowledge of structure. They do well when they can build on their own prior knowledge.

Advanced students' language skills are adequate for most social survival communication needs. However, they still make errors in structure and vocabulary and have occasional difficulty with abstract concepts and complex structures. They read with considerable fluency but may have trouble with texts that are decontextualized, have complex sentence structure, or contain abstract vocabulary. They can produce texts independently for personal and academic purposes, though errors may persist.

Multi-Level Options in *Visions*

Throughout the *Visions A, B, C Teacher Editions*, **Multi-Level Options** are included for selected activities on the page. These **Multi-Level Options** provide alternative teaching suggestions and differentiated levels of activities for different proficiency levels. For *Introductory Visions*, an "accelerated" **Multi-Level Option** is presented in place of the advanced **Multi-Level Option**. This accommodates students who may be able to handle expanded or more advanced language. The first four units of *Introductory Visions* also present a "pre-literate" **Multi-Level Option** for students who may lack literacy in English and in their native language.

Accurate assessment and placement of students is critical to optimal growth and acceleration of instruction for English learners. This is especially critical at the secondary level where heavy demands for content knowledge are placed on students. Suggestions are made throughout the *Visions Teacher Editions* concerning how to deal with these situations, but it should not be taken as an endorsement of multi-level classroom placement.

12 Principles of Modifications for Special Needs in *Visions*

1. **Multi-Level Options, Modifications for Special Needs, Learning Style Suggestions:** Use these sections in the *Visions* Teacher Editions to accommodate diversity in student learning.
2. **Learning Objectives:** State the learning objectives in simple terms. (e.g., "We are going to learn about . . .")
3. **Instructions:** Give instructions in a mode other than solely verbally. Demonstrate, model, or act out instructions.
4. **Sequence of Steps:** For more involved activities or projects, give students a clear sequence of numbered steps to follow. Place a written list of steps to follow on their desk.
5. **Point System:** Use a point system for various parts of the lesson: This provides a sense of smaller steps of achievement. For example, Activity Book: Build Vocabulary (15); Reading (5); Elements of Text (5); Word Study (5); Grammar Focus (20); Writing (6); Spelling, Punctuation, Capitalization (15). The *Visions* Assessment Program test items may be used section by section.
6. **Multi-Sensory Techniques:** Incorporating multi-sensory techniques when teaching allows students to process information using more than one sense. This includes visual, auditory, tactile/kinesthetic, gustatory (taste), and olfactory (smell) learning.
7. **Build Vocabulary:** Write the important words from this section in the first column of a two- or three-column chart. Go over the easiest words first with the whole class. Use each new word in a sentence and have students guess the word meaning. You may also ask: "Is this an example of . . . ? Or is this an example of . . . ?" Write the meaning in the second column. A third column can be used to make a picture or symbol to remind students of the meaning of a word.
8. **Highlighting Vocabulary Words and Definitions:** When working from a list of vocabulary words and definitions, highlight the items as you complete them. This helps students focus on the remaining ones.
9. **Reading Selections:** Read the reading selections as a group. Increase interest by personalizing and relating the context of each reading selection to the students.
10. **Reading Comprehension:** Go over all reading comprehension questions together in class. Check that students understand what information the question asks them to supply.
11. **CNN® Videos:** These help tie the theme of the unit together and have high interest for many types of special education situations. *Visions* CNN® Videos have closed-captioning available.
12. **Assessment Program:** When planning a lesson, look first at what is being tested in each chapter and then make sure to cover those points in the lesson. Use Examview® Pro to modify the number and type of items tested in each chapter.

Accommodating Hearing Impaired or Deaf Students

1. Teach with pictures and visual prompts that represent the language and content of a lesson.
2. Make sure students' desks are situated to their benefit.
3. Be aware of the negative effects of mechanical equipment, such as motor humming or other excess noise.
4. Write main concepts and vocabulary from each lesson on the board or on chart paper for students to read.
5. Look at the students when speaking to them. Be clear and concise.
6. Ask students about content, beginning with simple, literal questions and gradually moving to more thoughtful questions. Use leading questions, which require fewer words. Use a variety of question types.
7. Color code sections of reading according to the questions *who, what, where, why, when,* and *how.* (For example, parts of the reading that answer *who* questions are blue.) Tell students which color section corresponds to each type of question.
8. Students should work with peers for reading, notetaking, and other activities.
9. Use graphic organizers to support the students in reading, vocabulary, and writing activities.
10. Make sure students are included in group activities. Assign a role in which they can be successful.

Accommodating Visually Impaired or Blind Students

1. Arrange students' desks to their benefit, and keep in mind their placement when participating in group activities or learning centers.
2. Be aware that students may be missing vital experiential background that the teacher will need to provide prior to teaching new material.
3. Always allow students sufficient time to process information, respond during discussion, complete activities and assignments, and take tests.
4. Provide handouts in appropriate media (e.g., Braille, large print, etc.).
5. Allow students to complete assignments in appropriate media or orally.
6. Be aware of the negative effects of using audiovisual materials (overhead projectors, videos, etc.). Students may experience increased difficulty if lights are dimmed during such activities.
7. Teacher may need to remain in one place when speaking so that students can follow the voice.
8. Students should work with peers for activities.
9. Make sure students are included in group activities. Assign a role in which they can be successful. Remind all students in the group that speakers must take turns and identify themselves before speaking.
10. Make sure the classroom has proper lighting for the students and there is enough space in their work area to accommodate any assistive devices.

Suggestions for Teaching with *Visions*

I. Teaching Listening and Speaking

For both listening and speaking activities, students need to be engaged. Many students tend to view listening as a passive activity. To help students understand that listening is an active skill that they can develop, encourage them to remain focused during listening activities. Reassure students that they may not understand everything they hear. Instruct students to listen for the main idea, using known vocabulary and context to determine meaning. Create opportunities for authentic listening and speaking interactions between students through cooperative learning strategies. Support students when they have an opportunity to take risks as they express themselves for authentic purposes (Hedge, 2001), including giving opinions, describing things, giving instructions, describing a process, giving explanations, and supporting arguments (Gibbons, 1993).

Speaking strategies introduced and modeled by the teacher will aid students to conduct meaningful conversation. These strategies also provide students with the mechanical language needed to manage pair/group activities.

Teaching Conversation and Speaking Strategies

Point out that these are clarifying questions and statements. Model these expressions for students. Use rising, question intonation for interrogative sentences. Have students practice in pairs/groups.

- **When you want someone to repeat something:** *Pardon? Excuse me? Would you repeat that?*
- **When someone is speaking too quickly:** *Could you please speak a little more slowly? Would you mind speaking a bit more slowly?*
- **When you don't understand a word:** *What does . . . mean? Could you explain what you mean by . . . ?*
- **To make a suggestion:** *What about . . . ? How about . . . ? We could . . . Why don't we . . . ? Maybe we should . . .*
- **To accept a suggestion:** *That's a great idea. Why don't we try that? That sounds like a good idea.*
- **To reject a suggestion:** *I'm not sure that's a good idea. I'm not sure that will work. I don't know about that.*
- **To get a turn in a conversation:** Model how to use these expressions to enter into the conversation when there is a pause.
  Could I say something? Can I ask a question? I have something to say. I have a question.
- **To check if you understood the speaker correctly:**
  Use echoing: Explain that echoing means repeating what someone else said.
  Kima has four cats. *Four cats?*
  My sister is flying to Australia tomorrow. *Australia?*
  Use paraphrasing: Explain that paraphrasing means repeating what someone said in your own words.
  You're saying that . . . Let me see if I understand. You said . . . What you mean . . . Is that right?
- **To show you understand what the speaker said:** Use short questions or rising intonation to confirm understanding.
  My family just got a new TV. *Did you?*
  I don't like ice cream. *You don't?*

- **To check if your listeners understood what you said:** Point out that it is a good idea to occasionally check and see if your listeners understand.
  Do you see what I mean? Do you follow me? Is that clear?
- **To lead a discussion:** Model and use role playing to make sure students understand the circumstances in which each of the strategies is appropriate. Have students practice using one or more in their pair and group work.
  Encouraging participation: Who would like to respond? Does anyone have anything to add?
  Bringing people in: Than, what do you think? Juan, do you want to add anything?
  Controlling a speaker: Let's hear what other people have to say.
  Speeding up the discussion: We only have a few minutes left. We need to move along.

II. Teaching Phonemic Awareness, Phonics, and Pronunciation

Students learning to read in English can be taught to decode, or sound out words, by applying their knowledge of letter and sound correspondence. In English, twenty-six letters and their combinations represent forty-four sounds. Students literate in Chinese for example, may have no experience with an alphabetic system of writing. Specific English phonemes do not exist in some other languages. (See charts on pp. 27–29.) Word boundaries are foreign in some languages as well. Students with exposure to oral English are often unaware of English word boundaries.

Unlike the typical kindergartener who arrives at school with an estimated 2,000-word vocabulary, the English language learner arrives with little or none. For phonemic awareness and phonics to be meaningful, texts much be rich in art or photos to illustrate the concept associated with the print word and its sounds. Phonemic awareness, phonics, decoding, and word recognition should be taught in combination with vocabulary and concept development. As outlined in the California Reading/Language Arts Framework (p. 33), high-utility letter sounds are scheduled early. Realizing the accelerated pace English language learners face, *Visions* also focuses on teaching high-utility words in context and teaching vocabulary significant to understanding a reading passage.

Direct instruction in pronunciation is an on-going task for teachers of English language learners. The student can be instructed to use a mirror. Some find the exaggerated facial movements by the teacher useful. The teacher can use his/her hand, as well as diagrams, to show tongue position for the production of various sounds. However, research indicates that after puberty, it is often difficult to attain native-like pronunciation in a second language. It is generally recommended that pronunciation correction be focused on intelligibility issues. If an error interferes with the listener's understanding, attention should be drawn to it. This can often be simply done through restating, using the correct form, or by asking a clarifying question: *Did you mean "will" or "wheel"?* Correction may not be appropriate if the goal is fluency or brainstorming, as one wants to keep student ideas flowing. However, in grammatical instruction, more attention can be drawn to correctly pronouncing the grammar point at hand.

Accurate intonation and stress impact comprehensibility. Explicit instruction is needed not only in the phonetic system of English, but also in the correct word stress and English intonational system. English language learners benefit greatly from calling attention to rhythm, rhyme, alliteration (Adams, 1998; Blachman, 2000; Snow, Burns and Griffin, 1998; Verhoeven, 1999). Clapping or tapping out patterns is useful for secondary students so that they can kinesthetically experience the stress patterns of their new language. The use of arrows to show changes in pitch, which change meaning in English, is an effective way to teach intonation.

Tip

The selections in the *Visions* audio program serve as oral language models as students listen. Their attention can be drawn to correct pronunciation, word boundaries, intonation, and stress. Reading aloud with the recording encourages students to pronounce words correctly and with meaningful expression.

III. Teaching Vocabulary

The Effects of Vocabulary on Reading Comprehension

Research identifies limited vocabulary knowledge as the greatest impediment to reading comprehension (Levine & Reves in Anderson, 1999). Research also shows that vocabulary instruction promotes gains in word knowledge and in reading comprehension (Anderson, 1999; Garcia, 2000; Blachowitz and Fisher, 2000; Beck & McKeown, 1991; Nation, 1990). English language learners need to learn at least 2,000 high-frequency words, which constitutes about 80 percent of the words native speakers of English normally encounter (Decarrico, 2001). For efficient methods of acquiring clusters of new words instead of individual words, Schmitt (1997) recommends learning word families and building word associations from roots and affixes.

To support reading comprehension, vocabulary instruction should (1) increase the number of words known and (2) increase the depth of this knowledge, including multiple meanings for words. An effective vocabulary curriculum should present new words in context and in relation to other words. It should also provide multiple encounters with a word in various contexts and involve instruction with both spoken and written forms. The curriculum should include instruction on word analysis strategies using, for example, prefixes, suffixes, and root words, as well as teach clusters of new words instead of individual words.

Building Vocabulary and Word Study Skills in *Visions*

To help students both increase the number, as well as the depth, of their knowledge of vocabulary words, *Visions* teaches the following vocabulary-building and word study skills:

- Understanding word meaning, including multiple-meaning words.
- Relating new vocabulary to prior experience.
- Learning word families and content-area vocabulary through the introduction of topical vocabulary, such as science terms, with vivid verbs and contextualized words that scaffold the chapter reading.
- Using multiple reference aids (thesaurus, synonym finder, dictionary, software).
- Developing vocabulary and remembering words by association with a visual (drawing).
- Recognizing and using figurative language and modifiers.
- Recognizing and using contractions.
- Using air spelling to help students spell unfamiliar words by visualizing them.
- Using word identification strategies such as context clues, roots, and affixes.
- Developing organization techniques and strategies for learning or remembering new vocabulary, including word squares, note-taking, and maintaining a personal dictionary.

In addition, *Visions* also incorporates the following features into its vocabulary program:

Cognates: Cognates are words that "look alike" or "sound alike" from one language to another. There are about 4,000 cognates among the most frequently used words in Spanish and English. The number increases with technical terms. Sixty percent of English words have Greek or Latin roots (Moats, 2001). False cognates are word pairs that look like they might mean the same thing but do not. For example, "éxito," which means "success" in Spanish, and the English word "exit" are false cognates. To make efficient use of teaching vocabulary, it makes sense to tap students' existing knowledge by using cognates to increase their English vocabulary base.

Cognate awareness helps increase vocabulary and reading comprehension. Cognate awareness builds on prior knowledge, increases efficiency of vocabulary teaching, and connects to academic vocabulary. For a list of Spanish-English cognates, see pp. 397-399 in the *Introductory Visions* Teacher Edition.

Personal Dictionary: A personal dictionary is an individual dictionary of vocabulary words and their corresponding pictures, synonyms, or definitions that are important to an individual learner. (See p. 102 for the Personal Dictionary blackline master.) Students should dedicate a page to each letter of the alphabet and designate about a dozen pages for theme or category words such as foods, family members, or things found in the home. The personal dictionary becomes a valuable reference resource for students when writing or doing seatwork or homework activities.

Word Walls: A word wall is a group of carefully chosen and meaningful words displayed in the classroom. A word wall is a tool that supports both interactive group activities and individual students working independently. Word walls can help students spell frequently used sight words and recognize word patterns and categories. Word walls also help students apply phonics rules.

A word wall should be written in large print and displayed in the classroom where all students can see it. Students should be able to refer to it at any time for support with any activity.

Five new words should be introduced at a time. Select words that will help the students with reading and, by teaching spelling, be a resource for writing. The list of most frequently used sight words in *Introductory Visions* (p. 364) and the vocabulary lists at the end of each chapter are sources of word wall words. Color-coding words by using colored paper or colored makers can help show categories or make easily confused words (such as *their* and *there*) stand out. Introduce and practice the words through interactive activities such as chanting and writing.

School-Home Connection Newsletter

Each unit of *Visions* contains a newsletter that informs families about what their student learned, and encourages the family to support student achievement. A letter to each student's family, signed by the teacher, asks the family to work on an activity with the student. The student then shares this activity with the class. The activities place emphasis on practicing vocabulary learned in *Visions*. It is important to be sensitive to individual students' family situations.

Vocabulary Development Activities and Instructions

Activity	Instructions
Simon Says	One player is Simon, the person who gives commands. The other players must stand up and follow Simon's commands. Each command begins with "Simon says." For example: "Simon says touch your arm." Other players must follow the command, and if they fail to do so, they must sit down. If the command given does not begin with "Simon says," students must not obey the command. Those who follow such a command must sit down. The last person left standing is the winner.
I Spy	One player observes an item in clear view and calls out "I spy something that begins with the letter…" The rest of the players must call out the names of objects they see beginning with the letter until they guess the item.
Twenty Questions	One player thinks of a word. Other players need to guess what the word is by asking no more than 20 yes/no questions.
Bingo	Make Bingo cards with five rows and five columns. In each square write a letter, sound, or vocabulary word that students have been studying. Hand out the Bingo cards. Call out letters, sounds, or vocabulary words one at a time. Have students cross off each letter, word, or sound if they have it on their cards. The winner is the first player to cross off five squares in a row, either horizontally, vertically, or diagonally.
Charades	One player is given a word and must act it out so that the others can guess the word. The player may also give clues. For example, he or she may show with his or her fingers how many syllables are in the word.
Picture Dictionary	Make cards with vocabulary words. One player takes a card and must draw pictures to help the other players on his or her team guess the word. Points are given for each word the team guesses correctly. Set a time limit for each turn. At the end of the time, the opposing team may try to guess the correct word to win points.
Word Building	Using the Letter Tiles Blackline Masters (pp. 91–94), assemble a large pile of letters. Divide the letters between two teams. Teams make as many words as they can with the letters they have. Give each team one point for every three-letter word, two points for every four-letter word, etc. The team with the most points wins the game.
Hangman	Think of a word. Draw a "hanging stand" with one blank for each letter of the word you are thinking of. Students call out letters, one at a time. If the letter is in the word, write it in the correct blank. If not, draw one part of the hangman, starting with the head. The game is over either when students guess the word or when enough incorrect letter guesses have been made to complete the hangman.
Go Fish	Create a set of cards that has pairs of matching words and/or pictures. Shuffle the cards, and hand out five cards to each student. The object is to ask for and complete pairs of cards. For example, a student who has only one card with the word *book* might ask the other student, "Do you have a *book*?" The other student says "go fish," or gives the card. To "go fish," a student draws a new card from the center pile of cards. When students get a pair, they put the pair down on the table.

IV. Teaching Grammar

Research strongly suggests that pre-adolescent and adolescent English language learners need to focus on grammar to help them develop accuracy in their academic use of the language. Students often welcome analytic descriptions of grammatical patterns and rules in their writing. They also appreciate having their errors noted at appropriate moments and being taught useful substitutions and explanations. It is important to not rely on grammar drills and mechanical practice, which has not proved effective in achieving mastery. Instead, provide students with ample opportunity for meaningful practice to yield long-term success.

- Expose students to high-quality literature that provides syntactic challenges.
- Have students write as frequently as possible, and provide them with feedback on both content and use of language.
- Select and teach elements of grammar that students encounter in their content reading and need in the revision stage of their writing.
- Use students' writing as diagnostic tools to determine aspects of grammar they need to learn or are ready to learn, and make these a part of instruction.
- Teach students to use grammatical conventions and terminology to provide a common "language" of grammar.
- Emphasize aspects of grammar that help students to communicate more effectively and to use conventional mechanics and appropriate language. (Adapted from Celce-Murcia, 1991.)

V. Teaching Reading

Reading Comprehension

Reading involves making meaning from print. Students can be helped to build reading comprehension in a variety of ways. Guiding questions give students goals for their reading. A preview of chapter headings and sections provides students with an idea of what to expect. Teachers can engage students in monitoring comprehension by helping them to paraphrase and summarize chunks of text as they read. Helping students to figure out what is going to happen next or what type of information may be provided next is an example of a simple but effective reading comprehension strategy (Anderson, 1999; Carrell, Devine, and Eskey, 1988; Pressley, 2000; Pritchard, 1990).

Reading Log: A reading log is a way of recording the books a student independently reads over a given period of time—a week, a month, or a school term. It provides an opportunity for students to process what they have read by responding to readings and recording their reactions. Reading logs can be adapted to any reading level. (See p. 106 for the Reading Log blackline master.)

Audio for Reading Selections: In *Visions*, students learn reading with the audio program. Students can read along in the Student Book as they listen to a selection from the *Visions* audio program. This technique helps build reading fluency. (See pp. 17–18 for other Reading Fluency Strategies.)

Reading Fluency Strategies

Visions reading fluency activities help build confident readers. Teachers should model each reading strategy first.

PROCEDURE	DESCRIPTION	RESEARCH & BENEFIT
RAPID WORD RECOGNITION | the	you	my	or	my	of | |------|------|------|------|------|------| | have | or | you | my | have | my | | give | of | have | give | or | give | | my | the | of | have | the | have | | of | have | the | of | you | or | *Introductory Visions. p. 99*	1. With a partner, each read the words in the box 3 times aloud. 2. Next, read the words aloud for one minute. 3. Your partner can time you.	Rapidly recognizing words helps to increase students' reading speed and free learners to comprehend text. *National Reading Panel* 2002 Mather, N., Goldstein, S. *Reading Fluency* (2001). Learning Disabilities and Challenging Behaviors: A Guide to Intervention and Classroom Management. Brooks Publishing Co.
KEY PHRASES | or fork | or core | or pit | or stem | |------|------|------|------| | or core | or fork | or core | or pit | | or stem | or skin | or stem | or fork | | or pit | or stem | or pit | or skin | | or skin | or pit | or fork | or fork | *Introductory Visions. p. 269*	1. With a partner, each alternate taking turns reading the words in the box aloud 3 times. 2. Next, read the words aloud for one minute. *Visions Basic Activity Book, p. 62* *Visions A, p. 22* *Visions B, p. 10*	Reading key phrases will help students learn to read faster and discourage word-by-word reading. *National Reading Panel 2002.* Anderson, N. (1999). *Exploring Second Language Reading.* Heinle, Boston, MA
CHUNKING Dividing sentences into phrases for the purpose of not reading word by word. How to Get the Nutrition You Need You should eat food from all six groups to get the nutrition you need. The pyramid tells you how many servings to eat from each group. *Introductory Visions. p. 279*	1. Teacher takes a familiar text and divides it into natural phrases. 2. Teacher models reading each phrase aloud. 3. Class reads aloud. 4. Students each read phrases with a partner 3 times.	Encourages students to stop reading word-by-word. Anderson, N. (1999). *Exploring Second Language Reading.* Heinle, Boston, MA
ECHO READING An activity where the teacher model-reads a text, a sentence at a time, as the student tracks. The student then echoes or imitates the skilled reader. *Introductory Visions. p. 133*	1. Teacher reads aloud with expression a sentence at a time. 2. The class then reads (echoes) what the teacher read.	• Provides opportunities for learners to read with expression. • Allows all students access to reading. California Department of Education. *Strategic Thinking and Learning,* Sacramento, CA 2001
ADJUSTING YOUR READING RATE Reading rate depends upon the type of material you are reading. 1. Memorizing is the slowest reading rate. 2. Reading Quotations is done at a medium rate. 3. Scanning requires the fastest. *Introductory Visions. p. 209*	1. Teacher models adjusting reading rate for a particular reading. 2. Students each practice alternating reading with a partner 3 times.	• Students become aware of the need to adjust their reading rate depending on the purpose. • Helps students study and complete assignments. Mather, N., Goldstein, S. *Reading Fluency* (2001). Learning Disabilities and Challenging Behaviors: A Guide to Intervention and Classroom Management. Brooks Publishing Co.

Reading Fluency Strategies *(cont.)*

Visions reading fluency activities help build confident readers. Teachers should model each reading strategy first.

PROCEDURE	DESCRIPTION	RESEARCH & BENEFIT
AUDIO CD READING Listening and reading along with good readers. It involves learning how and when to change pitch, which words to stress, when to pause, and at what pace to read. Audio CD reading is also referred to as audio CD listening. *Introductory Visions. p. 175*	1. Teacher selects 2 paragraphs from the Audio CD. 2. Students follow along in their student books. 3. Students listen to the phrases, pauses, and expression on the CD. 4. Students reread with expression two paragraphs three times aloud in their lowest voices.	Helps students practice reading with expression, stress, and pitch. Mather, N., Goldstein, S. *Reading Fluency* (2001). Learning Disabilities and Challenging Behaviors: A Guide to Intervention and Classroom Management. Brooks Publishing Co.
CHORAL READ ALOUD A method where students read aloud together for 10–15 minutes.	1. Teacher selects high-interest text. 2. Partners sit next to each other. 3. Point to the word with your index finger. 4. Read at a slightly faster pace than the student. 5. Encourage student to keep up with you. 6. Remind students to keep their eyes on the book.	Successful decoding requires the reader to connect the flow of spoken language with the flow of the text. *National Reading Panel 2002* Mather, N., Goldstein, S. *Reading Fluency* (2001). Learning Disabilities and Challenging Behaviors: A Guide to Intervention and Classroom Management. Brooks Publishing Co.
REPEATED READING Repeated reading is rereading a short familiar passage three times until satisfactory fluency is reached. It is usually done with a partner. It is useful for nonautomatic readers who read word-by-word.	1. Teacher selects several paragraphs of familiar text up to 100 words. 2. Students practice with a partner each reading aloud softly three times. 3. Partners time each other for 1 minute. 4. Goal is to read 85 to 100 words per minute.	• Increases fluency and automaticity for slow readers. • Frees up students' attention for comprehension. • Repeated reading was found to be the only method which has consistent support in increasing fluency. *National Reading Panel 2002*
SILENT READING Independent silent reading is reading silently for a period of time at a student's own pace, and usually with a book of their choosing. *Introductory Visions. p. 307*	1. Student self-selects a book. 2. Student is responsible for reading 20-30 minutes each day. 3. Learners read at their own pace. 4. Students keep a record of their reading.	• Helps student personally interact with the text. • Allows freedom to choose own reading material. • Helps students learn how reading fits into their lives. Day & Bamford. *Top Ten Principles for Teaching Extensive Reading. Reading in a Foreign Language.* Vol. 14, No. 2 Oct. 2002. U. of Hawaii.

Reading Comprehension in *Visions*

Question/Answer Relationships (QAR): Research shows that understanding Question/Answer Relationships increases student achievement (Raphael). The QAR strategy helps students classify questions and locate answers to them (California Department of Education, *Strategic Teaching and Learning*. CDE Press: Sacramento, CA. 2000). QAR recognizes that reading is a dynamic process involving the reader, the text, and the context. This strategy teaches students to recognize the relationship between a specific type of question and where they can go in the text to find an answer to it. This is a critical skill for enhancing comprehension in content areas.

There are four types of QAR questions:

1. **Right There:** This is a literal question that checks factual recall. Students find the words used to create the question and look at the other words in that sentence.
2. **Think and Search:** This requires information from more than one sentence or paragraph. Students must integrate information from different parts of the text. (Inferential skills.)
3. **Author and You:** Students answer this question with a combination of background knowledge and information from the text. (Interpretive skills.)
4. **On Your Own:** This question draws on students' background knowledge.

VI. Teaching Writing

When teaching students how to write, show them that writing has a purpose and an audience. When students understand that writing is meaningful, they are more engaged and find it a rewarding activity. In *Visions*, students analyze types of text structure used in various writing models. The writing process is used throughout. Students are given opportunities to interact with others, which is an important part of learning to write. This way, students can share and compare writing with peers, and can learn from each other's writing. In addition, technology is integrated into the writing process, so students can edit and publish their work on the computer.

Visions uses a process approach to writing, which takes students step-by-step to the end product. The phases of process writing include prewriting, drafting, revising, editing, and publishing. By breaking writing down into discrete steps, the writer is able to concentrate on one task at a time and receive feedback throughout the writing process (Peregoy and Boyle, 2001).

Spelling

Spelling instruction supports both reading and writing skills. Students who receive direct instruction in word analysis and how to analyze speech sounds and spell words are more successful in reading and writing (Whittlesea, 1987). Spelling instruction supports students as they advance from being emergent to proficient readers (Ehri, 1997) (Pinnell, & Fountas, 1998) (Templeton, & Morris, 2000). As students progress, they can use their knowledge of letter cluster patterns that form sounds and words, and apply them in both reading and writing.

Graphic Organizers

For an activity as complex as writing, students need a clear framework within which they can organize their ideas and express themselves. Useful scaffolds and graphic organizers to guide students through the writing process are included as blackline masters in this Teacher Resource Book.

Student Portfolios

Writing portfolios track student development. As students build their portfolios, the range of their writing skills can be well represented. The portfolio allows students to be writers who set personal goals and monitor their own progress. A Portfolio Assessment form is included in the *Introductory Visions* Assessment Program on p. 207.

Research

Visions includes teaching how to use the library and the Internet for research. *Visions* approaches the Internet with the understanding that students may already be familiar with it, and builds on that knowledge as students are guided through a research project. More traditional sources of information, such as first-person interviews and a library for books and encyclopedias, are also used for learning research skills in *Visions*.

VII. Teaching Viewing

Teaching viewing is essential to developing students' visual literacy. This applies to watching films, other electronic media, and digital images, as well as to reading charts, maps, diagrams, cartoons, illustrations, photographs, and works of art created for a variety of purposes. A viewing activity can be as simple as identifying items in a collage or as complex as critiquing a Web site. Teaching viewing helps students learn to "read" these visual texts. Students need to develop visual language skills in order to use viewing as an effective tool for learning. The objective is for students to be able to view a visual text, make critical judgments and interpretations, engage in a discussion, and draw conclusions.

VIII. Teaching Technology

Technology can be integrated into the classroom in many ways. One area that is particularly compatible with the use of technology is writing. Introduce students to fundamental tools of word-processing programs that can help them develop their writing. Features such as spell check, dictionary, thesaurus, or a grammar check may be useful to students. Show students how to highlight text or apply color to text. Color is also useful in peer editing for inserting questions and suggestions to the author. Using a printer to publish students' work gives students a chance to see their ideas on a neat, printed page. If the technology is available to the classroom, scanning photos to illustrate student writing is a great enhancement.

The Internet can be a valuable and versatile classroom resource. Some students may already have experience with the Internet. Build on this prior knowledge when teaching about the Internet. As students learn to search the Internet, emphasize that key word searches are useful because URLs may change, and new Web sites are launched every day.

The use of technology is integrated into the *Visions* program in a variety of ways. For example, students practice looking for links and downloading information. *Visions* also incorporates technology into learning with a Web site, http://elt.thomson.com/visions, and CD-ROM. These applications may be used for self-study, remediation, and extra practice.

Language Transfer and Interference Charts

Cambodian

English Structure	Language Transfer Issue	Example of Transfer Error	Cambodian Language Structure
Adjectives	Placement of adjectives after nouns	Lena lives in a house big. *Lena lives in a big house.*	Adjectives commonly follow the nouns they modify
	No change of form for comparative adjectives	He is tall than me. *He is taller than me.*	Adjectives don't change form for this purpose
	Avoidance of –er and -est	The most funny joke. *The funniest joke.*	Comparatives and superlatives formed with a separate word
	Difficulty with –ed and –ing forms	The class was interested. *The class was interesting.*	No active and passive meanings for corresponding adjective forms
Adverbs	Use of adjectives in place of adverbs	Speak quiet. *Speak quietly.*	No suffixes for adverb forms; adjectives used after verbs
Articles	Overuse or omission of articles	She is lawyer. *She is a lawyer.*	Article use differs from English
Infinitives & Gerunds	Use of present tense verbs instead of gerund and infinitive forms	I enjoy play tennis. *I enjoy playing tennis.*	No gerund form
Nouns	Consistent use of singular noun form for plurals	He has three sister. *He has three sisters.*	No plural form for nouns; no plural form after a number
	Plural forms used for noncount nouns	Where is your luggages? *Where is your luggage?*	No distinction between count and noncount nouns
	Possessive nouns formed with *of* phrase or avoidance of using *'s*	This is the bag of Marisa. *This is Marisa's bag.*	Noun possessor follows object; a character forms possessive
Pronouns	Difficulty differentiating between subject and object pronouns	Her told I. *She told me.*	No distinction between subject and object pronouns
	Difficulty with singular pronouns	Marie? No, he is not here. *Marie? No, she is not here.*	No gender difference in third person singular pronouns
Verbs	Use of present tense for all tenses; no subject-verb agreement; no inflection to show person or number	She go tomorrow. *She will go tomorrow.*	Verb does not change to show tense; tense indicated by context
	Omission of *to be*	You tall girl. *You are a tall girl.*	When *be* is implied it is omitted
	Use of present perfect in place of past perfect	Yesterday I have gone there. *Yesterday I went there.*	A past marker (e.g., yesterday) indicates a completed action
Questions	Repeat verb to answer yes/no questions	Do you speak English? Speak. For negative: No speak. *Do you speak English? Yes.*	Affirmative repeats the verb; negative response repeats the verb with equivalent of *no*
	Omission of *do* or *did* in questions	What you have? *What do you have?*	No word for *do/did* in questions
	Avoidance of inverted question forms in yes/no questions in favor of tag questions or intonation	The pizza is good, yes? *Is the pizza good?*	No subject-verb inversion in questions

Pages 21–26: Adapted from Raimes, Ann. *Keys for Writers*, Third Edition. "Language Transfer: Tip Sheets for Ten Languages." Houghton Mifflin Company. 2005. 31 Jan. 2005 <http://college.hmco.com/english/raimes/keys_writers/3e/instructors/esl/tips.html>

Chinese

English Structure	Language Transfer Issue	Example of Transfer Error	Chinese Language Structure
Adjectives	Difficulty differentiating noun and adjective forms	Everyone wants free. *Everyone wants freedom.*	Some nouns and adjectives share the same form
	Difficulty with –ed and –ing forms	The class was interested. *The class was interesting.*	No active and passive meanings for corresponding adjective forms
Adverbs	Placement of adverbs before verbs	You hard work. *You work hard.*	Adverbs and adverbial phrases can precede verb
Articles	Omission of indefinite articles	I saw movie. *I saw a movie.* She is teacher. *She is a teacher.*	No indefinite articles; none used before a profession
Infinitives & Gerunds	Difficulty differentiating gerund and infinitive forms	I enjoy play tennis. *I enjoy playing tennis.*	No gerund form
Nouns	Consistent use of singular noun form for plurals	He has three sister. *He has three sisters.*	No plural form for nouns; no plural form after a number
	Plural forms used for noncount nouns	Where is your luggages? *Where is your luggage?*	No distinction between count and noncount nouns
	Names written last name first, no comma	Chan [last] Homan [first] *Chan, Homan* or *Homan Chan*	Family names precede first names
Pronouns	Difficulty differentiating between subject and object pronouns	Her told I. *She told me.*	No distinction between subject and object pronouns
	Omission of subject pronoun	Is cold. *It is cold.*	Subject pronoun can be omitted when subject is understood
	Difficulty with singular pronouns	Marie? No, he is not here. *Marie? No, she is not here.*	No gender difference in third person singular pronouns
	Confusion with possessive pronouns	I like she house. *I like her house.*	Character used between noun and pronoun to form possessive
	Omission of pronouns in clauses	If not have a car, I can't go. *If I don't have a car, I can't go.*	Sentence beginning with subordinate clause can omit subject
Verbs	Use of present tense for all tenses; no subject-verb agreement; no inflection to show person or number	She go tomorrow. *She will go tomorrow.*	Verb does not change to show tense; tense indicated by context
	Omission of *to be*	You tall girl. *You are a tall girl.*	Omit *to be* with adjectives and prepositional phrases
	Confusion with transitive and intransitive verbs	Oscar is married with Linda. *Oscar is married to Linda.*	Verbs that do, and do not take a direct object differ from English
	Consistent placement of subject before verb	He is hungry and so I is. *He is hungry and so am I.*	Subject and verb order rarely changes
Questions	Avoidance of inverted question forms in yes/no questions in favor of tag questions or intonation	The pizza is good, yes? *Is the pizza good?*	No subject-verb inversion in questions
	Repeat verb to answer yes/no questions	Do you speak English? Speak. For negative: No speak. *Do you speak English? Yes.*	Affirmative repeats the verb; negative response repeats the verb with *no* or *not*
	Awkward question formation	She is (is not) teacher? *Is (Isn't) she a teacher?*	Verb can be followed by its negative to form a question
	Question words placed at the end of question	Tell me she said what? *What did she say?*	Question words can be placed in the position of the answer

Haitian Creole

English Structure	Language Transfer Issue	Example of Transfer Error	Haitian Creole Language Structure
Adjectives	Placement of adjectives after nouns	Lena lives in a house big. *Lena lives in a big house.*	Adjectives commonly follow the nouns they modify
Adverbs	Use of adjectives in place of adverbs	Speak quiet. *Speak quietly.*	No suffixes for adverb forms; adjectives used after verbs
Articles	Omission or overuse of articles	I like the games. *I like games.*	Article use differs from English
	Inconsistent use of indefinite article with a profession	She is lawyer. *She is a lawyer.*	Indefinite article is usually omitted; it's optional if *to be* is used
	One used in place of indefinite article	I saw one movie. *I saw a movie.*	No indefinite articles
Infinitives & Gerunds	Use of present tense verbs instead of gerund and infinitive forms	I enjoy play tennis. *I enjoy playing tennis.*	Speakers tend to favor present tense over gerund or infinitive
Nouns	Use of an addition word rather than -s for plurals	He has three sister. *He has three sisters.*	Plural marker placed after noun; no plural form after a number
	Plural forms used for noncount nouns	Where is your luggages? *Where is your luggage?*	No distinction between count and noncount nouns
	Possessive nouns formed with *of* phrase or avoidance of using *'s*	This is the bag of Marisa. *This is Marisa's bag.*	Noun possessor follows object
Pronouns	Difficulty differentiating between subject and object pronouns	Her told I. *She told me.*	No distinction between subject and object pronouns
	Difficulty with singular pronouns	Marie? No, he is not here. *Marie? No, she is not here.*	No gender difference in third person singular pronouns
	Confusion with possessive pronouns	That dog is me. *That is my dog.*	Possessive pronoun follows noun
Verbs	Use of present tense for all tenses No subject-verb agreement	She go tomorrow. *She will go tomorrow.*	Verb does not change to show tense; tense indicated by context
	Avoidance of passive voice	Sell books here. *Books are sold here.*	No passive voice
	No tense change within a sentence	When I'm tired, I sleep. *When I'm tired, I will sleep.*	Verb tense does not change in a sentence
	Reliance on present tense	I do it later. *I will do it later.*	Present tense can be used in place of future and present perfect tenses
	Omission of *to be*	You tall girl. *You are a tall girl.*	Omit *to be* with adjectives, places, and prepositional phrases
	Inconsistent subject-verb agreement	Pierre have three daughters. *Pierre has three daughters.*	Verb is not inflected to show person or number
	Consistent placement of subject before verb	He is hungry and so I is. *He is hungry and so am I.*	Subject and verb order rarely changes
Questions	Omission of *do* or *did* in questions	What you have? *What do you have?*	No word for *do/did* in questions
	Avoidance of inverted question forms in yes/no questions in favor of tag questions or intonation	The pizza is good, yes? *Is the pizza good?*	No subject-verb inversion in questions
Negatives	Overuse of double negatives	I don't have none. *I don't have any.*	Double negatives used frequently

Hmong

English Structure	Language Transfer Issue	Example of Transfer Error	Hmong Language Structure
Adjectives	Placement of adjectives after nouns	Lena lives in a house big. *Lena lives in a big house.*	Adjectives follow the nouns they modify
	No change of form for comparative adjectives	The most funny joke. *The funniest joke.*	Comparatives and superlatives formed with a separate word
Adverbs	Extra adjective or verb used in place of an adverb or verb	I run run fast. *I run fast.* Speak quiet. *Speak quietly.*	Adverbs are not used; adjectives used after verbs
Articles	Overuse or omission of articles	Do you like the dogs? *Do you like dogs?*	Article use differs from English; definite article can be omitted
	One used in place of indefinite article	I saw one movie. *I saw a movie.*	No indefinite articles
Infinitives	*For* used in infinitive phrases	He left for go to school. *He left to go to school.*	A prepositional form is used for the infinitive that translates as *for*
Gerunds	Difficulty using the gerund form	I enjoy play tennis. *I enjoy playing tennis.*	No gerund form
Nouns	Consistent use of singular noun form for plurals	He has three sister. *He has three sisters.*	No plural form for nouns; no plural form after a number
	Plural forms used for noncount nouns	Where is you luggages? *Where is your luggage?*	No distinction between count and noncount nouns
	Possessive nouns formed with *of* phrase or avoidance of using *'s*	This is the bag of Marisa. *This is Marisa's bag.*	Noun possessor follows object; a character forms possessive
	Names written last name first, no comma	Chan [last] Homan [first] *Chan, Homan* or *Homan Chan*	Family names precede first names
Pronouns	Difficulty differentiating between subject and object pronouns	Her told I. *She told me.*	No distinction between subject and object pronouns
	Subject pronoun is omitted	Is cold. *It is cold.*	Subject pronoun can be omitted when subject is understood
	Difficulty with some gendered pronouns	Call Kim and ask it for help. *Call Kim and ask her for help.*	No gender difference in third person singular pronouns
	Confusion with possessive pronouns	I like she house. *I like her house.*	Character used between noun and pronoun to form possessive
	Difficulty distinguishing between various pronouns	The bag is I. *The bag is mine.* It is I dog. *It is my dog.*	No distinction between simple, compound, subject, object and reflexive pronouns
	Redundant use of pronouns	My sister, she lives in Hanoi. *My sister lives in Hanoi.*	States noun and uses pronoun in description
Verbs	Use of present tense for all tenses; no subject-verb agreement; no inflection to show person or number	She go tomorrow. *She will go tomorrow.*	Verb does not change to show tense; tense indicated by context
	Omission of *to be*	You tall girl. *You are a tall girl.*	Omit *to be* with adjectives, places, prepositional phrases
	Placement of two main verbs in the same clause without conjunctions	I went to the ATM took out cash. *I went to the ATM and took out cash.*	Has serial verbs, which can be connected without conjunctions
Questions	Repeat verb to answer yes/no questions	Do you speak English? Speak. For negative: No speak. *Do you speak English? Yes.*	Affirmative repeats the verb; negative response repeats the verb with *no* or *not*
	Question phrase placed at end of declarative sentence	The pizza is good, yes? *Is the pizza good?*	Can form questions by adding a phrase to a declarative sentence

Spanish

English Structure	Language Transfer Issue	Example of Transfer Error	Spanish Language Structure
Adjectives	Placement of adjectives after nouns	Lena lives in a house big. *Lena lives in a big house.*	Adjectives commonly follow the nouns they modify
	Adjectives made plural	She has beautifuls children. *She has beautiful children.*	Adjectives show number and gender
	Avoidance of *-er* and *-est*	The most funny joke. *The funniest joke.*	Comparatives and superlatives formed with a separate word
	Difficulty with *-ed* and *-ing* forms	The class was interested. *The class was interesting.*	No active and passive meanings for corresponding adjective forms
Articles	Omission and overuse of articles	Jason likes the birds. *Jason likes birds.*	Articles use differs from English; definite articles are often omitted
	Definite article placed before profession	The Doctor Sanchez is kind. *Doctor Sanchez is kind.*	Definite article can be used with a profession
	Definite article used for parts of the body	My father hurt the back. *My father hurt his back.*	Definite articles used for parts of the body
Infinitives	*For* used in infinitive phrases	He left for go to school. *He left to go to school.*	A prepositional form used that translates as *for*
Gerunds	Difficulty applying the gerund form	I enjoy play tennis. *I enjoy playing tennis.*	No gerund form
Nouns	Omission of *-s* to form plural	He has three sister. *He has three sisters.*	No plural form after a number
	Plural forms used for noncount nouns	Where is your luggages? *Where is your luggage?*	Some count, noncount nouns differ from English
	Possessive nouns formed with *of* phrase	This is the bag of Marisa. *This is Marisa's bag.*	Possessive nouns formed with *of* phrase
	Addition of *-es* to make plural words ending in consonants and *y*	bookes books dayes days	*-es* is added to nouns ending in consonants and *y* to form plural
Pronouns	Difficulty differentiating between subject and object pronouns	Her told I. *She told me.*	No distinction between subject and object pronouns
	Omission of subject pronoun	Is cold. *It is cold.*	Subject pronoun omitted when subject is understood
	Problems with gendered pronoun reference	The car is fast. He is new. *The car is fast. It is new.*	Nouns have gender
	Difficulty differentiating between human and nonhuman relative pronouns	The man which lives next door. *The man who lives next door.*	No distinction of human and nonhuman relative pronouns
	Omission of the pronoun *one*	Elena likes the red. *Elena likes the red one.*	Adjective is used instead of noun
Verbs	Reliance on present tense	I do it later. *I will do it later.*	Present tense used in place of future and present perfect tenses
	Confusion of present and simple past forms of regular verbs	He give it to me to keep. *He gave it to me to keep.*	Tense affects end of word only
	Past continuous used for recurring action in the past	As a child I was playing a lot. *As a child I played a lot.*	Past continuous used instead of *used to* or simple past in English
	Have used instead of *be* to describe state of being	I have thirst. *I am thirsty.*	*Have* expresses states of being
Questions	Omission of *do* or *did* in questions	What you have? *What do you have?*	No word for *do/did* in questions
	Omission and overuse of auxiliary verbs in questions	What they found? *What did they find?* Who did find it? *Who found it?*	No auxiliaries used in questions
Negatives	Overuse of double negatives	I don't have none. *I don't have any.*	Double negatives used frequently

Vietnamese

English Structure	Language Transfer Issue	Example of Transfer Error	Vietnamese Language Structure
Adjectives	Placement of adjectives after nouns	Lena lives in a house big. *Lena lives in a big house.*	Adjectives commonly follow the nouns they modify
	No change of form for comparative adjectives	The most funny joke. *The funniest joke.*	Comparatives and superlatives formed with a separate word
Adverbs	An extra adjective or verb used in place of an adverb or verb	I run run fast. *I run fast.* Speak quiet. *Speak quietly.*	Adverbs are not used; adjectives are used after verbs
Articles	Inconsistent use of indefinite article with a profession	She is lawyer. *She is a lawyer.*	Indefinite article omitted before a profession
	One used in place of indefinite article	I saw one movie. *I saw a movie.*	No indefinite articles
Gerunds	Difficulty applying the gerund and infinitive form	I enjoy play tennis. *I enjoy playing tennis.*	No gerund form
Nouns	Consistent use of singular noun form for plurals	He has three sister. *He has three sisters.*	No plural form for nouns; no plural form after a number
	Plural forms used for noncount nouns	Where is you luggages? *Where is your luggage?*	No distinction between count and noncount nouns
	Possessive nouns formed with *of* phrase or avoidance of using *'s*	This is the bag of Marisa. *This is Marisa's bag.*	Noun possessor follows object; a character forms possessive
	Names written last name first, no comma	Chan [last] Homan [first] *Chan, Homan* or *Homan Chan*	Family names precede first names
	Titles, Mr., Ms., etc., used with first name	Mr. Homan Chan likes to sail. *Mr. Homan owns a boat.*	First name is preferred when repeating a person's name
Pronouns	Difficulty differentiating between subject and object pronouns	Her told I. *She told me.*	No distinction between subject and object pronouns
	Subject pronoun is omitted	Is cold. *It is cold.*	Subject pronoun can be omitted when subject is understood
	Omission of possessive pronouns; extra words used to form possessive pronouns; confusion with possessive and personal pronouns	She hurt leg. *She hurt her leg.* I like she car. *I like her car.* It's the pen of her. *It's her pen.* That is dog I. *That is my dog.*	Possessive pronouns are: omitted when relationship is clear; formed by a separate character; indistinct from personal pronouns
	Difficulty with singular pronouns	Marie? No, he is not here. *Marie? No, she is not here.*	No gender difference in third person singular pronouns
	Absence of object pronouns	It's sweet, so he likes. *It's sweet, so he likes it.*	Direct objects can be omitted
	Redundant use of pronouns	My sister, she lives in Hanoi. *My sister lives in Hanoi.*	States noun and uses pronoun in description
	Repetition of noun instead of using pronoun	I like fish, I eat fish every day. *I like fish, I eat it every day.*	Repetition of nouns is common
Verbs	Use of present tense for all tenses; no subject-verb agreement; no change to show person or number	She go tomorrow. *She will go tomorrow.*	Verb does not change to show tense; tense indicated by context
	Omission of *to be*	You tall girl. *You are a tall girl.*	Omit *to be* with adjectives, places, prepositional phrases
	Punctuation and conjunctions omitted between some verbs	I wash dry the dishes. *I wash and dry the dishes.*	Some verbs can be used without punctuation or conjunctions
Questions	Avoidance of inverted question forms in yes/no questions in favor of tag questions or intonation	The pizza is good, yes? *Is the pizza good?*	No subject-verb inversion in questions
	Awkward question formation	She is (is not) teacher? *Is (Isn't) she a teacher?*	Verb can be followed by its negative to form a question
Commands	Use of *go* at the end of a command	Fix my car, go! *Fix my car!*	*go* used for emphasis at the end of a sentence

Sound-Symbol (Phonology) Transfer and Interference Chart

The symbol X pinpoints sounds that are difficult to produce or perceive for speakers of the following languages.

Consonants	Cambodian	Chinese	Haitian Creole	Hmong	Spanish	Vietnamese
/b/ as in bell		X		X		
/k/ as in car and king				X		
/d/ as in day		X				
/g/ as in go	X	X		X		
/h/ as in hat			X			
/j/ as in joke		X		X	X	X
/p/ as in pen				X		
/r/ as in red		X	X	X	X	
/s/ as in sun				X		
/t/ as in teach				X		X
/v/ as in vain	X	X			X	
/w/ as in wall	X			X	X	
/z/ as in zebra	X	X		X	X	
/kw/ as in quick				X		
/ks/ as in x-ray		X		X		

Short Vowels	Cambodian	Chinese	Haitian Creole	Hmong	Spanish	Vietnamese
Short a as in bat		X			X	X
Short e as in let		X	X	X	X	
Short i as in sit		X	X	X	X	X
Short o as in cot				X	X	
Short u as in nut		X	X	X	X	

Long Vowels	Cambodian	Chinese	Haitian Creole	Hmong	Spanish	Vietnamese
Long a as in late		X		X		
Long e as in me		X				
Long i as in rice		X				
Long o as in old		X		X		
Long u as in blue		X				

Vowel Patterns	Cambodian	Chinese	Haitian Creole	Hmong	Spanish	Vietnamese
oo as in look	X		X	X	X	X
aw as in law					X	

Diphthongs	Cambodian	Chinese	Haitian Creole	Hmong	Spanish	Vietnamese
oy as in toy				X		
ow as in now					X	

r-controlled vowels	Cambodian	Chinese	Haitian Creole	Hmong	Spanish	Vietnamese
ir as in bird	X	X	X	X	X	X
ar as in card	X	X	X	X	X	X
or as in torn	X	X	X	X	X	X
air as in fair	X	X	X	X	X	X
ear as in fear	X	X	X	X	X	X

Sound-Symbol (Phonology) Transfer and Interference Chart *(cont.)*

Consonant Digraphs	Cambodian	Chinese	Haitian Creole	Hmong	Spanish	Vietnamese
sh as in shoe	X	X			X	X
ch as in chair				X		X
th as in thin	X	X	X	X	X	X
ng as in ring			X	X	X	

Consonant Blends	Cambodian	Chinese	Haitian Creole	Hmong	Spanish	Vietnamese
bl, tr, dr and others blue, try, dry		X		X		X
ld, nt, rt, and others bald, ant, art	X	X	X	X		X

Sound-Symbol (Phonics) Transfer and Interference Chart

This chart pinpoints sound-symbol transfer issues for the following four languages that use the Roman alphabet. The symbol X identifies symbols that do not represent a corresponding sound to English in the writing system of the primary language.

Consonants	Haitian Creole	Hmong	Spanish	Vietnamese
b as in bet		X		
c as in cut as in cell	X	X X		X X
d as in dog				
f as in fun				
g as in goal as in giant		X X	X	
h as in hat			X	
j as in joke		X	X	X
k as in kite		X		
l as in light				
m as in moon				
n as in noon				
p as in pen				
qu as in quick	X	X	X	
r as in red		X	X	
s as in son		X		
t as in teach		X		
v as in vain			X	
w as in wall		X		X
x as in x-ray	X	X		X
y as in yes				
z as in zebra		X	X	X

Consonants Digraphs	Haitian Creole	Hmong	Spanish	Vietnamese
ch as in chair	X			
sh as in shoe			X	
th as in thin			X	

Sound-Symbol (Phonics) Transfer and Interference Chart
(cont.)

Vowels, Vowel Patterns	Haitian Creole	Hmong	Spanish	Vietnamese
a as in cat		X	X	
a as in late			X	X
ai as in rain	X	X	X	X
ay as in say	X	X	X	
au as in auto	X	X	X	X
aw as in law	X	X	X	X
e as in let	X	X	X	
ee as in feed	X	X	X	X
ea as in sea	X	X	X	X
ew as in new	X	X	X	X
i as in hit	X	X	X	
i as in ice	X	X	X	X
o as in pot	X	X	X	
o as in hope	X	X	X	X
oo as in noon	X	X	X	X
oo as in hook	X	X	X	
oa as in float	X	X	X	X
ow as in low	X	X	X	X
ow as in now	X	X	X	X
ou as in round	X	X	X	X
oi as in oil	X	X		
oy as in toy	X	X		X
u as in up	X	X	X	X
u as in tune			X	X
ui as in suit	X	X	X	X
ue as in true	X	X	X	X
y as in cry	X	X	X	X
ar as in car	X	X		
er as in fern	X	X	X	
ir as in bird	X	X	X	
or as in corn		X	X	
ur as in turn		X	X	

Word Study

English and Spanish have some fundamental linguistic characteristics in common, such as using prefixes and suffixes that can change word meaning and part of speech. The following chart pinpoints some prefixes and suffixes that serve similar functions in both languages. The example words used below have similar meaning but are not necessarily cognates.

Prefixes

Prefix	English Prefix Example		Spanish Prefix or Word	
not	dis-	disagreeable	des-	desagradable
	in-	inoffensive	in-	inofensivo
	non-	nonreturnable	no	no retornable
	un-	unfair	in-	injusto
again	re-	review	re-	revista
before	pre-	preview	pre-	preestreno

Suffixes

Function	English Suffix		Spanish Suffix or Word	
Makes verb into adjective	-able	acceptable	-able	aceptable
Means "with" Makes noun into adjective form	-ful	careful	-oso/a	cuidadoso/a
Makes verb into a noun	-ion	decision	-ion	decision
	-tion	presentation	-cion	presentacion
	-ment			
Means "without" Makes noun into adjective form	-less	bottomless	sin	sin fondo sin = without fondo = bottom
Makes adjective into an adverb	-ly	finally	-mente	finalmente
Makes adjective into a noun	-ness	happiness	-idad	fecilidad

Class _____ Date _____

UNIT A At School

CHAPTER 1 • Language and Vocabulary

Chapter Materials

Activity Book: pp. 4–5
Audio: Unit A, Chapter 1
Student Handbook
Teacher Resource Book: Suggestions and Techniques, pp. 1–20; Lesson Plan, p. 31; Blackline Masters, pp. 75–128; Activity Book Answer Key

Teacher Resource CD-ROM
Transparency 1
The Heinle Picture Dictionary/CD-ROM
Web site: http://elt.thomson.com/visions

➤ See the Teacher's Edition wrap-around for complete teaching suggestions for each section.

Period 1

- **Unit Opener** (pp. 2–3) 15 MIN.
  Preview the unit contents and chapter vocabulary. Use Transparency 1 to teach vocabulary in context.
- **Build Vocabulary** (p. 2) 30 MIN.
  Present the chapter vocabulary by listening to the audio and completing the activities. New vocabulary will be recycled throughout the unit. When playing the audio, give students visual cues during the activity by pointing to your ear when it is time for them to listen, and then by pointing to the class when it is time for them to repeat. Encourage everyone to speak.
- **Homework:** Have students practice writing the new vocabulary words in their notebooks.

Period 2

- **Warm Up** 5 MIN.
  Write on the board: *My name is _____. What is your name?* Have students practice asking and telling their names. This will familiarize them with your name and enable them to learn their classmates' names.
- **Listen, Speak, Interact** (pp. 4–5) 40 MIN.
  Practice listening and speaking skills in controlled and guided activities as well as in authentic conversations. Introduce vocabulary for identifying people. Listen to the dialogues and complete the activities. Encourage students to monitor their own speech by comparing their speech to the text and to that of other students as they practice the dialogues. Repeat the dialogues several times so students have the opportunity to work with different partners. Make sure students are reading the dialogues correctly and are inserting their own personal information.
- **Homework:** Activity Book (p. 4)

Period 3

- **Check Homework** 5 MIN.
  OR
- **Warm Up** 5 MIN.
  Review the vocabulary on pp. 2–3. Model asking and answering the question: "What is this? This is a(n) _____."
- **Listen, Speak, Interact** (pp. 6–7) 40 MIN.
  Practice listening and speaking skills in controlled and guided activities as well as in authentic conversations. Introduce vocabulary for greeting and introducing people. Listen to the dialogues and complete the activities. Encourage students to monitor their own speech by comparing their speech to the text and to that of other students as they practice the dialogues. Repeat the dialogues several times so students have the opportunity to work with different partners. Make sure students are reading the dialogues correctly and are inserting their own personal information.
- **Homework:** Activity Book (p. 5)

Class _____ Date _____

UNIT A At School

CHAPTER 2 • Letters, Sounds, Words

Chapter Materials
Activity Book: pp. 6–11
Audio: Unit A, Chapter 2
Student Handbook
Teacher Resource Book: Suggestions and Techniques, pp. 1–20; Lesson Plan, p. 32; Blackline Masters, pp. 75–128; Activity Book Answer Key

Teacher Resource CD-ROM
Transparencies 2, 3, 4, 5, 10, 11, 12, 13
The Heinle Picture Dictionary/CD-ROM
Web site: http://elt.thomson.com/visions

➤ See the Teacher's Edition wrap-around for complete teaching suggestions for each section.

Period 1

- **Check Homework** 5 MIN.
  OR
- **Warm Up** 5 MIN.
  Write on the board: 1) *Hello.* 2) *Good-bye.* Ask: "When do you say Hello? When do you say Good-bye?"
- **Sounds and Words** (pp. 8–11) 40 MIN.
  Bring to class familiar objects with labels such as food packages or newspaper ads. Have students identify the letters and/or words. Make sure to bring objects that reinforce the letters/sounds taught in this lesson. Introduce the initial consonants **b, c, f, g**; complete the activities (p. 8). Introduce the initial consonants **m, p, s, t**; complete the activities (p. 9). Introduce the final consonants **b, f, g**; complete the activities (p. 10). Introduce the final consonants **m, p, s, t**; complete the activities (p. 11). Use Transparencies 2 and 3 to teach students how to distinguish consonants in initial, medial, and final positions. Point out and exaggerate, if needed, how specific letter sounds are made. Make sure students can distinguish each sound before having them produce the sounds themselves. Do a letter dictation for new letters/sounds. Slowly dictate the upper- and lowercase letters just taught. Time permitting, ask students to find and identify the letters/sounds on items in the classroom such as posters, signs, books, etc.
- **Homework:** Activity Book (pp. 6–8)

Period 2

- **Check Homework** 5 MIN.
  OR
- **Warm Up** 5 MIN.
  Write on the board: *Say the first sound:* 1) *bag* 2) *cat* 3) *fan* 4) *gas* 5) *man* 6) *pan* 7) *sad* 8) *tag. Say the last sound:* 1) *cab* 2) *beef* 3) *leg* 4) *gum* 5) *cup* 6) *bus* 7) *tag.*
- **Sounds and Words** (pp. 12–15) 40 MIN.
  Bring to class familiar objects with labels such as food packages or newspaper ads. Have students identify the letters and/or words. Make sure to bring objects that reinforce the letters/sounds taught in this lesson. Introduce short **a**; complete the activities (p. 12). Introduce short **e**; complete the activities (p. 13). Introduce short **i, o, u**; complete the activities (pp. 14–15). Use Transparencies 4 and 5 to teach short vowels and sound changes to make new words. Do a letter dictation for new letters/sounds. Slowly dictate the upper- and lowercase letters just taught. Time permitting, ask students to find and identify the letters/sounds on items in the classroom such as posters, signs, books, etc.
- **Homework:** Activity Book (pp. 9–11)

Class _____ Date _____

UNIT A At School

CHAPTER 3 • Reading and Writing Project, Review

Chapter Materials

Activity Book: pp. 12–23
Audio: Unit A, Chapter 3
Student Handbook
Student CD-ROM: Unit A
Teacher Resource Book: Suggestions and Techniques, pp. 1–20; Lesson Plan, p. 33; Blackline Masters, pp. 75–128; School-Home Connection Newsletters, pp. 129–135; Activity Book Answer Key

Teacher Resource CD-ROM
Assessment Program: Unit A Test, pp. 9–14; Resources, Checklists, Rubrics, pp. 183–207
Assessment CD-ROM: Unit A Test
Transparencies 6, 7, 8, 9, 10, 11, 12, 13, 14, 15, 16, 17, 18, 19
The Heinle Picture Dictionary/CD-ROM
Web site: http://elt.thomson.com/visions

➤ See the Teacher's Edition wrap-around for complete teaching suggestions for each section.

Period 1

- **Check Homework** 5 MIN.
  OR
- **Warm Up** 5 MIN.
  Write on the board: *Say the words: 1) pin 2) can 3) pet 4) top 5) cup*
- **Reading** (p. 16) 15 MIN.
  Complete the reading activities, focusing on sight words.
- **Writing** (pp. 17–19) 25 MIN.
  Use Transparencies 6–8 and 10–13 to teach printing (lowercase and uppercase). Use Transparencies 14–18 to teach cursive writing (lowercase and uppercase). Use the writing lines on Transparency 9 to demonstrate writing. Have students practice print and cursive letters by completing the activities. Monitor students' writing. Some non-literate students may need assistance holding their pens/pencils or properly positioning the paper. Encourage students to make their letters the same size and to space the letters equally. For extra practice writing, have the class work on Activity Book pages 14–16 (printing) and/or pages 18–20 (cursive writing) in class.
- **Homework:** Activity Book (pp. 12–13)

Period 2

- **Check Homework** 5 MIN.
  OR
- **Warm Up** 5 MIN.
  Write on the board: *Say the words: 1) bag–bat 2) pen–ten 3) man–map 4) tub–cup*
- **Projects** (p. 20) 40 MIN.
  Projects require students to integrate and apply the new skills learned in the unit. Introduce the assignments of alphabetizing names and/or meeting the principal.
- **Homework:** Activity Book (p. 21); Have students complete their projects and study for the Unit A Test.

Period 3

- **Review** (p. 21) 15 MIN.
  Review the unit contents. Use Transparency 17 or 18 to play Bingo and review the unit vocabulary. Use Transparency 19 for Unit A Sentence Builders to review the unit vocabulary.
- **Unit A Test** (Assessment Program, pp. 9–14) 30 MIN.
  After the Unit A Test, reassess student learning. Record strong and weak areas based on the unit test. Review weak areas before the Unit A–D Exam.
- **Homework:** Activity Book (pp. 22–23)

Class _____ Date _____

UNIT B In the Classroom

CHAPTER 1 • Language and Vocabulary

Chapter Materials
Activity Book: pp. 24–28
Audio: Unit B, Chapter 1
Student Handbook
Teacher Resource Book: Suggestions and Techniques, pp. 1–20; Lesson Plan, p. 34; Blackline Masters, pp. 75–128; Activity Book Answer Key
Teacher Resource CD-ROM
Transparencies 20, 21, 22
The Heinle Picture Dictionary/CD-ROM
Web site: http://elt.thomson.com/visions

▶ See the Teacher's Edition wrap-around for complete teaching suggestions for each section.

Period 1

- **Unit Opener** (pp. 22–23) 10 MIN.
  Preview the unit contents and chapter vocabulary. Use Transparency 20 to teach vocabulary in context.
- **Build Vocabulary** (p. 22) 15 MIN.
  Present the chapter vocabulary by listening to the audio and completing the activities. New vocabulary will be recycled throughout the unit. Encourage students to follow your example of first listening to the words and then pointing to them. Encourage everyone to speak. Refrain from correcting pronunciation errors at this point. Repeat the activities several times if necessary.
- **Listen, Speak, Interact** (pp. 24–25) 20 MIN.
  Practice listening and speaking skills in controlled and guided activities as well as in authentic conversations. Have students talk about objects in the classroom. Practice giving and following instructions by completing the activities. Encourage students to monitor their own speech by comparing their speech to the text and to that of other students as they practice the dialogues. Repeat the dialogues several times so students have the opportunity to work with different partners. Make sure students are reading the dialogues correctly and are inserting their own personal information.
- **Homework:** Activity Book (p. 24)

Period 2

- **Check Homework** 5 MIN.
  OR
- **Warm Up** 5 MIN.
  Write on the board: *Name three things you see in the classroom.*

- **Build Vocabulary** (pp. 26–27) 40 MIN.
  Introduce vocabulary for numbers and colors. Use Transparencies 21 and 22 to teach numbers. For additional practice writing numbers, have the class work on Activity Book pages 26 and 27 in class. Listen to the dialogues and complete the activities. Encourage students to follow your example of first listening to the words and then pointing to them. Encourage everyone to speak. Refrain from correcting pronunciation errors at this point. Repeat the activities several times if necessary.
- **Homework:** Activity Book (p. 25)

Period 3

- **Check Homework** 5 MIN.
  OR
- **Warm Up** 5 MIN.
  Write on the board: *Name something blue. Name something green. Name something yellow.*
- **Listen, Speak, Interact** (pp. 28–29) 40 MIN.
  Practice listening and speaking skills in controlled and guided activities as well as in authentic conversations. Have students talk about personal information (age, nationality) by completing the activities. Encourage students to monitor their own speech by comparing their speech to the text and to that of other students as they practice the dialogues. Repeat the dialogues several times so students have the opportunity to work with different partners. Make sure students are reading the dialogues correctly and are inserting their own personal information.
- **Homework:** Activity Book (p. 28)

Class _____   Date _____

UNIT B In the Classroom

CHAPTER 2 • Letters, Sounds, Words

Chapter Materials
Activity Book: pp. 29–33
Audio: Unit B, Chapter 2
Student Handbook
Teacher Resource Book: Suggestions and Techniques, pp. 1–20; Lesson Plan, p. 35; Blackline Masters, pp. 75–128; Activity Book Answer Key

Teacher Resource CD-ROM
Transparencies 10, 11, 12, 13, 23, 24, 25, 26
The Heinle Picture Dictionary/CD-ROM
Web site: http://elt.thomson.com/visions

➤ See the Teacher's Edition wrap-around for complete teaching suggestions for each section.

Period 1

- **Check Homework** 5 MIN.
  OR
- **Warm Up** 5 MIN.
  Write on the board: *How old are you? Where are you from? What is your nationality?*
- **Sounds and Words** (pp. 30–33) 40 MIN.
  Bring to class familiar objects with labels such as food packages or newspaper ads. Have students identify the letters and/or words. Make sure to bring objects that reinforce the letters/sounds taught in this lesson. Introduce the initial consonants **d, j, l** (p. 30); complete the activities. Introduce the initial consonants **n, r, v** (p. 31); complete the activities. Introduce the final consonants **d, l, n, r, x** (pp. 32–33); complete the activities. Use Transparencies 23 and 24 to teach students how to distinguish more consonants in initial, medial, and final positions. Make sure students can distinguish each sound before having them produce the sounds themselves. Do a letter dictation for new letters/sounds. Slowly dictate the upper- and lowercase letters just taught. Time permitting, ask students to find and identify the letters on items in the classroom such as posters, signs, books, etc.
- **Homework:** Activity Book (pp. 29–30)

Period 2

- **Check Homework** 5 MIN.
  OR
- **Warm Up** 5 MIN.
  Write on the board: *Say the words: 1) dog–jog–lip 2) net–rug–vet 3) bed–pencil–sun–car–six*

- **Sounds and Words** (pp. 34–37) 40 MIN.
  Bring to class familiar objects with labels such as food packages or newspaper ads. Have students identify the letters and/or words. Make sure to bring objects that reinforce the letters/sounds taught in this lesson. Introduce long **a** (p. 34); complete the activities. Introduce long **i** (p. 35); complete the activities. Introduce long **o** (p. 36); complete the activities. Introduce long **u** (p. 37); complete the activities. Use Transparencies 25 and 26 to teach long vowels and sound changes to make new words. Make sure students can distinguish each sound before having them produce the sounds themselves. Do a letter dictation for new letters/sounds. Slowly dictate the upper- and lowercase letters just taught. Time permitting, ask students to find and identify the letters/sounds on items in the classroom such as posters, signs, books, etc.
- **Homework:** Activity Book (pp. 31–33)

Class _____ Date _____

UNIT B In the Classroom

CHAPTER 3 • Reading and Writing Project, Review

Chapter Materials

Activity Book: pp. 34–39
Audio: Unit B, Chapter 3
Student Handbook
Student CD-ROM: Unit B
Teacher Resource Book: Suggestions and Techniques, pp. 1–20; Lesson Plan, p. 36; Blackline Masters, pp. 75–128; School-Home Connection Newsletters, pp. 136–142; Activity Book Answer Key

Teacher Resource CD-ROM
Assessment Program: Unit B Test, pp. 15–20; Resources, Checklists, Rubrics, pp. 183–207
Assessment CD-ROM: Unit B Test
Transparencies 9, 10, 11, 12, 13, 17, 18, 27
The Heinle Picture Dictionary/CD-ROM
Web site: http://elt.thomson.com/visions

➤ See the Teacher's Edition wrap-around for complete teaching suggestions for each section.

Period 1

- **Check Homework** 5 MIN.
  OR
- **Warm Up** 5 MIN.
  Write on the board: *Say the words: 1) cake–tape 2) dime–five 3) nose–bone 4) June–cute*
- **Reading** (p. 38) 20 MIN.
  Complete the pre-reading activity. Have students read the selection about the American flag. Read the selection aloud and have students follow along in their books. Ask for volunteers to read the selection aloud. Read the selection together as a class. Work with the class to answer the reading comprehension questions.
- **Writing** (p. 39) 20 MIN.
  Have students complete the writing activities. Monitor students' writing. Encourage students to make their letters the same size and to space the letters equally. Use the writing lines on Transparency 9 to demonstrate writing.
  • **Homework:** Activity Book (pp. 34–35)

Period 2

- **Check Homework** 5 MIN.
  OR
- **Warm Up** 5 MIN.
  Write on the board: *What are the colors of the American flag? What color are the stars? What colors are the stripes?*

- **Projects** (p. 40) 40 MIN.
  Projects require students to integrate and apply the new skills learned in the unit. Introduce the assignments of keeping a personal dictionary and/or creating a nationality bar chart.
- **Homework:** Activity Book (pp. 36–37); Have students complete their projects and study for the Unit B Test.

Period 3

- **Review** (p. 41) 15 MIN.
  Review the unit contents. Use Transparency 17 or 18 to play Bingo and review the unit vocabulary. Use Transparency 27 for Unit B Sentence Builders to review unit vocabulary.
- **Unit B Test** (Assessment Program, pp. 15–20) 30 MIN.
  After the Unit B Test, reassess student learning. Record strong and weak areas based on the unit test. Review weak areas before the Unit A–D Exam.
- **Homework:** Activity Book (pp. 38–39)

Class _____ Date _____

UNIT C Classmates

CHAPTER 1 • Language and Vocabulary

Chapter Materials
Activity Book: pp. 40–42
Audio: Unit C, Chapter 1
Student Handbook
Teacher Resource Book: Suggestions and Techniques, pp. 1–20; Lesson Plan, p. 37; Blackline Masters, pp. 75–128; Activity Book Answer Key

Teacher Resource CD-ROM
Transparency 28
The Heinle Picture Dictionary/CD-ROM
Web site: http://elt.thomson.com/visions

➤ See the Teacher's Edition wrap-around for complete teaching suggestions for each section.

Period 1

- **Unit Opener** (pp. 42–43) 10 MIN.
  Preview the unit contents and chapter vocabulary. Use Transparency 28 to teach vocabulary in context.
- **Build Vocabulary** (p. 42) 15 MIN.
  Present the chapter vocabulary by listening to the audio and completing the activities. New vocabulary will be recycled throughout the unit. Encourage everyone to speak. Refrain from correcting pronunciation errors at this point. Repeat the activities several times if necessary.
- **Listen, Speak, Interact** (pp. 44–45) 20 MIN.
  Practice listening and speaking skills in controlled and guided activities as well as in authentic conversations. Have students talk about clothing, compliments, and thanking by completing the activities. Encourage students to monitor their own speech by comparing their speech to the text and to that of other students as they practice the dialogues. Repeat the dialogues several times so students have the opportunity to work with different partners. Make sure students are reading the dialogues correctly and are inserting their own personal information.
- **Homework:** Activity Book (p. 40)

Period 2

- **Check Homework** 5 MIN.
  OR
- **Warm Up** 5 MIN.
  Write on the board: 1) *What clothes do you have on?* 2) *What color is your shirt?* 3) *What color are your shoes?*

- **Build Vocabulary** (pp. 46–47) 40 MIN.
  Introduce vocabulary for parts of the face and body. Listen to the dialogues and complete the activities. Encourage everyone to speak. Refrain from correcting pronunciation errors at this point. Repeat the activities several times if necessary.
- **Homework:** Activity Book (p. 41)

Period 3

- **Check Homework** 5 MIN.
  OR
- **Warm Up** 5 MIN.
  Review vocabulary using TPR. Name a body part and have students point to it. *Point to your ear. Point to your nose. Point to your mouth. Point to your eye. Point to your teeth. Point to your lips. Point to your cheek. Point to your hair.* etc.
- **Listen, Speak, Interact** (pp. 48–49) 40 MIN.
  Practice listening and speaking skills in controlled and guided activities as well as in authentic conversations. Have students talk about personal appearance. Practice giving and following instructions by completing the activities. Encourage students to monitor their own speech by comparing their speech to the text and to that of other students as they practice the dialogues. Repeat the dialogues several times so students have the opportunity to work with different partners. Make sure students are reading the dialogues correctly and are inserting their own personal information.
- **Homework:** Activity Book (p. 42)

Class _____ Date _____

UNIT C Classmates

CHAPTER 2 • Sounds, Words, Sentences

Chapter Materials

Activity Book: pp. 43–47
Audio: Unit C, Chapter 2
Student Handbook
Teacher Resource Book: Suggestions and Techniques, pp. 1–20; Lesson Plan, p. 38; Blackline Masters, pp. 75–128; Activity Book Answer Key

Teacher Resource CD-ROM
Transparencies 10, 11, 12, 13, 29, 30, 31, 32, 33, 34
The Heinle Picture Dictionary/CD-ROM
Web site: http://elt.thomson.com/visions

➤ See the Teacher's Edition wrap-around for complete teaching suggestions for each section.

Period 1

- **Check Homework** 5 MIN.
  OR
- **Warm Up** 5 MIN.
  Write on the board: *What color is your hair? What color are your eyes?*
- **Sounds and Words** (pp. 50–53) 40 MIN.
  Bring to class familiar objects with labels such as food packages or newspaper ads. Have students identify the letters and/or words. Make sure to bring objects that reinforce the letters/sounds taught in this lesson. Introduce the initial consonants **h, k, q** (p. 50); complete the activities. Introduce the initial consonants **w, y, z** (p. 51); complete the activities. Introduce the consonant digraphs **sh, ch, th, ng** (pp. 52–53); complete the activities. Use Transparencies 29 and 30 to teach more consonants in initial, medial, and final positions as well as consonant digraphs. Make sure students can distinguish each sound before having them produce the sounds themselves. Do a letter dictation for new letters/sounds. Slowly dictate the upper- and lowercase letters just taught. Time permitting, ask students to find and identify the letters/sounds on items in the classroom such as posters, signs, books, etc.
- **Homework:** Activity Book (pp. 43–44)

Period 2

- **Check Homework** 5 MIN.
  OR
- **Warm Up** 5 MIN.
  Write on the board: *Say the words: 1) hat–key–quarter 2) window–yes–zero 3) ship–fish 4) chin–bench 5) thirty–bath 6) ring*
- **Sounds and Words** (pp. 54–57) 40 MIN.
  Bring to class familiar objects with labels such as food packages or newspaper ads. Have students identify the letters and/or words. Make sure to bring objects that reinforce the letters/sounds taught in this lesson. Introduce the vowel digraphs **ai, ay, oa, ee, ea** (pp. 54–55); complete the activities. Introduce the vowel diphthongs **oi, oy** (p. 56); complete the activities. Introduce the vowel diphthongs **ou, ow** (p. 57); complete the activities. Introduce long **u** (p. 37); complete the activities. Use Transparencies 31–34 to teach vowel digraphs and sound changes to make new words. Make sure students can distinguish each sound before having them produce the sounds themselves. Do a letter dictation for new letters/sounds. Slowly dictate the upper- and lowercase letters just taught. Time permitting, ask students to find and identify the letters/sounds on items in the classroom such as posters, signs, books, etc.
- **Homework:** Activity Book (pp. 45–47)

Class _____ Date _____

UNIT C Classmates

CHAPTER 3 • Reading and Writing Project, Review

Chapter Materials

Activity Book: pp. 48–53
Audio: Unit C, Chapter 3
Student Handbook
Student CD-ROM: Unit C
Teacher Resource Book: Suggestions and Techniques, pp. 1–20; Lesson Plan, p. 39; Blackline Masters, pp. 75–128; School-Home Connection Newsletters, pp. 143–149; Activity Book Answer Key

Teacher Resource CD-ROM
Assessment Program: Unit C Test, pp. 21–26; Resources, Checklists, Rubrics, pp. 183–207
Assessment CD-ROM: Unit C Test
Transparencies 9, 10, 11, 12, 13, 17, 18, 35
The Heinle Picture Dictionary/CD-ROM
Web site: http://elt.thomson.com/visions

➤ See the Teacher's Edition wrap-around for complete teaching suggestions for each section.

Period 1

- **Check Homework** 5 MIN.
  OR
- **Warm Up** 5 MIN.
  Write on the board: *Say the words: 1) noise–enjoy 2) rain–pay–road–feet–leaf 3) house–down*
- **Reading** (p. 58) 20 MIN.
  Complete the pre-reading activity. Read the poem aloud and have students follow along in their books. Ask for volunteers to read the selection aloud. Read the selection together as a class. Have students answer the reading comprehension questions.
- **Writing** (p. 59) 20 MIN.
  Have students complete the writing activities. Monitor students' writing. Encourage students to make their letters the same size and to space the letters equally. Use the writing lines on Transparency 9 to demonstrate writing.
- **Homework:** Activity Book (pp. 48–49)

Period 2

- **Check Homework** 5 MIN.
  OR
- **Warm Up** 5 MIN.
  Write on the board: *1) Who are the people in the poem "Friends"? 2) What color are Jen's eyes? 3) What color is Tim's hair?*
- **Projects** (p. 60) 40 MIN.
  Projects require students to integrate and apply the new skills learned in the unit. Introduce the assignments of planning and putting on a fashion show and/or writing tongue twisters.
- **Homework:** Activity Book (pp. 50–51); Have students complete their projects and study for the Unit C Test.

Period 3

- **Review** (p. 61) 15 MIN.
  Review the unit contents. Use Transparency 17 or 18 to play Bingo and review the unit vocabulary. Use Transparency 35 for Unit C Sentence Builders to review the unit vocabulary.
- **Unit C Test** (Assessment Program, pp. 21–26) 30 MIN.
  After the Unit C Test, reassess student learning. Record strong and weak areas based on the unit test. Review weak areas before the Unit A–D Exam.
- **Homework:** Activity Book (pp. 52–53)

Class _____   Date _____

UNIT D Around the School

CHAPTER 1 • Language and Vocabulary

Chapter Materials
Activity Book: pp. 54–56
Audio: Unit D, Chapter 1
Student Handbook
Teacher Resource Book: Suggestions and Techniques, pp. 1–20; Lesson Plan, p. 40; Blackline Masters, pp. 75–128; Activity Book Answer Key
Teacher Resource CD-ROM
Transparency 36
The Heinle Picture Dictionary/CD-ROM
Web site: http://elt.thomson.com/visions

➤ See the Teacher's Edition wrap-around for complete teaching suggestions for each section.

Period 1

- **Unit Opener** (pp. 62–63) 10 MIN.
  Preview the unit contents and chapter vocabulary. Use Transparency 36 to teach vocabulary in context.
- **Build Vocabulary** (p. 62) 15 MIN.
  Present the chapter vocabulary by listening to the audio and completing the activities. New vocabulary will be recycled throughout the unit. Encourage everyone to speak. Refrain from correcting pronunciation errors at this point. Repeat the activities several times if necessary.
- **Listen, Speak, Interact** (pp. 64–65) 20 MIN.
  Practice listening and speaking skills in controlled and guided activities as well as in authentic conversations. Have students talk about needs and wants by completing the activities. Encourage students to monitor their own speech by comparing their speech to the text and to that of other students as they practice the dialogues. Repeat the dialogues several times so students have the opportunity to work with different partners. Make sure students are reading the dialogues correctly and are inserting their own personal information.
- **Homework:** Activity Book (p. 54)

Period 2

- **Check Homework** 5 MIN.
  OR
- **Warm Up** 5 MIN.
  Write on the board: *Name one thing you want. Name one thing you need.*

- **Build Vocabulary** (pp. 66–67) 40 MIN.
  Introduce vocabulary for location. Listen to the dialogues and complete the activities. Encourage everyone to speak. Refrain from correcting pronunciation errors at this point. Repeat the activities several times if necessary.
- **Homework:** Activity Book (p. 55)

Period 3

- **Check Homework** 5 MIN.
  OR
- **Warm Up** 5 MIN.
  Write on the board: *Where is your desk? Use prepositions of location to say where you sit.*
- **Listen, Speak, Interact** (pp. 68–69) 40 MIN.
  Practice listening and speaking skills in controlled and guided activities as well as in authentic conversations. Have students talk about asking for and giving directions by completing the activities. Encourage students to monitor their own speech by comparing their speech to the text and to that of other students as they practice the dialogues. Repeat the dialogues several times so students have the opportunity to work with different partners. Make sure students are reading the dialogues correctly and are inserting their own personal information.
- **Homework:** Activity Book (p. 56)

Class _____ Date _____

UNIT D Around the School

CHAPTER 2 • Sounds, Words, Sentences

Chapter Materials
Activity Book: pp. 57–61
Audio: Unit D, Chapter 2
Student Handbook
Teacher Resource Book: Suggestions and Techniques, pp. 1–20; Lesson Plan, p. 41; Blackline Masters, pp. 75–128; Activity Book Answer Key

Teacher Resource CD-ROM
Transparencies 10, 11, 12, 13, 37, 38, 39, 40, 41, 42, 43, 44, 45, 46, 47, 48
The Heinle Picture Dictionary/CD-ROM
Web site: http://elt.thomson.com/visions

➤ See the Teacher's Edition wrap-around for complete teaching suggestions for each section.

Period 1

- **Check Homework** 5 MIN.
  OR
- **Warm Up** 5 MIN.
  Write on the board: *What is on the first floor of our school? What is on the second floor of our school?*
- **Sounds and Words** (pp. 70–73) 40 MIN.
  Bring to class familiar objects with labels such as food packages or newspaper ads. Have students identify the letters and/or words. Make sure to bring objects that reinforce the letters/sounds taught in this lesson. Introduce initial l-blends **cl, fl, gl, sl** (p. 70); complete the activities. Introduce initial r-blends **br, cr, dr, tr** (p. 71); complete the activities. Introduce initial s-blends **sk, sn, st, sw** (p. 72); complete the activities. Introduce final consonant blends **nd, nk, nt, st** (p. 73); complete the activities. Use Transparencies 37–40 to teach initial, medial, and final blends. Make sure students can distinguish each sound before having them produce the sounds themselves. Do a letter dictation for new letters/sounds. Slowly dictate the upper- and lowercase letters just taught. Time permitting, ask students to find and identify the letters/sounds on items in the classroom such as posters, signs, books, etc.
- **Homework:** Activity Book (pp. 57–58)

Period 2

- **Check Homework** 5 MIN.
  OR
- **Warm Up** 5 MIN.
  Write on the board: *Say the words:*
  1) cloud–flag–glass–sleep 2) brush–crib–drink–tree
  3) skirt–snake–star–swim 4) hand–sink–ant–test
- **Sounds and Words** (pp. 74–77) 40 MIN.
  Bring to class familiar objects with labels such as food packages or newspaper ads. Have students identify the letters and/or words. Make sure to bring objects that reinforce the letters/sounds taught in this lesson. Introduce r-controlled vowels **ar, er, ir, ur** (pp. 74–75); complete the activities. Introduce compound words and head syllables (pp. 76–77); complete the activities. Use Transparencies 41–48 to teach r-controlled vowels and syllabication. Make sure students can distinguish each sound before having them produce the sounds themselves. Do a letter dictation for new letters/sounds. Slowly dictate the upper- and lowercase letters just taught. Time permitting, ask students to find and identify the letters/sounds on items in the classroom such as posters, signs, books, etc.
- **Homework:** Activity Book (pp. 59–61)

Class _____   Date _____

UNIT D Around the School

CHAPTER 3 • Reading and Writing Project, Review

Chapter Materials

Activity Book: pp. 62–67
Audio: Unit D, Chapter 3
Student Handbook
Student CD-ROM: Unit D
Teacher Resource Book: Suggestions and Techniques, pp. 1–20; Lesson Plan, p. 42; Blackline Masters, pp. 75–128; School-Home Connection Newsletters, pp. 150–156; Activity Book Answer Key

Teacher Resource CD-ROM
Assessment Program: Unit D Test, pp. 27–32; Units A–D Exam, pp. 33–40; Resources, Checklists, Rubrics, pp. 183–207
Assessment CD-ROM: Unit D Test, Units A–D Exam
Transparencies 9, 10, 11, 12, 13, 17, 18, 49
The Heinle Picture Dictionary/CD-ROM
Web site: http://elt.thomson.com/visions

➤ See the Teacher's Edition wrap-around for complete teaching suggestions for each section.

Period 1

- **Check Homework** 5 MIN.
  OR
- **Warm Up** 5 MIN.
  Write on the board: *Say the words: car–bird–her–fur*
- **Reading** (p. 78) 20 MIN.
  Complete the pre-reading activity. Read the selection "The Jefferson High News" aloud and have students follow along in their books. Ask for volunteers to read the selection aloud. Read the selection together as a class. Work with the class to answer the reading comprehension questions.
- **Writing** (p. 79) 20 MIN.
  Have students complete the writing activities. Monitor students' writing. Encourage students to make their letters the same size and to space the letters equally. Use the writing lines on Transparency 9 to demonstrate writing.
- **Homework:** Activity Book (pp. 62–63)

Period 2

- **Check Homework** 5 MIN.
  OR
- **Warm Up** 5 MIN.
  Write on the board: *Think about the newspaper article from yesterday. What place in our school has many books? What place in our school is for playing basketball? What place in our school is for lunch?*

- **Projects** (p. 80) 40 MIN.
  Projects require students to integrate and apply the new skills learned in the unit. Introduce the assignments of creating a floor plan of your school and/or having a spelling bee.
- **Homework:** Activity Book (pp. 64–65); Have students complete their projects and study for the Unit D Test.

Period 3

- **Review** (p. 81) 15 MIN.
  Review the unit contents. Use Transparency 17 or 18 to play Bingo and review the unit vocabulary. Use Transparency 49 for Unit D Sentence Builders to review the unit vocabulary.
- **Unit D Test** (Assessment Program, pp. 27–32) 30 MIN.
  After the Unit D Test, reassess student learning. Record strong and weak areas based on the unit test. Review weak areas before the Unit A–D Exam.
- **Homework:** Activity Book (pp. 66–67); Have students study for the Unit A–D Exam.

Period 4

- **Unit A–D Exam** (Assessment Program, pp. 33–40) 45 MIN.

42 LESSON PLANS Unit D • Chapter 3

Class _____   Date _____

UNIT 1 A Day at School

CHAPTER 1 • In the School Office

Chapter Materials
Activity Book: pp. 68–75
Audio: Unit 1, Chapter 1
Student Handbook
Teacher Resource Book: Suggestions and Techniques, pp. 1–20; Lesson Plan, p. 43; Blackline Masters, pp. 75–128; Activity Book Answer Key
Teacher Resource CD-ROM

Assessment Program: Unit 1, Chapter 1 Quiz, pp. 41–43; Resources, Checklists, Rubrics, pp. 183–207
Assessment CD-ROM: Unit 1, Chapter 1 Quiz
Transparencies 9, 17, 18, 50, 51, 52, 53, 54, 55, 57, 58
The Heinle Basic Newbury House Dictionary/CD-ROM
Web site: http://elt.thomson.com/visions

➤ See the Teacher's Edition wrap-around for complete teaching suggestions for each section.

Period 1

- **Unit Opener** (pp. 82–83) 10 MIN.
  Preview the unit contents. Complete the "View the Picture" activity using Transparency 50.
- **Chapter Opener** (p. 84) 10 MIN.
  Preview the chapter contents. Introduce the chapter vocabulary using Transparency 51.
- **Listen, Speak, Interact** (p. 85) 25 MIN.
  Introduce the dialogue and have students practice it in pairs.
- **Homework:** Have students practice writing the new vocabulary words in their notebooks.

Period 2

- **Check Homework** 5 MIN.
  OR
- **Warm Up** 5 MIN.
  Practice the dialogue on p. 85.
- **Build Vocabulary** (pp. 86–87) 20 MIN.
  Introduce words for days, months, and ordinal numbers and complete the activities.
- **Grammar Focus** (p. 88) 20 MIN.
  Present nouns and pronouns. Present the verb *be* in the simple present. Complete the activities.
- **Homework:** Activity Book (pp. 68–69)

Period 3

- **Check Homework** 5 MIN.
  OR
- **Warm Up** 5 MIN.
  Write on the board: *1) Name two nouns. 2) Name two pronouns. 3) What is a noun? What is a pronoun?*

- **Grammar Focus** (p. 89) 20 MIN.
  Present possessive adjectives and complete the activities.
- **Word Study** (p. 90) 10 MIN.
  Teach students how to recognize short vowels (**a, e, i, o, u**) (Transparency 54).
- **Capitalization and Punctuation** (p. 91) 10 MIN.
  Introduce capital letters and periods.
- **Homework:** Activity Book (pp. 70–73)

Period 4

- **Check Homework** 5 MIN.
  OR
- **Warm Up** 5 MIN.
  Write on the board: *Find the short vowels in these words: 1) class 2) desk 3) in 4) clock 5) up*
- **Writing** (p. 91) 20 MIN.
  Teach students how to write sentences. Introduce the Editing Checklist.
- **Project** (p. 92) 15 MIN.
  Introduce the assignment of making a class calendar.
- **Review** (p. 93) 5 MIN.
  Review the chapter contents.
- **Homework:** Activity Book (pp. 74–75); Have students study for the Unit 1, Chapter 1 Quiz.

Class _____ Date _____

UNIT 1 A Day at School

CHAPTER 2 • Information Forms

Chapter Materials

Activity Book: pp. 76–81
Audio: Unit 1, Chapter 2
Student Handbook
Teacher Resource Book: Suggestions and Techniques, pp. 1–20; Lesson Plan, p. 44; Blackline Masters, pp. 75–128; Activity Book Answer Key
Teacher Resource CD-ROM

Assessment Program: Unit 1, Chapter 2 Quiz, pp. 44–46; Resources, Checklists, Rubrics, pp. 183–207
Assessment CD-ROM: Unit 1, Chapter 2 Quiz
Transparencies 52, 55, 56, 57, 58
The Heinle Basic Newbury House Dictionary/CD-ROM
Web site: http://elt.thomson.com/visions

➤ See the Teacher's Edition wrap-around for complete teaching suggestions for each section.

Period 1

- **Unit 1, Chapter 1 Quiz** (Assessment Program, pp. 41–43) 25 MIN.
- **Use Prior Knowledge** (p. 94) 10 MIN.
  Activate prior knowledge by talking about emergency information and information your school needs about you.
- **Build Vocabulary** (p. 95) 10 MIN.
  Introduce words for emergency information.
- **Homework:** Activity Book (p. 76)

Period 2

- **Check Homework** 5 MIN.
  OR
- **Warm Up** 5 MIN.
  Write on the board: *Name two pieces of information on an Emergency Information Form.*
- **Text Structure** (p. 95) 10 MIN.
  Present the text features of information forms (key words and blank spaces).
- **Reading Strategy** (p. 96) 5 MIN.
  Teach the strategy of scanning for information.
- **Reading Selection** (pp. 96–97) 25 MIN.
  Complete the pre-reading questions. Have students read the selection and use the reading strategy.
- **Homework:** Activity Book (p. 77)

Period 3

- **Check Homework** 5 MIN.
  OR
- **Warm Up** (reading) 5 MIN.
  Write on the board: *What are two things you learned about information forms?*

- **Listen, Speak, Interact** (p. 97) 5 MIN.
  Have students discuss the class schedule.
- **Reading Comprehension** (p. 98) 10 MIN.
  Have students answer the questions.
- **Elements of Text** (p. 98) 5 MIN.
  Teach students how to compare and contrast information.
- **Build Reading Fluency** (p. 99) 10 MIN.
  Teach how to build reading fluency by using rapid word recognition for irregular sight words.
- **Punctuation** (p. 99) 10 MIN.
  Teach how to use commas in dates and addresses.
- **Homework:** Activity Book (pp. 78–79)

Period 4

- **Check Homework** 5 MIN.
  OR
- **Warm Up** 5 MIN.
  Write on the board: *Correct the errors: 1) September 21 2008 2) Sacramento. CA*
- **Writing** (pp. 100–101) 35 MIN.
  Teach how to fill out a form.
- **Review** (p. 101) 5 MIN.
- **Homework:** Activity Book (pp. 80–81); Have students study for the Unit 1, Chapter 2 Quiz.

Class _____ Date _____

UNIT 1 A Day at School

CHAPTER 3 • How to Solve a Word Problem

Chapter Materials

Activity Book: pp. 82–87
Audio: Unit 1, Chapter 3
Student Handbook
Teacher Resource Book: Suggestions and Techniques, pp. 1–20; Lesson Plan, p. 45; Blackline Masters, pp. 75–128; Activity Book Answer Key
Teacher Resource CD-ROM

Assessment Program: Unit 1, Chapter 3 Quiz, pp. 47–49; Resources, Checklists, Rubrics, pp. 183–207
Assessment CD-ROM: Unit 1, Chapter 3 Quiz
Transparencies 52, 56, 58, 59
The Heinle Basic Newbury House Dictionary/CD-ROM
Web site: http://elt.thomson.com/visions

➤ See the Teacher's Edition wrap-around for complete teaching suggestions for each section.

Period 1

- **Unit 1, Chapter 2 Quiz** (Assessment Program, pp. 44–46) 25 MIN.
- **Use Prior Knowledge** (p. 102) 10 MIN.
  Activate prior knowledge about math words and operations.
- **Build Vocabulary** (p. 103) 10 MIN.
  Introduce synonyms (Transparency 59) and question words.
- **Homework:** Activity Book (p. 82)

Period 2

- **Check Homework** 5 MIN.
  OR
- **Warm Up** 5 MIN.
  Write on the board: *Correct the errors in these sentences: 1) Six plus four equals two. 2) Twelve times three equals four.*
- **Text Structure** (p. 103) 10 MIN.
  Present the features of a math textbook (chapter title, explanation, highlighted words, diagrams, examples, exercises).
- **Reading Strategy** (p. 104) 5 MIN.
  Teach the strategy of setting a purpose when reading.
- **Reading Selection** (pp. 104–105) 25 MIN.
  Complete the pre-reading questions. Have students read the selection and use the reading strategy.
- **Homework:** Activity Book (p. 83)

Period 3

- **Check Homework** 5 MIN.
  OR
- **Warm Up** 5 MIN.
  Write on the board: *True or false? 1) A word problem uses words and data to ask a question. 2) In math problems, data is the words.*
- **Listen, Speak, Interact** (p. 105) 5 MIN.
  Have students talk about the word problems.
- **Reading Comprehension** (p. 106) 10 MIN.
  Have students answer the questions.
- **Elements of Text** (p. 106) 5 MIN.
  Teach how to use headings to find information.
- **Build Reading Fluency** (p. 107) 10 MIN.
  Teach how to build reading fluency by rapid word recognition for multisyllable math words.
- **Capitalization and Punctuation** (p. 107) 10 MIN.
  Introduce punctuation and capitalization for declarative and interrogative sentences.
- **Homework:** Activity Book (pp. 84–85)

Period 4

- **Check Homework** 5 MIN.
  OR
- **Warm Up** 5 MIN.
  Write on the board: *Where are the syllables? 1) subtract 2) equals 3) divide 4) addition*
- **Writing** (pp. 108–109) 35 MIN.
  Introduce the strategy of selecting a focus when writing. Teach how to write a word problem.
- **Review** (p. 109) 5 MIN.
  Review the chapter contents.
- **Homework:** Activity Book (pp. 86–87); Have students study for the Unit 1, Chapter 3 Quiz.

Class _____   Date _____

UNIT 1 A Day at School

APPLY AND EXPAND

End-of-Unit Materials

Student Handbook
Student CD-ROM, Unit 1
Teacher Resource Book: Suggestions and Techniques, pp. 1–20; Lesson Plan, p. 46; Blackline Masters, pp. 75–128; School-Home Connection Newsletter, pp. 157–163
Teacher Resource CD-ROM
Assessment Program: Unit 1 Test, pp. 50–55; Resources, Checklists, Rubrics, pp. 183–207

Assessment CD-ROM: Unit 1 Test
Transparency 52, 56, 60
The Heinle Basic Newbury House Dictionary/CD-ROM
Heinle Reading Library Mini-Reader Collection: *First Day of School*
Web site: http://elt.thomson.com/visions

➤ See the Teacher's Edition wrap-around for complete teaching suggestions for each section.

Period 1

- **Unit 1, Chapter 3 Quiz** (Assessment Program, pp. 47–49) 25 MIN.
- **Listening and Speaking Workshop** (p. 110) 20 MIN. Introduce the assignment of giving a math presentation. Have students prepare and practice their presentations.
- **Homework:** Have students review their presentations so that they will be familiar with them for Period 2.

Period 2

- **Listening and Speaking Workshop** (pp. 110–111) 30 MIN.
  Have students present and evaluate their math problems.
- **Viewing Workshop** (p. 111) 15 MIN.
  Have students compare and contrast the calendars.
- **Homework:** Have students complete the Viewing Workshop assignment.

Period 3

- **Writer's Workshop** (pp. 112–113) 45 MIN.
  Present the writing assignment of filling out a form.
- **Homework:** Have students revise and prepare the final version of their forms.

Period 4

- **Projects** (pp. 114–115) 45 MIN.
  Introduce the assignments of making a holiday chart and/or group writing.
- **Homework:** Have students study for the Unit 1 Test.

Period 5

- **Unit 1 Test** (Assessment Program, pp. 50–55) 45 MIN.
  After the Unit 1 Test, reassess student learning. Record strong and weak areas based on the unit test. Review weak areas before the Mid-Book Exam.

Class _____ Date _____

UNIT 2 Families

CHAPTER 1 • About My Family

Chapter Materials
Activity Book: pp. 88–95
Audio: Unit 2, Chapter 1
Student Handbook
Teacher Resource Book: Suggestions and Techniques, pp. 1–20; Lesson Plan, p. 47; Blackline Masters, pp. 75–128; Activity Book Answer Key
Teacher Resource CD-ROM

Assessment Program: Unit 2, Chapter 1 Quiz, pp. 56–58; Resources, Checklists, Rubrics, pp. 183–207
Assessment CD-ROM: Unit 2, Chapter 1 Quiz
Transparencies 9, 17, 18, 52, 58, 62, 63, 64, 65
The Heinle Basic Newbury House Dictionary/CD-ROM
Web site: http://elt.thomson.com/visions

➤ See the Teacher's Edition wrap-around for complete teaching suggestions for each section.

Period 1
- **Unit Opener** (pp. 116–117) 10 MIN.
  Preview the unit contents. Complete the "View the Picture" activity using Transparency 61.
- **Chapter Opener** (p. 118) 10 MIN.
  Preview the chapter contents. Introduce the chapter vocabulary using Transparency 62.
- **Listen, Speak, Interact** (p. 119) 25 MIN.
  Have students practice the dialogue.
- **Homework:** Have students review the new vocabulary words by writing them in their notebooks.

Period 2
- **Check Homework** 5 MIN.
  OR
- **Warm Up** 5 MIN.
  Write on the board: *Name three members of your family.*
- **Build Vocabulary** (pp. 120–121) 20 MIN.
  Introduce descriptive adjectives and antonyms (Transparency 63).
- **Grammar Focus** (p. 122) 20 MIN.
  Introduce contractions and negatives with *be* and the simple present of *have*. Complete the activities.
- **Homework:** Activity Book (pp. 88–89).

Period 3
- **Check Homework** 5 MIN.
  OR
- **Warm Up** 5 MIN.
  Write on the board: *Name three adjectives that describe your appearance (what you look like).*
- **Grammar Focus** (p. 123) 20 MIN.
  Introduce the simple present tense and complete the activities.
- **Word Study** (p. 124) 10 MIN.
  Present long vowels (**a, i, o, u**) and complete the activities (Transparency 64).
- **Spelling** (p. 125) 10 MIN.
  Introduce the spelling of regular plurals and complete the activities.
- **Homework:** Activity Book (pp. 90–93).

Period 4
- **Check Homework** 5 MIN.
  OR
- **Warm Up** 5 MIN.
  Write on the board: *Write the plural of these words: 1) brother 2) cousin 3) aunt*
- **Writing** (p. 125) 20 MIN.
  Teach students how to write a descriptive paragraph.
- **Project** (p. 126) 15 MIN.
  Have students prepare and present their family charts.
- **Review** (p. 127) 5 MIN.
  Review the chapter contents.
- **Homework:** Activity Book (pp. 94–95); Have students study for the Unit 2, Chapter 1 Quiz.

Class _____ Date _____

UNIT 2 Families

CHAPTER 2 • Two Family Poems

Chapter Materials

Activity Book: pp. 96–101
Audio: Unit 2, Chapter 2
Student Handbook
Teacher Resource Book: Suggestions and Techniques, pp. 1–20; Lesson Plan, p. 48; Blackline Masters, pp. 75–128; Activity Book Answer Key
Teacher Resource CD-ROM

Assessment Program: Unit 2, Chapter 2 Quiz, pp. 59–61; Resources, Checklists, Rubrics, pp. 183–207
Assessment CD-ROM: Unit 2, Chapter 2 Quiz
Transparencies 52, 56, 58, 59, 66, 67
The Heinle Basic Newbury House Dictionary/CD-ROM
Web site: http://elt.thomson.com/visions

➤ See the Teacher's Edition wrap-around for complete teaching suggestions for each section.

Period 1

- **Unit 2, Chapter 1 Quiz** (Assessment Program, pp. 56–58) 25 MIN.
- **Use Prior Knowledge** (p. 128) 10 MIN.
  Activate prior knowledge by talking about words for family members.
- **Build Vocabulary** (p. 129) 10 MIN.
  Introduce words for family members.
- **Homework:** Activity Book (p. 96)

Period 2

- **Check Homework** 5 MIN.
  OR
- **Warm Up** 5 MIN.
  Write on the board: *Complete these sentences. 1) Your mother's sister is your _____. 2) Your father's father is your _____. 3) Your uncle's daughter is your _____.*
- **Text Structure** (p. 129) 10 MIN.
  Present the text features of poems (rhyme, stanzas, descriptive language).
- **Reading Strategy** (p. 130) 5 MIN.
  Teach the strategy of identifying main idea and details.
- **Reading Selection** (pp. 130–131) 25 MIN.
  Complete the pre-reading questions. Have students read the selection and use the reading strategy.
- **Homework:** Activity Book (p. 97)

Period 3

- **Check Homework** 5 MIN.
  OR
- **Warm Up** 5 MIN.
  Write on the board: *What is a main idea? What are details?*

- **Listen, Speak, Interact** (p. 131) 5 MIN.
  Have students talk about the poems on pp. 130–131.
- **Reading Comprehension** (p. 132) 10 MIN.
  Have students answer the questions.
- **Elements of Literature** (p. 132) 5 MIN.
  Present rhyme and free verse in poems.
- **Build Reading Fluency** (p. 133) 10 MIN.
  Teach how to build reading fluency by reading aloud with intonation and expression.
- **Spelling** (p. 133) 10 MIN.
  Introduce the spelling of more regular plurals and complete the activities.
- **Homework:** Activity Book (pp. 98–99)

Period 4

- **Check Homework** 5 MIN.
  OR
- **Warm Up** 5 MIN.
  Write on the board: *Which words rhyme? 1) son 2) man 3) dog 4) win 5) log 6) fun 7) tan*
- **Writing** (pp. 134–135) 35 MIN.
  Teach students how to write a poem using the model provided.
- **Review** (p. 135) 5 MIN.
  Review the chapter contents.
- **Homework:** Activity Book (pp. 100–101); Have students study for the Unit 2, Chapter 2 Quiz.

Class _____ Date _____

UNIT 2 Families

CHAPTER 3 • Classifying Animals

Chapter Materials
Activity Book: pp. 102–107
Audio: Unit 2, Chapter 3
Student Handbook
Teacher Resource Book: Suggestions and Techniques, pp. 1–20; Lesson Plan, p. 49; Blackline Masters, pp. 75–128; Activity Book Answer Key
Teacher Resource CD-ROM

Assessment Program: Unit 2, Chapter 3 Quiz, pp. 62–64; Resources, Checklists, Rubrics, pp. 183–207
Assessment CD-ROM: Unit 2, Chapter 3 Quiz
Transparencies 52, 56, 58, 65, 66, 67
The Heinle Basic Newbury House Dictionary/CD-ROM
Web site: http://elt.thomson.com/visions

➤ See the Teacher's Edition wrap-around for complete teaching suggestions for each section.

Period 1

- **Unit 2, Chapter 2 Quiz** (Assessment Program, pp. 59–61) 25 MIN.
- **Use Prior Knowledge** (p. 136) 10 MIN.
  Activate prior knowledge by talking about animals.
- **Build Vocabulary** (p. 137) 10 MIN.
  Introduce words for animals and complete the activities.
- **Homework:** Activity Book (p. 102)

Period 2

- **Check Homework** 5 MIN.
  OR
- **Warm Up** 5 MIN.
  Write on the board: *What animals have feathers? What animals have fur? What animals have scales?*
- **Text Structure** (p. 137) 10 MIN.
  Present the text features of a science textbook (headings, facts, graphics with captions, key words).
- **Reading Strategy** (p. 138) 5 MIN.
  Teach the strategy of identifying main idea and details.
- **Reading Selection** (pp. 138–139) 25 MIN.
  Complete the pre-reading questions. Have students read the selection and use the reading strategy.
- **Homework:** Activity Book (p. 103)

Period 3

- **Check Homework** 5 MIN.
  OR
- **Warm Up** 5 MIN.
  Write on the board: *Name three categories used to classify animals.*
- **Listen, Speak, Interact** (p. 139) 5 MIN.
  Have students talk about fish, mammals, birds, and reptiles.
- **Reading Comprehension** (p. 140) 10 MIN.
  Have students answer the questions.
- **Elements of Text** (p. 140) 5 MIN.
  Teach how to read a bar graph.
- **Build Reading Fluency** (p. 141) 10 MIN.
  Teach how to build reading fluency by scanning to locate information.
- **Spelling** (p. 141) 10 MIN.
  Introduce the spelling of regular and irregular plurals and complete the activities.
- **Homework:** Activity Book (pp. 104–105)

Period 4

- **Check Homework** 5 MIN.
  OR
- **Warm Up** 5 MIN.
  Write on the board: *Correct the errors in these words: 1) mouses 2) fishes 3) boies*
- **Writing** (pp. 142–143) 35 MIN.
  Introduce the writing strategy of choosing a main idea and teach students how to write a descriptive paragraph.
- **Review** (p. 143) 5 MIN.
  Review the chapter contents.
- **Homework:** Activity Book (pp. 106–107); Have students study for the Unit 2, Chapter 3 Quiz.

Class _____ Date _____

UNIT 2 Families

APPLY AND EXPAND

End-of-Unit Materials

Student Handbook
Student CD-ROM, Unit 2
Teacher Resource Book: Suggestions and Techniques, pp. 1–20; Lesson Plan, p. 50; Blackline Masters, pp. 75–128; School-Home Connection Newsletter, pp. 164–170
Teacher Resource CD-ROM
Assessment Program: Unit 2 Test, pp. 65–70; Resources, Checklists, Rubrics, pp. 183–207

Assessment CD-ROM: Unit 2 Test
Transparencies 52, 55, 56, 57, 65, 67
The Heinle Basic Newbury House Dictionary/CD-ROM
Heinle Reading Library Mini-Reader Collection: *Here is My Family*
Web site: http://elt.thomson.com/visions

➤ See the Teacher's Edition wrap-around for complete teaching suggestions for each section.

Period 1

- **Unit 2, Chapter 3 Quiz** (Assessment Program, pp. 62–64) 25 MIN.
- **Listening and Speaking Workshop** (pp. 144) 20 MIN. Introduce the assignment of giving a descriptive presentation. Have students brainstorm, take notes, prepare graphic aids, plan, and practice their presentations (steps 1–5).
- **Homework:** Have students review their presentations so that they will be familiar with them for Period 2.

Period 2

- **Listening and Speaking Workshop** (p. 145) 20 MIN. Have students present and evaluate their descriptive presentations (steps 6–7).
- **Viewing Workshop** (p. 145) 25 MIN. Introduce the assignment of comparing and contrasting two families.
- **Homework:** Have students finish the Viewing Workshop assignment.

Period 3

- **Writer's Workshop** (pp. 146–147) 45 MIN. Present the writing assignment of writing a descriptive paragraph. Have students brainstorm, draft, and edit their paragraphs.

- **Homework:** Have students revise and prepare the final version of their descriptive paragraphs.

Period 4

- **Projects** (pp. 148–149) 45 MIN. Introduce the assignments of making animal classification posters, rhyme cards, and/or group writing.
- **Homework:** Have students study for the Unit 2 Test.

Period 5

- **Unit 2 Test** (Assessment Program, pp. 65–70) 45 MIN. After the Unit 2 Test, reassess student learning. Record strong and weak areas based on the unit test. Review weak areas before the Mid-Book Exam.

Class _____ Date _____

UNIT 3 After School

CHAPTER 1 • After-School Activities

Chapter Materials

Activity Book: pp. 108–115
Audio: Unit 3, Chapter 1
Student Handbook
Teacher Resource Book: Suggestions and Techniques, pp. 1–20; Lesson Plan, p. 51; Blackline Masters, pp. 75–128; Activity Book Answer Key
Teacher Resource CD-ROM

Assessment Program: Unit 3, Chapter 1 Quiz, pp. 71–73; Resources, Checklists, Rubrics, pp. 183–207
Assessment CD-ROM: Unit 3, Chapter 1 Quiz
Transparencies 9, 17, 18, 52, 53, 58, 60, 66, 68, 69, 70, 71
The Heinle Basic Newbury House Dictionary/CD-ROM
Web site: http://elt.thomson.com/visions

➤ See the Teacher's Edition wrap-around for complete teaching suggestions for each section.

Period 1

- **Unit Opener** (pp. 150–151) 10 MIN.
  Preview the unit contents. Complete the "View the Picture" activity using Transparency 68.
- **Chapter Opener** (p. 152) 10 MIN.
  Preview the chapter contents. Introduce the chapter vocabulary using Transparency 69.
- **Listen, Speak, Interact** (p. 153) 25 MIN.
  Have students talk about their after-school activities.
- **Homework:** Have students review the new vocabulary by writing sentences with the new vocabulary words.

Period 2

- **Check Homework** 5 MIN.
  OR
- **Warm Up** 5 MIN.
  Write on the board: *What are three things you do after school?*
- **Build Vocabulary** (pp. 154–155) 20 MIN.
  Introduce words for after-school activities and telling time.
- **Grammar Focus** (p. 156) 20 MIN.
  Present the simple past tense of regular and irregular verbs and complete the activities.
- **Homework:** Activity Book (pp. 108–109)

Period 3

- **Check Homework** 5 MIN.
  OR
- **Warm Up** 5 MIN.
  Write on the board: *What is the simple past tense of these verbs? 1) play 2) write 3) study 4) read 5) learn*
- **Grammar Focus** (p. 157) 20 MIN.
  Present negatives of regular and irregular verbs (including *be*) in the simple past and complete the activities.
- **Word Study** (p. 158) 10 MIN.
  Teach students how to recognize long vowel sounds (**ee, ea**) (Transparency 70).
- **Spelling** (p. 159) 10 MIN.
  Introduce spelling the simple past of verbs ending in consonant + **y**.
- **Homework:** Activity Book (pp. 110–113)

Period 4

- **Check Homework** 5 MIN.
  OR
- **Warm Up** 5 MIN.
  Write on the board: *Correct the spelling of these verbs: 1) hurryed 2) carryed 3) dryed*
- **Writing** (p. 159) 20 MIN.
  Teach students how to write a friendly letter.
- **Project** (p. 160) 15 MIN.
  Have students prepare and display their activity collages.
- **Review** (p. 161) 5 MIN.
  Review the chapter contents.
- **Homework:** Activity Book (pp. 114–115); Have students study for the Unit 3, Chapter 1 Quiz.

Class _____   Date _____

UNIT 3 After School

CHAPTER 2 • Tomás Cleans the Car, a narrative by Tom Friedman

Chapter Materials

Activity Book: pp. 116–121
Audio: Unit 3, Chapter 2
Student Handbook
Teacher Resource Book: Suggestions and Techniques, pp. 1–20; Lesson Plan, p. 52; Blackline Masters, pp. 75–128; Activity Book Answer Key
Teacher Resource CD-ROM

Assessment Program: Unit 3, Chapter 2 Quiz, pp. 74–76; Resources, Checklists, Rubrics, pp. 183–207
Assessment CD-ROM: Unit 3, Chapter 2 Quiz
Transparencies 52, 56, 58, 59, 72, 73, 74, 75
The Heinle Basic Newbury House Dictionary/CD-ROM
Web site: http://elt.thomson.com/visions

➤ See the Teacher's Edition wrap-around for complete teaching suggestions for each section.

Period 1
- **Unit 3, Chapter 1 Quiz** (Assessment Program, pp. 71–73) 25 MIN.
- **Use Prior Knowledge** (p. 162) 10 MIN.
  Activate prior knowledge by talking about after-school jobs.
- **Build Vocabulary** (p. 163) 10 MIN.
  Introduce synonyms and new vocabulary.
- **Homework:** Activity Book (p. 116)

Period 2
- **Check Homework** 5 MIN.
  OR
- **Warm Up** 5 MIN.
  Write on the board: *Name synonyms for 1) big 2) small 3) pretty.*
- **Text Structure** (p. 163) 10 MIN.
  Present the text features of narratives (characters, setting, plot).
- **Reading Strategy** (p. 164) 5 MIN.
  Teach the strategy of identifying sequence.
- **Reading Selection** (pp. 164–165) 25 MIN.
  Complete the pre-reading questions. Have students read the selection and use the reading strategy.
- **Homework:** Activity Book (p. 117)

Period 3
- **Check Homework** 5 MIN.
  OR
- **Warm Up** 5 MIN.
  Write on the board: *Who cleaned Tomás's mother's car?*
- **Listen, Speak, Interact** (p. 166) 5 MIN.
  Have students perform a role-play of the story "Tomás Cleans the Car."
- **Reading Comprehension** (p. 166) 10 MIN.
  Have students answer the questions.
- **Elements of Literature** (p. 166) 5 MIN.
  Teach how to identify and retell the plot.
- **Build Reading Fluency** (p. 167) 10 MIN.
  Teach how to build reading fluency using rapid word recognition for compound words and contractions.
- **Punctuation** (p. 167) 10 MIN.
  Introduce quotation marks and commas and complete the activities.
- **Homework:** Activity Book (pp. 118–119)

Period 4
- **Check Homework** 5 MIN.
  OR
- **Warm Up** 5 MIN.
  Write on the board: *When do you use quotation marks? Where do you use commas?*
- **Writing** (pp. 168–169) 35 MIN.
  Introduce the writing strategy of using sequence to organize writing. Teach students how to write a narrative.
- **Review** (p. 169) 5 MIN.
  Review the chapter contents.
- **Homework:** Activity Book (pp. 120–121); Have students study for the Unit 3, Chapter 2 Quiz.

Class _____   Date _____

UNIT 3 After School

CHAPTER 3 • The First Amendment

Chapter Materials

Activity Book: pp. 122–127
Audio: Unit 3, Chapter 3
Student Handbook
Teacher Resource Book: Suggestions and Techniques, pp. 1–20; Lesson Plan, p. 53; Blackline Masters, pp. 75–128; Activity Book Answer Key
Teacher Resource CD-ROM

Assessment Program: Unit 3, Chapter 3 Quiz, pp. 77–79; Resources, Checklists, Rubrics, pp. 183–207
Assessment CD-ROM: Unit 3, Chapter 3 Quiz
Transparencies 52, 55, 56, 58, 65, 66
The Heinle Basic Newbury House Dictionary/CD-ROM
Web site: http://elt.thomson.com/visions

➤ See the Teacher's Edition wrap-around for complete teaching suggestions for each section.

Period 1

- **Unit 3, Chapter 2 Quiz** (Assessment Program, pp. 74–76) 25 MIN.
- **Use Prior Knowledge** (p. 170) 10 MIN.
  Activate prior knowledge by talking about reasons people come to the United States.
- **Build Vocabulary** (p. 171) 10 MIN.
  Teach students how to use a dictionary to find definitions.
- **Homework:** Activity Book (p. 122)

Period 2

- **Check Homework** 5 MIN.
  OR
- **Warm Up** 5 MIN.
  Write on the board: *Correct the errors in these sentences: 1) I jog home yesterday after school. 2) She plaied the guitar and her friend singed. 3) He writed a letter to his grandmother.*
- **Text Structure** (p. 171) 10 MIN.
  Present the text features of expository text (title, headings, index, glossary).
- **Reading Strategy** (p. 172) 5 MIN.
  Teach the strategy of summarizing.
- **Reading Selection** (pp. 172–173) 25 MIN.
  Complete the pre-reading questions. Have students read the selection and use the reading strategy.
- **Homework:** Activity Book (p. 123)

Period 3

- **Check Homework** 5 MIN.
  OR
- **Warm Up** 5 MIN.
  Write on the board: *Name two reasons people come to the United States.*
- **Listen, Speak, Interact** (p. 173) 5 MIN.
  Have students talk about which freedoms are important to them.
- **Reading Comprehension** (p. 174) 10 MIN.
  Have students answer the questions.
- **Elements of Text** (p. 174) 5 MIN.
  Teach how to use an index to find information.
- **Build Reading Fluency** (p. 175) 10 MIN.
  Teach how to build reading fluency by reading along with an audio recording.
- **Punctuation** (p. 175) 10 MIN.
  Introduce the use of commas in a series and complete the activities.
- **Homework:** Activity Book (pp. 124–125)

Period 4

- **Check Homework** 5 MIN.
  OR
- **Warm Up** 5 MIN.
  Write on the board: *Correct the errors in these sentences: 1) Yesterday after school I did my homework cleaned my room and watched TV. 2) The First Amendment guarantees Freedom of Religion Freedom of Speech Freedom of Press and Freedom of Assembly.*
- **Writing** (pp. 176–177) 35 MIN.
  Introduce the writing strategy of using a topic sentence and supporting details. Teach students how to write an expository paragraph.
- **Review** (p. 177) 5 MIN.
  Review the chapter contents.
- **Homework:** Activity Book (pp. 126–127); Have students study for the Unit 3, Chapter 3 Quiz.

Class _____ Date _____

UNIT 3 After School

APPLY AND EXPAND

End-of-Unit Materials

Student Handbook
Student CD-ROM, Unit 3
Teacher Resource Book: Suggestions and Techniques, pp. 1–20; Lesson Plan, p. 54; Blackline Masters, pp. 75–128; School-Home Connection Newsletter, pp. 171–177
Teacher Resource CD-ROM
Assessment Program: Unit 3 Test, pp. 80–85; Resources, Checklists, Rubrics, pp. 183–207

Assessment CD-ROM: Unit 3 Test
Transparencies 52, 56, 73, 74, 75, 76
The Heinle Basic Newbury House Dictionary/CD-ROM
Heinle Reading Library Mini-Reader Collection: *After School Work*
Web site: http://elt.thomson.com/visions

➤ See the Teacher's Edition wrap-around for complete teaching suggestions for each section.

Period 1

- **Unit 3, Chapter 3 Quiz** (Assessment Program, pp. 77–79) 25 MIN.
- **Listening and Speaking Workshop** (p. 178) 20 MIN.
  Introduce the assignment of presenting your favorite activities. Have students brainstorm, organize, make posters, plan, and practice their presentations (steps 1–5).
- **Homework:** Have students review their presentations so that they will be familiar with them for Period 2.

Period 2

- **Listening and Speaking Workshop** (pp. 179) 20 MIN.
  Have students present and evaluate their favorite activities (steps 6–7).
- **Viewing Workshop** (p. 179) 25 MIN.
  Introduce the assignment of identifying after-school activities in the community.
- **Homework:** Have students complete the Viewing Workshop assignment.

Period 3

- **Writer's Workshop** (pp. 180–181) 45 MIN.
  Present the writing assignment of writing a narrative. Have students brainstorm, draft, and edit their narratives.
- **Homework:** Have students revise and prepare the final version of their narratives.

Period 4

- **Projects** (pp. 182–183) 45 MIN.
  Introduce the assignments of making freedom posters, role-playing stories about a first amendment freedom, and/or group writing.
- **Homework:** Have students study for the Unit 3 Test.

Period 5

- **Unit 3 Test** (Assessment Program, pp. 80–85) 45 MIN.
  After the Unit 3 Test, reassess student learning. Record strong and weak areas based on the unit test. Review weak areas before the Mid-Book Exam.

Class _____ Date _____

UNIT 4 Home

CHAPTER 1 • A House or an Apartment

Chapter Materials

Activity Book: pp. 128–135
Audio: Unit 4, Chapter 1
Student Handbook
Teacher Resource Book: Suggestions and Techniques, pp. 1–20; Lesson Plan, p. 55; Blackline Masters, pp. 75–128; Activity Book Answer Key
Teacher Resource CD-ROM

Assessment Program: Unit 4, Chapter 1 Quiz, pp. 86–88; Resources, Checklists, Rubrics, pp. 183–207
Assessment CD-ROM: Unit 4, Chapter 1 Quiz
Transparencies 9, 17, 18, 52, 58, 65, 77, 78, 79
The Heinle Basic Newbury House Dictionary/CD-ROM
Web site: http://elt.thomson.com/visions

▶ See the Teacher's Edition wrap-around for complete teaching suggestions for each section.

Period 1

- **Unit Opener** (pp. 184–185) 10 MIN.
  Preview the unit contents. Complete the "View the Picture" activity using Transparency 77.
- **Chapter Opener** (p. 186) 10 MIN.
  Preview the chapter contents. Introduce the chapter vocabulary using Transparency 78.
- **Listen, Speak, Interact** (p. 187) 25 MIN.
  Have students talk about where they live.
- **Homework:** Have students review the new vocabulary words by writing sentences in their notebooks that contain these words.

Period 2

- **Check Homework** 5 MIN.
  OR
- **Warm Up** 5 MIN.
  Write on the board: *What is your favorite room in your house?*
- **Build Vocabulary** (pp. 188–189) 20 MIN.
  Introduce words for rooms and furniture. Introduce *there is/there are*.
- **Grammar Focus** (p. 190) 20 MIN.
  Present yes/no questions and short answers with *be* in the simple present and simple past.
- **Homework:** Activity Book (pp. 128–129)

Period 3

- **Check Homework** 5 MIN.
  OR
- **Warm Up** 5 MIN.
  Write on the board: *Correct the errors in these sentences: 1) There is three bedrooms in my house. 2) There are one kitchen in my apartment.*

- **Grammar Focus** (p. 191) 20 MIN.
  Present yes/no questions and short answers with verbs other than *be* in the simple present and simple past.
- **Word Study** (p. 192) 10 MIN.
  Present compound words and complete the activities (Transparency 79).
- **Punctuation** (p. 193) 10 MIN.
  Introduce possessives with apostrophes and complete the activities.
- **Homework:** Activity Book (pp. 130–133)

Period 4

- **Check Homework** 5 MIN.
  OR
- **Warm Up** 5 MIN.
  Write on the board: *Complete these sentences: 1) I watch TV in _____. 2) We cook in _____. 3) I sleep in _____.*
- **Writing** (p. 193) 20 MIN.
  Teach students how to write a descriptive paragraph.
- **Project** (p. 194) 15 MIN.
  Introduce the assignment of making a favorite room poster. Have students prepare and present their posters.
- **Review** (p. 195) 5 MIN.
  Review the chapter contents.
- **Homework:** Activity Book (pp. 134–135); Have students study for the Unit 4, Chapter 1 Quiz.

Class _____ Date _____

UNIT 4 Home

CHAPTER 2 • A House of My Own, a personal narrative by Sandra Cisneros

Chapter Materials

Activity Book: pp. 136–141
Audio: Unit 4, Chapter 2
Student Handbook
Teacher Resource Book: Suggestions and Techniques, pp. 1–20; Lesson Plan, p. 56; Blackline Masters, pp. 75–128; Activity Book Answer Key
Teacher Resource CD-ROM

Assessment Program: Unit 4, Chapter 2 Quiz, pp. 89–91; Resources, Checklists, Rubrics, pp. 183–207
Assessment CD-ROM: Unit 4, Chapter 2 Quiz
Transparencies 17, 52, 56, 58, 65, 67, 71
The Heinle Basic Newbury House Dictionary/CD-ROM
Web site: http://elt.thomson.com/visions

➤ See the Teacher's Edition wrap-around for complete teaching suggestions for each section.

Period 1

- **Unit 4, Chapter 1 Quiz** (Assessment Program, pp. 86–88) 25 MIN.
- **Use Prior Knowledge** (p. 196) 10 MIN.
  Activate prior knowledge about sensory details.
- **Build Vocabulary** (p. 197) 10 MIN.
  Introduce multiple-meaning words.
- **Homework:** Activity Book (p. 136)

Period 2

- **Check Homework** 5 MIN.
  OR
- **Warm Up** 5 MIN.
  Write on the board: *What are two meanings of the word flat?*
- **Text Structure** (p. 197) 10 MIN.
  Present the text features of a personal narrative (experiences, personal details, first-person pronouns).
- **Reading Strategy** (p. 198) 5 MIN.
  Teach the strategy of making predictions.
- **Reading Selection** (pp. 198–199) 25 MIN.
  Complete the pre-reading questions. Have students read the selection and use the reading strategy.
- **Homework:** Activity Book (p. 137)

Period 3

- **Check Homework** 5 MIN.
  OR
- **Warm Up** 5 MIN.
  Write on the board: *What kind of home do you live in?*
- **Listen, Speak, Interact** (p. 199) 5 MIN.
  Have students talk about their predictions about "A House of My Own."
- **Reading Comprehension** (p. 200) 10 MIN.
  Have students answer the questions.
- **Elements of Literature** (p. 200) 5 MIN.
  Present similes and complete the activity.
- **Build Reading Fluency** (p. 201) 10 MIN.
  Introduce how to build reading fluency by reading key phrases.
- **Spelling** (p. 201) 10 MIN.
  Introduce homophones and complete the activity.
- **Homework:** Activity Book (pp. 138–139)

Period 4

- **Check Homework** 5 MIN.
  OR
- **Warm Up** 5 MIN.
  Write on the board: *Name two homophones we learned.*
- **Writing** (pp. 202–203) 35 MIN.
  Introduce the writing strategy of using descriptive words and sensory details. Teach students how to write a personal narrative.
- **Review** (p. 203) 5 MIN.
  Review the chapter contents.
- **Homework:** Activity Book (pp. 140–141); Have students study for the Unit 4, Chapter 2 Quiz.

Class _____ Date _____

UNIT 4 Home

CHAPTER 3 • Perimeter and Area

Chapter Materials
Activity Book: pp. 142–147
Audio: Unit 4, Chapter 3
Student Handbook
Teacher Resource Book: Suggestions and Techniques, pp. 1–20; Lesson Plan, p. 57; Blackline Masters, pp. 75–128; Activity Book Answer Key
Teacher Resource CD-ROM

Assessment Program: Unit 4, Chapter 3 Quiz, pp. 92–94; Resources, Checklists, Rubrics, pp. 183–207
Assessment CD-ROM: Unit 4, Chapter 3 Quiz
Transparencies 52, 56, 58, 96
The Heinle Basic Newbury House Dictionary/CD-ROM
Web site: http://elt.thomson.com/visions

➤ See the Teacher's Edition wrap-around for complete teaching suggestions for each section.

Period 1

- **Unit 4, Chapter 2 Quiz** (Assessment Program, pp. 89–91) 25 MIN.
- **Use Prior Knowledge** (p. 204) 10 MIN.
  Activate prior knowledge by talking about taking measurements.
- **Build Vocabulary** (p. 205) 10 MIN.
  Introduce math terms and complete the activity.
- **Homework:** Activity Book (p. 142)

Period 2

- **Check Homework** 5 MIN.
  OR
- **Warm Up** 5 MIN.
  Write on the board: *Name two measures used in the United States.*
- **Text Structure** (p. 205) 10 MIN.
  Present the text features of math word problems (diagrams, key words, data).
- **Reading Strategy** (p. 206) 5 MIN.
  Teach the strategy of stating the purpose in reading.
- **Reading Selection** (pp. 206–207) 25 MIN.
  Complete the pre-reading questions. Have students read the selection and use the reading strategy.
- **Homework:** Activity Book (p. 143)

Period 3

- **Check Homework** 5 MIN.
  OR
- **Warm Up** 5 MIN.
  Write on the board: *How do you find the perimeter of a room? How do you find the area of a room?*
- **Listen, Speak, Interact** (p. 207) 5 MIN.
  Have students talk about solving math word problems.
- **Reading Comprehension** (p. 208) 10 MIN.
  Have students answer the questions.
- **Elements of Text** (p. 208) 5 MIN.
  Teach the types of graphic aids.
- **Build Reading Fluency** (p. 209) 10 MIN.
  Introduce how to build reading fluency by scanning to locate information.
- **Spelling and Punctuation** (p. 209) 10 MIN.
  Introduce abbreviations for measurement and complete the activity.
- **Homework:** Activity Book (pp. 144–145)

Period 4

- **Check Homework** 5 MIN.
  OR
- **Warm Up** 5 MIN.
  Write on the board: *What are the abbreviations for 1) inch 2) foot 3) yard?*
- **Writing** (pp. 210–211) 35 MIN.
  Introduce the writing strategy of selecting a focus. Teach students how to write a math word problem.
- **Review** (p. 211) 5 MIN.
  Review the chapter contents.
- **Homework:** Activity Book (pp. 146–147); Have students study for the Unit 4, Chapter 3 Quiz.

Class _____ Date _____

UNIT 4 Home

APPLY AND EXPAND

End-of-Unit Materials

Student Handbook
Student CD-ROM, Unit 4
Teacher Resource Book: Suggestions and Techniques, pp. 1–20; Lesson Plan, p. 58; Blackline Masters, pp. 75–128; School-Home Connection Newsletter, pp. 178–184
Teacher Resource CD-ROM
Assessment Program: Unit 4 Test, pp. 95–100; Mid-Book Exam, pp. 101–108; Resources, Checklists, Rubrics, pp. 183–207

Assessment CD-ROM: Unit 4 Test
Transparencies 52, 56, 57, 73, 75
The Heinle Basic Newbury House Dictionary/CD-ROM
Heinle Reading Library Mini-Reader Collection:
Teenagers in the Morning
Web site: http://elt.thomson.com/visions

➤ See the Teacher's Edition wrap-around for complete teaching suggestions for each section.

Period 1

- **Unit 4, Chapter 3 Quiz** (Assessment Program, pp. 92–94) 25 MIN.
- **Listening and Speaking Workshop** (p. 212) 20 MIN.
  Introduce the assignment of responding to your favorite reading. Have students choose their favorite readings and practice explaining why they chose the readings (steps 1–3).
- **Homework:** Have students review their presentations so that they will be familiar with them for Period 2.

Period 2

- **Listening and Speaking Workshop** (p. 213) 20 MIN.
  Have students present and evaluate their literary responses (steps 4–5).
- **Viewing Workshop** (p. 213) 25 MIN.
  Introduce the assignment of comparing and contrasting houses.
- **Homework:** Have students complete the Viewing Workshop assignment.

Period 3

- **Writer's Workshop** (pp. 214–215) 45 MIN.
  Present the writing assignment of writing a personal narrative. Have students brainstorm, draft, and edit their personal narratives.
- **Homework:** Have students revise and prepare the final version of their personal narratives.

Period 4

- **Projects** (pp. 216–217) 45 MIN.
  Introduce the assignments of preparing a plan to fix up a room, making a compound word wallchart, and/or group writing.
- **Homework:** Have students study for the Unit 4 Test.

Period 5

- **Unit 4 Test** (Assessment Program, pp. 95–100) 45 MIN.
  After the Unit 4 Test, reassess student learning. Record strong and weak areas based on the unit test. Review weak areas before the Mid-Book Exam.
- **Homework:** Have students study for the Mid-Book Exam.

Period 6

- **Mid-Book Exam** (Assessment Program, pp. 101–108) 45 MIN.

Class _____ Date _____

UNIT 5 The Community

CHAPTER 1 • Places in the Community

Chapter Materials

Activity Book: pp. 148–155
Audio: Unit 5, Chapter 1
Student Handbook
Teacher Resource Book: Suggestions and Techniques, pp. 1–20; Lesson Plan, p. 59; Blackline Masters, pp. 75–128; Activity Book Answer Key
Teacher Resource CD-ROM

Assessment Program: Unit 5, Chapter 1 Quiz, pp. 109–111; Resources, Checklists, Rubrics, pp. 183–207
Assessment CD-ROM: Unit 5, Chapter 1 Quiz
Transparencies 9, 17, 18, 52, 58, 65, 80, 81, 82, 83
The Heinle Basic Newbury House Dictionary/CD-ROM
Web site: http://elt.thomson.com/visions

➤ See the Teacher's Edition wrap-around for complete teaching suggestions for each section.

Period 1

- **Unit Opener** (pp. 218–219) 10 MIN.
  Preview the unit contents. Complete the "View the Picture" activity using Transparency 80.
- **Chapter Opener** (p. 220) 10 MIN.
  Preview the chapter contents. Introduce the chapter vocabulary using Transparency 81.
- **Listen, Speak, Interact** (p. 221) 25 MIN.
  Have students talk about getting from place to place.
- **Homework:** Have students review the new vocabulary words by using them to create a dialogue.

Period 2

- **Check Homework** 5 MIN.
  OR
- **Warm Up** 5 MIN.
  Write on the board: *How did you get to school today?*
- **Build Vocabulary** (pp. 222–223) 20 MIN.
  Introduce multiple-meaning words for directions, signs (Transparency 82), and prepositions of place.
- **Grammar Focus** (p. 224) 20 MIN.
  Introduce the present continuous and complete the activities.
- **Homework:** Activity Book (pp. 148–149)

Period 3

- **Check Homework** 5 MIN.
  OR
- **Warm Up** 5 MIN.
  Write on the board: *Correct the errors in these sentences: 1) I is taking the bus. 2) She are riding her bike. 3) They walking home.*

- **Grammar Focus** (p. 225) 20 MIN.
  Teach imperatives and complete the activities.
- **Word Study** (p. 226) 10 MIN.
  Teach students how to pronounce digraphs and complete the activities (Transparency 83).
- **Capitalization** (p. 227) 10 MIN.
  Introduce capital letters for places and geographical names and complete the activities.
- **Homework:** Activity Book (pp. 150–153)

Period 4

- **Check Homework** 5 MIN.
  OR
- **Warm Up** 5 MIN.
  Write on the board: *Correct the errors in these sentences: 1) I live on washington street. 2) Many people come to california for vacation. 3) The atlantic ocean has many beautiful beaches.*
- **Writing** (p. 227) 20 MIN.
  Teach students how to write a descriptive narrative.
- **Project** (p. 228) 15 MIN.
  Introduce the assignment of making a brochure for your bus line.
- **Review** (p. 229) 5 MIN.
  Review the chapter contents.
- **Homework:** Activity Book (pp. 154–155); Have students study for the Unit 5, Chapter 1 Quiz.

Class _____   Date _____

UNIT 5 The Community

CHAPTER 2 • *East City Community News*

Chapter Materials

Activity Book: pp. 156–161
Audio: Unit 5, Chapter 2
Student Handbook
Teacher Resource Book: Suggestions and Techniques, pp. 1–20; Lesson Plan, p. 60; Blackline Masters, pp. 75–128; Activity Book Answer Key
Teacher Resource CD-ROM

Assessment Program: Unit 5, Chapter 2 Quiz, pp. 112–114; Resources, Checklists, Rubrics, pp. 183–207
Assessment CD-ROM: Unit 5, Chapter 2 Quiz
Transparencies 52, 56, 58, 66, 76
The Heinle Basic Newbury House Dictionary/CD-ROM
Web site: http://elt.thomson.com/visions

➤ See the Teacher's Edition wrap-around for complete teaching suggestions for each section.

Period 1

- **Unit 5, Chapter 1 Quiz** (Assessment Program, pp. 109–111) 25 MIN.
- **Use Prior Knowledge** (p. 230) 10 MIN.
  Activate prior knowledge by talking about newspapers.
- **Build Vocabulary** (p. 231) 10 MIN.
  Introduce word families and complete the activity.
- **Homework:** Activity Book (p. 156)

Period 2

- **Check Homework** 5 MIN.
  OR
- **Warm Up** 5 MIN.
  Write on the board: *What are two things you find in newspapers?*
- **Text Structure** (p. 231) 10 MIN.
  Present the text features of newspaper articles and letters to the editor (title, author, kind of writing, photos).
- **Reading Strategy** (p. 232) 5 MIN.
  Teach the strategy of recognizing facts and opinions.
- **Reading Selection** (pp. 232–233) 25 MIN.
  Complete the pre-reading questions. Have students read the selection and use the reading strategy.
- **Homework:** Activity Book (p. 157)

Period 3

- **Check Homework** 5 MIN.
  OR
- **Warm Up** (reading) 5 MIN.
  Write on the board: *True or False? A newspaper article contains opinions.*
- **Listen, Speak, Interact** (p. 233) 5 MIN.
  Have students talk about facts and opinions in the reading selections.
- **Reading Comprehension** (p. 234) 10 MIN.
  Have students answer the questions.
- **Elements of Text** (p. 234) 5 MIN.
  Present *wh* questions and complete the activity.
- **Build Reading Fluency** (p. 235) 10 MIN.
  Introduce how to build reading fluency by locating information in headings.
- **Spelling** (p. 235) 10 MIN.
  Introduce irregular sight words (*who, what, why, was, were, says, said*).
- **Homework:** Activity Book (pp. 158–159)

Period 4

- **Check Homework** 5 MIN.
  OR
- **Warm Up** 5 MIN.
  Write on the board: *Read these words aloud:* 1) who 2) why 3) were 4) says 5) said
- **Writing** (pp. 236–237) 35 MIN.
  Introduce the writing strategy of selecting a focus. Teach students how to write a letter to the editor.
- **Review** (p. 237) 5 MIN.
  Review the chapter contents.
- **Homework:** Activity Book (pp. 160–161); Have students study for the Unit 5, Chapter 2 Quiz.

Class _____ Date _____

UNIT 5 The Community

CHAPTER 3 • Resources in the United States

Chapter Materials

Activity Book: pp. 162–167
Audio: Unit 5, Chapter 3
Student Handbook
Teacher Resource Book: Suggestions and Techniques, pp. 1–20; Lesson Plan, p. 61; Blackline Masters, pp. 75–128; Activity Book Answer Key
Teacher Resource CD-ROM

Assessment Program: Unit 5, Chapter 3 Quiz, pp. 115–117; Resources, Checklists, Rubrics, pp. 183–207
Assessment CD-ROM: Unit 5, Chapter 3 Quiz
Transparency 52, 56, 57, 58, 84
The Heinle Basic Newbury House Dictionary/CD-ROM
Web site: http://elt.thomson.com/visions

➤ See the Teacher's Edition wrap-around for complete teaching suggestions for each section.

Period 1

- **Unit 5, Chapter 2 Quiz** (Assessment Program, pp. 112–114) 25 MIN.
- **Use Prior Knowledge** (p. 238) 10 MIN.
  Activate prior knowledge by talking about maps.
- **Build Vocabulary** (p. 239) 10 MIN.
  Introduce words and symbols for resources.
- **Homework:** Activity Book (p. 162)

Period 2

- **Check Homework** 5 MIN.
  OR
- **Warm Up** 5 MIN.
  Write on the board: *Correct the errors in these sentences: 1) We is go to the post office to send a letter. 2) She are go to the library to get a new book. 3) He am go to the movie theater with his friend.*
- **Text Structure** (p. 239) 10 MIN.
  Present the text features of a social studies textbook (headings, graphics, keys).
- **Reading Strategy** (p. 240) 5 MIN.
  Teach the strategy of restating facts and details.
- **Reading Selection** (pp. 240–241) 25 MIN.
  Complete the pre-reading questions. Have students read the selection and use the reading strategy.
- **Homework:** Activity Book (p. 163)

Period 3

- **Check Homework** 5 MIN.
  OR
- **Warm Up** 5 MIN.
  Write on the board: *Name two resources from our state.*
- **Listen, Speak, Interact** (p. 241) 5 MIN.
  Have students talk about resources in the United States.
- **Reading Comprehension** (p. 242) 10 MIN.
  Have students answer the questions.
- **Elements of Text** (p. 242) 5 MIN.
  Teach how to use headings to find information.
- **Build Reading Fluency** (p. 243) 10 MIN.
  Teach how to build reading fluency by silent reading.
- **Capitalization and Punctuation** (p. 243) 10 MIN.
  Introduce capitalization and punctuation in titles of newspapers, books, and articles.
- **Homework:** Activity Book (pp. 164–165)

Period 4

- **Check Homework** 5 MIN.
  OR
- **Warm Up** 5 MIN.
  Write on the board: *True or False? The headings in your textbooks tell you what information is in the section.*
- **Writing** (pp. 244–245) 35 MIN.
  Introduce the writing strategy of developing a newspaper article by including facts and details to support the topic sentence. Teach students how to write a newspaper article.
- **Review** (p. 245) 5 MIN.
  Review the chapter contents.
- **Homework:** Activity Book (pp. 166–167); Have students study for the Unit 5, Chapter 3 Quiz.

Class _____   Date _____

UNIT 5 The Community

APPLY AND EXPAND

End-of-Unit Materials

Student Handbook
Student CD-ROM, Unit 5
Teacher Resource Book: Suggestions and Techniques, pp. 1–20; Lesson Plan, p. 62; Blackline Masters, pp. 75–128; School-Home Connection Newsletter, pp. 185–191
Teacher Resource CD-ROM
Assessment Program: Unit 5 Test, pp. 118–123; Resources, Checklists, Rubrics, pp. 183–207

Assessment CD-ROM: Unit 5 Test
Transparencies 52, 56, 71, 73, 85, 86
The Heinle Basic Newbury House Dictionary/CD-ROM
Heinle Reading Library Mini-Reader Collection:
  Saturday Afternoon
Web site: http://elt.thomson.com/visions

➤ See the Teacher's Edition wrap-around for complete teaching suggestions for each section.

Period 1

- **Unit 5, Chapter 3 Quiz** (Assessment Program, pp. 115–117) 25 MIN.
- **Listening and Speaking Workshop** (p. 246) 20 MIN. Introduce the assignment of conducting an interview. Have students brainstorm and practice their interviews (steps 1–2).
- **Homework:** Have students review their presentations so that they will be familiar with them for Period 2.

Period 2

- **Listening and Speaking Workshop** (pp. 246–247) 20 MIN. Have students present and evaluate their interviews (steps 3–4).
- **Viewing Workshop** (p. 247) 25 MIN. Introduce the assignment of comparing and contrasting features of books, dictionaries, atlases, and/or magazines.
- **Homework:** Have students complete the Viewing Workshop assignment.

Period 3

- **Writer's Workshop** (pp. 248–249) 45 MIN. Present the writing assignment of creating a class newspaper. Have students brainstorm, draft, and edit their newspaper articles.
- **Homework:** Have students revise and prepare the final version of their articles for the class newspaper.

Period 4

- **Projects** (pp. 250–251) 45 MIN. Introduce the assignments of touring a newspaper, making a community wall map, and/or group writing.
- **Homework:** Have students study for the Unit 5 Test.

Period 5

- **Unit 5 Test** (Assessment Program, pp. 118–123) 45 MIN. After the Unit 5 Test, reassess student learning. Record strong and weak areas based on the unit test. Review weak areas before the End-of-Book Exam.

Class _____ Date _____

UNIT 6 Food

CHAPTER 1 • What's on the Menu?

Chapter Materials

Activity Book: pp. 168–175
Audio: Unit 6, Chapter 1
Student Handbook
Teacher Resource Book: Suggestions and Techniques, pp. 1–20; Lesson Plan, p. 63; Blackline Masters, pp. 75–128; Activity Book Answer Key
Teacher Resource CD-ROM

Assessment Program: Unit 6, Chapter 1 Quiz, pp. 124–126; Resources, Checklists, Rubrics, pp. 183–207
Assessment CD-ROM: Unit 6, Chapter 1 Quiz
Transparencies 9, 17, 18, 52, 57, 58, 60, 66, 67, 84, 88, 96
The Heinle Basic Newbury House Dictionary/CD-ROM
Web site: http://elt.thomson.com/visions

➤ See the Teacher's Edition wrap-around for complete teaching suggestions for each section.

Period 1

- **Unit Opener** (pp. 252–253) 10 MIN.
  Preview the unit contents. Complete the "View the Picture" activity using Transparency 87.
- **Chapter Opener** (p. 254) 10 MIN.
  Preview the chapter contents. Introduce the chapter vocabulary using Transparency 88.
- **Listen, Speak, Interact** (p. 255) 25 MIN.
  Have students talk about food.
- **Homework:** Have students review the new vocabulary words by writing a paragraph about food.

Period 2

- **Check Homework** 5 MIN.
  OR
- **Warm Up** 5 MIN.
  Write on the board: *What did you eat for dinner last night?*
- **Build Vocabulary** (pp. 256–257) 20 MIN.
  Introduce words for food and food adjectives.
- **Grammar Focus** (p. 258) 20 MIN.
  Introduce count and noncount nouns and complete the activities.
- **Homework:** Activity Book (pp. 168–169)

Period 3

- **Check Homework** 5 MIN.
  OR
- **Warm Up** 5 MIN.
  Write on the board: *Write "count" or "noncount" beside each noun: 1) sandwich 2) juice 3) soup 4) peach 5) bread*

- **Grammar Focus** (p. 259) 20 MIN.
  Present the modals *would* and *should* and complete the activities.
- **Word Study** (p. 260) 10 MIN.
  Present syllabication and complete the activities.
- **Punctuation** (p. 261) 10 MIN.
  Introduce exclamation points and complete the activities.
- **Homework:** Activity Book (pp. 170–173)

Period 4

- **Check Homework** 5 MIN.
  OR
- **Warm Up** 5 MIN.
  Write on the board: *Correct the errors in these sentences: 1) I want a glass of juice. I should like a glass of fresh orange juice. 2) He doesn't like fish. He wouldn't eat the grilled salmon.*
- **Writing** (p. 261) 20 MIN.
  Teach students how to write an expository composition.
- **Project** (p. 262) 15 MIN.
  Introduce the assignment of making a class recipe book.
- **Review** (p. 263) 5 MIN.
  Review the chapter contents.
- **Homework:** Activity Book (pp. 174–175); Have students study for the Unit 6, Chapter 1 Quiz.

Class _____ Date _____

UNIT 6 Food

CHAPTER 2 • How to Eat a Poem by Eve Merriam

Chapter Materials

Activity Book: pp. 176–181
Audio: Unit 6, Chapter 2
Student Handbook
Teacher Resource Book: Suggestions and Techniques, pp. 1–20; Lesson Plan, p. 64; Blackline Masters, pp. 75–128; Activity Book Answer Key
Teacher Resource CD-ROM

Assessment Program: Unit 6, Chapter 2 Quiz, pp. 127–129; Resources, Checklists, Rubrics, pp. 183–207
Assessment CD-ROM: Unit 6, Chapter 2 Quiz
Transparencies 52, 56, 57, 58, 60, 67, 84
The Heinle Basic Newbury House Dictionary/CD-ROM
Web site: http://elt.thomson.com/visions

➤ See the Teacher's Edition wrap-around for complete teaching suggestions for each section.

Period 1

- **Unit 6, Chapter 1 Quiz** (Assessment Program, pp. 124–126) 25 MIN.
- **Use Prior Knowledge** (p. 264) 10 MIN.
  Activate prior knowledge by talking about multiple-meaning words.
- **Build Vocabulary** (p. 265) 10 MIN.
  Introduce words for setting the table.
- **Homework:** Activity Book (p. 176)

Period 2

- **Check Homework** 5 MIN.
  OR
- **Warm Up** 5 MIN.
  Write on the board: *True or False? 1) Knives are silverware. 2) A napkin is not a dish. 3) A spoon is a dish.*
- **Text Structure** (p. 265) 10 MIN.
  Present the text features of poems (sensory words, repetition, rhythm).
- **Reading Strategy** (p. 266) 5 MIN.
  Teach the strategy of understanding mental images.
- **Reading Selection** (p. 266–267) 25 MIN.
  Complete the pre-reading activities. Have students read the selection and use the reading strategy.
- **Homework:** Activity Book (p. 177)

Period 3

- **Check Homework** 5 MIN.
  OR
- **Warm Up** (reading) 5 MIN.
  Write on the board: *What are two mental images from the poem "How to Eat a Poem"?*
- **Listen, Speak, Interact** (p. 267) 5 MIN.
  Have students talk about fruit.
- **Reading Comprehension** (p. 268) 10 MIN.
  Have students answer the questions.
- **Elements of Literature** (p. 268) 5 MIN.
  Present metaphors and complete the activity.
- **Build Reading Fluency** (p. 269) 10 MIN.
  Introduce how to build reading fluency by using chunking.
- **Spelling** (p. 269) 10 MIN.
  Review spelling words with short and long vowel sounds.
- **Homework:** Activity Book (pp. 178–179)

Period 4

- **Check Homework** 5 MIN.
  OR
- **Warm Up** 5 MIN.
  Write on the board: *What are two words that have the long* a *sound and two words that have the short* u *sound?*
- **Writing** (pp. 270–271) 35 MIN.
  Introduce multiple-paragraph compositions. Teach students how to write an expository composition.
- **Review** (p. 271) 5 MIN.
  Review the chapter contents.
- **Homework:** Activity Book (pp. 180–181); Have students study for the Unit 6, Chapter 2 Quiz.

Class _____ Date _____

UNIT 6 Food

CHAPTER 3 • The Food Guide Pyramid

Chapter Materials

Activity Book: pp. 182–187
Audio: Unit 6, Chapter 3
Student Handbook
Teacher Resource Book: Suggestions and Techniques, pp. 1–20; Lesson Plan, p. 65; Blackline Masters, pp. 75–128; Activity Book Answer Key
Teacher Resource CD-ROM

Assessment Program: Unit 6, Chapter 3 Quiz, pp. 130–132; Resources, Checklists, Rubrics, pp. 183–207
Assessment CD-ROM: Unit 6, Chapter 3 Quiz
Transparencies 52, 55, 56, 58, 66, 84
The Heinle Basic Newbury House Dictionary/CD-ROM
Web site: http://elt.thomson.com/visions

➤ See the Teacher's Edition wrap-around for complete teaching suggestions for each section.

Period 1

- **Unit 6, Chapter 2 Quiz** (Assessment Program, pp. 127–129) 25 MIN.
- **Use Prior Knowledge** (p. 272) 10 MIN.
  Activate prior knowledge by talking about healthy foods.
- **Build Vocabulary** (p. 273) 10 MIN.
  Introduce using context to find meanings.
- **Homework:** Activity Book (p. 182)

Period 2

- **Check Homework** 5 MIN.
  OR
- **Warm Up** 5 MIN.
  Write on the board: *Name two healthy foods and two unhealthy foods.*
- **Text Structure** (p. 273) 10 MIN.
  Introduce the features of diagrams in expository text.
- **Reading Strategy** (p. 274) 5 MIN.
  Teach the strategy of recognizing cause and effect.
- **Reading Selection** (pp. 274–277) 25 MIN.
  Complete the pre-reading questions. Have students read the selection and use the reading strategy.
- **Homework:** Activity Book (p. 183)

Period 3

- **Check Homework** 5 MIN.
  OR
- **Warm Up** 5 MIN.
  Write on the board: *Name one thing you learned about good nutrition.*
- **Listen, Speak, Interact** (p. 277) 5 MIN.
  Have students talk about eating healthy food.
- **Reading Comprehension** (p. 278) 10 MIN.
  Have students answer the questions.
- **Elements of Text** (p. 278) 5 MIN.
  Present signpost words and complete the activity.
- **Build Reading Fluency** (p. 279) 10 MIN.
  Teach how to build reading fluency by chunking and reading like natural speech.
- **Punctuation** (p. 279) 10 MIN.
  Review periods, question marks, and exclamation points.
- **Homework:** Activity Book (pp. 184–185)

Period 4

- **Check Homework** 5 MIN.
  OR
- **Warm Up** 5 MIN.
  Write on the board: *Signpost words show cause and effect. Name two signpost words you learned.*
- **Writing** (pp. 280–281) 35 MIN.
  Introduce the writing strategy of selecting and maintaining a focus by grouping related ideas. Teach students how to write an expository composition.
- **Review** (p. 281) 5 MIN.
  Review the chapter contents.
- **Homework:** Activity Book (pp. 186–187); Have students study for the Unit 6, Chapter 3 Quiz.

Class _____ Date _____

UNIT 6 Food

APPLY AND EXPAND

End-of-Unit Materials

Student Handbook
Student CD-ROM, Unit 6
Teacher Resource Book: Suggestions and Techniques,
   pp. 1–20; Lesson Plan, p. 66; Blackline Masters,
   pp. 75–128; School-Home Connection Newsletter,
   pp. 192–198
Teacher Resource CD-ROM
Assessment Program: Unit 6 Test, pp. 133–138;
   Resources, Checklists, Rubrics, pp. 183–207

Assessment CD-ROM: Unit 6 Test
Transparencies 52, 56, 60, 84, 89
The Heinle Basic Newbury House Dictionary/CD-ROM
Heinle Reading Library Mini-Reader Collection: *Friends at Lunch*
Web site: http://elt.thomson.com/visions

➤ See the Teacher's Edition wrap-around for complete teaching suggestions for each section.

Period 1

- **Unit 6, Chapter 3 Quiz** (Assessment Program, pp. 130–132) 25 MIN.
- **Listening and Speaking Workshop** (p. 282) 20 MIN. Introduce the assignment of presenting an oral report about nutrition. Have students brainstorm, create a poster, and practice their oral reports (steps 1–4).
- **Homework:** Have students review their presentations so that they will be familiar with them for Period 2.

Period 2

- **Listening and Speaking Workshop** (p. 283) 20 MIN. Have students present and evaluate their oral reports (steps 5–6).
- **Viewing Workshop** (p. 283) 25 MIN. Introduce the assignment of distinguishing facts and opinions in advertisements.
- **Homework:** Have students complete the Viewing Workshop assignment.

Period 3

- **Writer's Workshop** (pp. 284–285) 45 MIN. Present the writing assignment of writing an expository composition. Have students brainstorm, draft, and edit their expository compositions.
- **Homework:** Have students revise and prepare the final version of their expository compositions.

Period 4

- **Projects** (pp. 286–287) 45 MIN. Introduce the assignments of making a restaurant menu, making a chart of websites on healthy foods, and/or group writing.
- **Homework:** Have students study for the Unit 6 Test.

Period 5

- **Unit 6 Test** (Assessment Program, pp. 133–138) 45 MIN. After the Unit 6 Test, reassess student learning. Record strong and weak areas based on the unit test. Review weak areas before the End-of-Book Exam.

Class _____   Date _____

UNIT 7 Money

CHAPTER 1 • Clothes and Prices

Chapter Materials
Activity Book: pp. 188–195
Audio: Unit 7, Chapter 1
Student Handbook
Teacher Resource Book: Suggestions and Techniques, pp. 1–20; Lesson Plan, p. 67; Blackline Masters, pp. 75–128; Activity Book Answer Key
Teacher Resource CD-ROM

Assessment Program: Unit 7, Chapter 1 Quiz, pp. 139–141; Resources, Checklists, Rubrics, pp. 183–207
Assessment CD-ROM: Unit 7, Chapter 1 Quiz
Transparencies 52, 58, 60, 91
The Heinle Basic Newbury House Dictionary/CD-ROM
Web site: http://elt.thomson.com/visions

➤ See the Teacher's Edition wrap-around for complete teaching suggestions for each section.

Period 1

- **Unit Opener** (pp. 288–289) 10 MIN.
  Preview the unit contents. Complete the "View the Picture" activity using Transparency 90.
- **Chapter Opener** (p. 290) 10 MIN.
  Preview the chapter contents. Introduce the chapter vocabulary using Transparency 91.
- **Listen, Speak, Interact** (p. 291) 25 MIN.
  Have students talk about buying clothing.
- **Homework:** Have students review the new vocabulary words by writing a short narrative about money.

Period 2

- **Check Homework** 5 MIN.
  OR
- **Warm Up** 5 MIN.
  Write on the board: *What are the names of three American coins? What are the names of coins from other countries?*
- **Build Vocabulary** (pp. 292–293) 20 MIN.
  Introduce comparative and superlative adjectives and complete the activities.
- **Grammar Focus** (p. 294) 20 MIN.
  Present the future tense with *will* and complete the activities.
- **Homework:** Activity Book (pp. 188–189)

Period 3

- **Check Homework** 5 MIN.
  OR
- **Warm Up** 5 MIN.
  Write on the board: *Name three things you will do this weekend.*

- **Grammar Focus** (p. 295) 20 MIN.
  Present the future tense with *be + going to* and complete the activities.
- **Word Study** (p. 296) 10 MIN.
  Present the prefixes **re**, **un**, **pre**, and **dis** and complete the activities.
- **Spelling** (p. 297) 10 MIN.
  Introduce how to spell words with **qu** and complete the activity.
- **Homework:** Activity Book (pp. 190–193)

Period 4

- **Check Homework** 5 MIN.
  OR
- **Warm Up** 5 MIN.
  Write on the board: *Write a sentence with one of these words: 1) equals 2) queen 3) question 4) quick 5) quiet. Read your sentence to the class.*
- **Writing** (p. 297) 20 MIN.
  Teach students how to write checks.
- **Project** (p. 298) 15 MIN.
  Introduce the assignment of designing an ad. Have students create and present their ads to the class.
- **Review** (p. 299) 5 MIN.
  Review the chapter contents.
- **Homework:** Activity Book (pp. 194–195); Have students study for the Unit 7, Chapter 1 Quiz.

Class _____ Date _____

UNIT 7 Money

CHAPTER 2 • The Midas Touch

Chapter Materials

Activity Book: pp. 196–201
Audio: Unit 7, Chapter 2
Student Handbook
Teacher Resource Book: Suggestions and Techniques, pp. 1–20; Lesson Plan, p. 68; Blackline Masters, pp. 75–128; Activity Book Answer Key
Teacher Resource CD-ROM

Assessment Program: Unit 7, Chapter 2 Quiz, pp. 142–144; Resources, Checklists, Rubrics, pp. 183–207
Assessment CD-ROM: Unit 7, Chapter 2 Quiz
Transparencies 9, 17, 18, 52, 56, 58, 74
The Heinle Basic Newbury House Dictionary/CD-ROM
Web site: http://elt.thomson.com/visions

➤ See the Teacher's Edition wrap-around for complete teaching suggestions for each section.

Period 1

- **Unit 7, Chapter 1 Quiz** (Assessment Program, pp. 139–141) 25 min.
- **Use Prior Knowledge** (p. 300) 10 MIN.
  Activate prior knowledge by making predictions about the reading selection.
- **Build Vocabulary** (p. 301) 10 MIN.
  Introduce signpost words.
- **Homework:** Activity Book (p. 196)

Period 2

- **Check Homework** 5 MIN.
  OR
- **Warm Up** 5 MIN.
  Write on the board: *Correct the errors in these sentences: 1) My shoes are expensiver than my shirt. 2) Those are the most ugliest hats in the store.*
- **Text Structure** (p. 301) 10 MIN.
  Present the text features of myths (characters, plot, lesson/moral).
- **Reading Strategy** (p. 302) 5 MIN.
  Teach the strategy of making a prediction.
- **Reading Selection** (pp. 302–305) 25 MIN.
  Complete the pre-reading activities. Have students read the selection and use the reading strategy.
- **Homework:** Activity Book (p. 197)

Period 3

- **Check Homework** 5 MIN.
  OR
- **Warm Up** 5 MIN.
  Write on the board: *Complete these sentences: 1) Dionysus gave King Midas one _____ for releasing his follower. 2) King Midas wished to turn everything he touched into _____. 3) King Midas was miserable and _____.*

- **Listen, Speak, Interact** (p. 305) 5 MIN.
  Have students talk about the timeline of the myth.
- **Reading Comprehension** (p. 306) 10 MIN.
  Have students answer the questions.
- **Elements of Text** (p. 306) 5 MIN.
  Teach how to understand characters (traits, motivation).
- **Build Reading Fluency** (p. 307) 10 MIN.
  Introduce how to build reading fluency by distinguishing between the main idea and details.
- **Capitalization** (p. 307) 10 MIN.
  Introduce capital letters for holidays and special events and complete the activities.
- **Homework:** Activity Book (pp. 198–199)

Period 4

- **Check Homework** 5 MIN.
  OR
- **Warm Up** 5 MIN.
  Write on the board: *Who are two main characters of the myth "The Midas Touch"?*
- **Writing** (pp. 308–309) 35 MIN.
  Introduce the writing strategy of giving context and providing concrete details. Teach students how to write a personal narrative.
- **Review** (p. 309) 5 MIN.
  Review the chapter contents.
- **Homework:** Activity Book (pp. 200–201); Have students study for the Unit 7, Chapter 2 Quiz.

Class _____ Date _____

UNIT 7 Money

CHAPTER 3 • Making a Budget

Chapter Materials

Activity Book: pp. 202–207
Audio: Unit 7, Chapter 3
Student Handbook
Teacher Resource Book: Suggestions and Techniques, pp. 1–20; Lesson Plan, p. 69; Blackline Masters, pp. 75–128; Activity Book Answer Key
Teacher Resource CD-ROM

Assessment Program: Unit 7, Chapter 3 Quiz, pp. 145–147; Resources, Checklists, Rubrics, pp. 183–207
Assessment CD-ROM: Unit 7, Chapter 3 Quiz
Transparencies 52, 56, 58, 75, 84
The Heinle Basic Newbury House Dictionary/CD-ROM
Web site: http://elt.thomson.com/visions

➤ See the Teacher's Edition wrap-around for complete teaching suggestions for each section.

Period 1

- **Unit 7, Chapter 2 Quiz** (Assessment Program, pp. 142–144) 25 MIN.
- **Use Prior Knowledge** (p. 310) 10 MIN.
  Activate prior knowledge by talking about budgets.
- **Build Vocabulary** (p. 311) 10 MIN.
  Teach students how to use a dictionary to learn new words.
- **Homework:** Activity Book (p. 202)

Period 2

- **Check Homework** 5 MIN.
  OR
- **Warm Up** 5 MIN.
  Write on the board: *What magazines do you know? What do they look like?*
- **Text Structure** (p. 311) 10 MIN.
  Present the text features of magazine articles (visual aids, bulleted lists, boxes, color, fonts).
- **Reading Strategy** (p. 312) 5 MIN.
  Teach the strategy of understanding the author's purpose.
- **Reading Selection** (pp. 312–315) 25 MIN.
  Complete the pre-reading questions. Have students read the selection and use the reading strategy.
- **Homework:** Activity Book (p. 203)

Period 3

- **Check Homework** 5 MIN.
  OR
- **Warm Up** 5 MIN.
  Write on the board: *True or False? 1) Your budget is the money you earn. 2) Your savings is the money you spend. 3) A debt is money you owe someone.*
- **Listen, Speak, Interact** (p. 315) 5 MIN.
  Have students talk about their short-term and long-term goals.
- **Reading Comprehension** (p. 316) 10 MIN.
  Have students answer the questions.
- **Elements of Text** (p. 316) 5 MIN.
  Teach students how to interpret pie charts.
- **Build Reading Fluency** (p. 317) 10 MIN.
  Introduce how to build reading fluency by using rapid word recognition on words with *r*-controlled vowels.
- **Spelling** (p. 317) 10 MIN.
  Introduce spelling words with *r*-controlled vowels and complete the activities.
- **Homework:** Activity Book (pp. 204–205)

Period 4

- **Check Homework** 5 MIN.
  OR
- **Warm Up** 5 MIN.
  Write on the board: *Name two things you learned about budgets.*
- **Writing** (pp. 318–319) 35 MIN.
  Introduce the writing strategy of grouping related ideas and maintaining a consistent focus. Teach students how to write an expository composition.
- **Review** (p. 319) 5 MIN.
  Review the chapter contents.
- **Homework:** Activity Book (pp. 206–207); Have students study for the Unit 7, Chapter 3 Quiz.

Class _____ Date _____

UNIT 7 Money

APPLY AND EXPAND

End-of-Unit Materials

Student Handbook
Student CD-ROM, Unit 7
Teacher Resource Book: Suggestions and Techniques, pp. 1–20; Lesson Plan, p. 70; Blackline Masters, pp. 75–128; School-Home Connection Newsletter, pp. 199–205
Teacher Resource CD-ROM

Assessment Program: Unit 7 Test, pp. 148–153; Resources, Checklists, Rubrics, pp. 183–207
Assessment CD-ROM: Unit 7 Test
Transparencies 52, 56, 57, 66, 71, 75, 84
The Heinle Basic Newbury House Dictionary/CD-ROM
Heinle Reading Library Mini-Reader Collection: *Working at the Supermarket*
Web site: http://elt.thomson.com/visions

➤ See the Teacher's Edition wrap-around for complete teaching suggestions for each section.

Period 1

- **Unit 7, Chapter 3 Quiz** (Assessment Program, pp. 145–147) 25 MIN.
- **Listening and Speaking Workshop** (p. 320) 20 MIN. Introduce the assignment of presenting a role-play. Have students choose the characters, brainstorm and organize their ideas, write the dialogue on index cards, and practice their role-plays (steps 1–4).
- **Homework:** Have students review their role-plays so that they will be familiar with them for Period 2.

Period 2

- **Listening and Speaking Workshop** (pp. 320–321) 20 MIN. Have students present and evaluate their role-plays (steps 5–6).
- **Viewing Workshop** (p. 321) 25 MIN. Introduce the assignment of comparing and contrasting a story and a video.
- **Homework:** Have students complete the Viewing Workshop assignment.

Period 3

- **Writer's Workshop** (pp. 322–323) 45 MIN. Present the writing assignment of writing an opinion composition. Have students brainstorm, draft, and edit their opinion compositions.
- **Homework:** Have students revise and prepare the final version of their opinion compositions.

Period 4

- **Projects** (pp. 324–325) 45 MIN. Introduce the assignments of making a budget and/or group writing.
- **Homework:** Have students study for the Unit 7 Test.

Period 5

- **Unit 7 Test** (Assessment Program, pp. 148–153) 45 MIN. After the Unit 7 Test, reassess student learning. Record strong and weak areas based on the unit test. Review weak areas before the End-of-Book Exam.

Class _____ Date _____

UNIT 8 Jobs and Careers
CHAPTER 1 • People at Work

Chapter Materials

Activity Book: pp. 208–215
Audio: Unit 8, Chapter 1
Student Handbook
Teacher Resource Book: Suggestions and Techniques, pp. 1–20; Lesson Plan, p. 71; Blackline Masters, pp. 75–128; Activity Book Answer Key
Teacher Resource CD-ROM

Assessment Program: Unit 8, Chapter 1 Quiz, pp. 154–156; Resources, Checklists, Rubrics, pp. 183–207
Assessment CD-ROM: Unit 8, Chapter 1 Quiz
Transparencies 9, 17, 18, 52, 56, 58, 66, 86, 92, 93
The Heinle Basic Newbury House Dictionary/CD-ROM
Web site: http://elt.thomson.com/visions

▶ See the Teacher's Edition wrap-around for complete teaching suggestions for each section.

Period 1

- **Unit Opener** (pp. 326–327) 10 MIN.
  Preview the unit contents. Complete the "View the Picture" activity using Transparency 92.
- **Chapter Opener** (p. 328) 10 MIN.
  Preview the chapter contents. Introduce the chapter vocabulary using Transparency 93.
- **Listen, Speak, Interact** (p. 329) 25 MIN.
  Have students talk about jobs.
- **Homework:** Have students review the new vocabulary words by writing a short narrative about jobs and careers.

Period 2

- **Check Homework** 5 MIN.
  OR
- **Warm Up** 5 MIN.
  Write on the board: *What jobs do you want to learn more about?*
- **Build Vocabulary** (pp. 330–331) 20 MIN.
  Introduce names of tools and equipment and descriptive adjectives to describe people at work.
- **Grammar Focus** (p. 332) 20 MIN.
  Introduce the modal *can* and complete the activities.
- **Homework:** Activity Book (pp. 208–209)

Period 3

- **Check Homework** 5 MIN.
  OR
- **Warm Up** 5 MIN.
  Write on the board: *Complete the sentences with these words: hard-working, enthusiastic, patient*
  1) An _____ person is very excited about her job.
  2) A _____ person works hard and does a good job.
  3) A _____ person isn't bothered by interruptions.

- **Grammar Focus** (p. 333) 20 MIN.
  Introduce object pronouns and complete the activities.
- **Word Study** (p. 334) 10 MIN.
  Present suffixes **ly, ful,** and **ment** and complete the activities.
- **Punctuation** (p. 335) 10 MIN.
  Introduce commas and colons in letters.
- **Homework:** Activity Book (pp. 210–213)

Period 4

- **Check Homework** 5 MIN.
  OR
- **Warm Up** 5 MIN.
  Write on the board: *Name two adverbs that end in* -ly. *Name two adjectives that end in* -ful.
- **Writing** (p. 335) 20 MIN.
  Teach students how to write a business letter.
- **Project** (p. 336) 15 MIN.
  Introduce the assignment of inviting a guest speaker to class.
- **Review** (p. 337) 5 MIN.
  Review the chapter contents.
- **Homework:** Activity Book (pp. 214–215); Have students study for the Unit 8, Chapter 1 Quiz.

Class _____   Date _____

UNIT 8 Jobs and Careers
CHAPTER 2 • Three Scientists

Chapter Materials

Activity Book: pp. 216–221
Audio: Unit 8, Chapter 2
Student Handbook
Teacher Resource Book: Suggestions and Techniques, pp. 1–20; Lesson Plan, p. 72; Blackline Masters, pp. 75–128; Activity Book Answer Key
Teacher Resource CD-ROM

Assessment Program: Unit 8, Chapter 2 Quiz, pp. 157–159; Resources, Checklists, Rubrics, pp. 183–207
Assessment CD-ROM: Unit 8, Chapter 2 Quiz
Transparencies 52, 56, 58, 60, 89
The Heinle Basic Newbury House Dictionary/CD-ROM
Web site: http://elt.thomson.com/visions

➤ See the Teacher's Edition wrap-around for complete teaching suggestions for each section.

Period 1

- **Unit 8, Chapter 1 Quiz** (Assessment Program, pp. 154–156) 25 min.
- **Use Prior Knowledge** (p. 338) 10 MIN.
  Activate prior knowledge by talking about areas of scientific study.
- **Build Vocabulary** (p. 339) 10 MIN.
  Introduce words with Latin roots and complete the activity.
- **Homework:** Activity Book (p. 216)

Period 2

- **Check Homework** 5 MIN.
  OR
- **Warm Up** 5 MIN.
  Write on the board: *Name two science words with Latin roots.*
- **Text Structure** (p. 339) 10 MIN.
  Present the features of a biography (events, actions, dates, sequence).
- **Reading Strategy** (p. 340) 5 MIN.
  Teach the strategy of paraphrasing to recall major points.
- **Reading Selection** (p. 340–343) 25 MIN.
  Complete the pre-reading activities. Have students read the selection and use the reading strategy.
- **Homework:** Activity Book (p. 217)

Period 3

- **Check Homework** 5 MIN.
  OR
- **Warm Up** (reading) 5 MIN.
  Write on the board: *Name two things you learned about Gregor Mendel, Irène Curie, or Franklin Chang-Diaz.*
- **Listen, Speak, Interact** (p. 343) 5 MIN.
  Have students talk about Gregor Mendel, Irène Curie, and Franklin Chang-Diaz.
- **Reading Comprehension** (p. 344) 10 MIN.
  Have students answer the questions.
- **Elements of Text** (p. 344) 5 MIN.
  Teach students how to describe a process.
- **Build Reading Fluency** (p. 345) 10 MIN.
  Introduce how to build reading fluency by reading aloud chunks of words.
- **Spelling** (p. 345) 10 MIN.
  Introduce the suffixes *er, or, ist* and complete the activity.
- **Homework:** Activity Book (pp. 218–219)

Period 4

- **Check Homework** 5 MIN.
  OR
- **Warm Up** 5 MIN.
  Write on the board: *What are two words with the suffix –er? What are two words with the suffix –ist?*
- **Writing** (pp. 346–347) 35 MIN.
  Introduce the writing strategy of collecting information and taking notes. Teach students how to write a biography.
- **Review** (p. 347) 5 MIN.
  Review the chapter contents.
- **Homework:** Activity Book (pp. 220–221); Have students study for the Unit 8, Chapter 2 Quiz.

Class _____   Date _____

UNIT 8 Jobs and Careers

CHAPTER 3 • Research on the Internet

Chapter Materials

Activity Book: pp. 222–227
Audio: Unit 8, Chapter 3
Student Handbook
Teacher Resource Book: Suggestions and Techniques, pp. 1–20; Lesson Plan, p. 73; Blackline Masters, pp. 75–128; Activity Book Answer Key
Teacher Resource CD-ROM

Assessment Program: Unit 8, Chapter 3 Quiz, pp. 160–162; Resources, Checklists, Rubrics, pp. 183–207
Assessment CD-ROM: Unit 8, Chapter 3 Quiz
Transparencies 52, 56, 58, 72, 89, 94, 95
The Heinle Basic Newbury House Dictionary/CD-ROM
Web site: http://elt.thomson.com/visions

➤ See the Teacher's Edition wrap-around for complete teaching suggestions for each section.

Period 1

- **Unit 8, Chapter 2 Quiz** (Assessment Program, pp. 157–159) 25 MIN.
- **Use Prior Knowledge** (p. 348) 10 MIN.
  Activate prior knowledge by talking about the Internet (Transparency 94).
- **Build Vocabulary** (p. 349) 10 MIN.
  Introduce multiple-meaning words for Internet terms.
- **Homework:** Activity Book (p. 222)

Period 2

- **Check Homework** 5 MIN.
  OR
- **Warm Up** 5 MIN.
  Write on the board: *Fill in the blanks with these words: mouse, web, engine*
  1) We found lots of information about jobs on the _____.
  2) I used a search _____ to find information about veterinarians. 3) Use the _____ to point and click on a word.
- **Text Structure** (p. 349) 10 MIN.
  Present the text features of technical manuals (table of contents, numbered lists, graphic aids, FAQs, troubleshooting pages, index).
- **Reading Strategy** (p. 350) 5 MIN.
  Teach the strategy of taking notes to understand and remember.
- **Reading Selection** (pp. 350–353) 25 MIN.
  Complete the pre-reading questions. Have students read the selection and use the reading strategy.
- **Homework:** Activity Book (p. 223)

Period 3

- **Check Homework** 5 MIN.
  OR
- **Warm Up** 5 MIN.
  Write on the board: *When do you use a search engine? What do you do if you bookmark a Web page?*
- **Listen, Speak, Interact** (p. 353) 5 MIN.
  Have students talk about careers they want to research on the Internet.
- **Reading Comprehension** (p. 354) 10 MIN.
  Have students answer the questions.
- **Elements of Text** (p. 354) 5 MIN.
  Present features of Web sites and encyclopedias.
- **Build Reading Fluency** (p. 355) 10 MIN.
  Introduce how to build reading fluency by using rapid word recognition of multisyllable words.
- **Punctuation** (p. 355) 10 MIN.
  Introduce parentheses and complete the activities.
- **Homework:** Activity Book (pp. 224–225)

Period 4

- **Check Homework** 5 MIN.
  OR
- **Warm Up** 5 MIN.
  Write on the board: *Name three things you learned about doing research on the Internet.*
- **Writing** (pp. 356–357) 35 MIN.
  Introduce the writing strategy of using logical order to describe the steps in a process using Transparency 95. Teach students how to write a research report on a scientific process.
- **Review** (p. 357) 5 MIN.
  Review the chapter contents.
- **Homework:** Activity Book (pp. 226–227); Have students study for the Unit 8, Chapter 3 Quiz.

Class _____ Date _____

UNIT 8 Jobs and Careers

APPLY AND EXPAND

End-of-Unit Materials

Student Handbook
Student CD-ROM, Unit 8
Teacher Resource Book: Suggestions and Techniques, pp. 1–20; Lesson Plan, p. 74; Blackline Masters, pp. 75–128; School-Home Connection Newsletter, pp. 206–212
Teacher Resource CD-ROM
Assessment Program: Unit 8 Test, pp. 163–168; End-of-Book Test, pp. 169–176; Resources, Checklists, Rubrics, pp. 183–207

Assessment CD-ROM: Unit 8 Test
Transparencies 10, 11, 12, 13, 52, 56, 66, 70, 72, 73, 74, 79, 83, 85, 96
The Heinle Basic Newbury House Dictionary/CD-ROM
Heinle Reading Library Mini-Reader Collection: *Career Day at School*
Web site: http://elt.thomson.com/visions

➤ See the Teacher's Edition wrap-around for complete teaching suggestions for each section.

Period 1

- **Unit 8, Chapter 3 Quiz** (Assessment Program, pp. 160–162) 25 MIN.
- **Listening and Speaking Workshop** (p. 358) 20 MIN. Introduce the assignment of giving a "how-to" presentation. Have students brainstorm and organize the steps in the process, prepare graphic aids, organize their presentations, and practice their presentations (steps 1–5).
- **Homework:** Have students review their presentations so that they will be familiar with them for Period 2.

Period 2

- **Listening and Speaking Workshop** (p. 359) 20 MIN. Have students present and evaluate their "how-to" presentations (steps 6–7) (Transparency 96).
- **Viewing Workshop** (p. 359) 25 MIN. Introduce the assignment of researching jobs in the newspaper and on the Internet.
- **Homework:** Have students complete the Viewing Workshop assignment.

Period 3

- **Writer's Workshop** (pp. 360–361) 45 MIN. Present the writing assignment of writing an autobiography. Have students brainstorm, draft, and edit their autobiographies.
- **Homework:** Have students revise and prepare the final version of their autobiographies.

Period 4

- **Projects** (pp. 362–363) 45 MIN. Introduce the assignments of creating a research manual, role-playing a job interview, and/or group writing.
- **Homework:** Have students study for the Unit 8 Test.

Period 5

- **Unit 8 Test** (Assessment Program, pp. 163–168) 45 MIN. After the Unit 8 Test, reassess student learning. Record strong and weak areas based on the unit test. Review weak areas before the End-of-Book Exam.

Period 6

- **End-of-Book Test** (Assessment Program, pp. 169–176) 45 MIN.

Bingo (3 x 3 Card)

Use this Bingo game to match oral words to printed words and to identify and distinguish letters, sounds, and words.

1. In each space, write a letter, sound, or vocabulary word.
2. Your teacher calls out the letters, sounds, or vocabulary words one at a time.
3. Cross off the letter, sound, or word if you have it on your card.
4. The winner is the first student to cross off the squares in a row horizontally, vertically, or diagonally.

	FREE SPACE	

Name _____ Date _____

Bingo (5 x 5 Card)

Use this Bingo game to match oral words to printed words and to identify and distinguish letters, sounds, and words.

1. In each space, write a letter, sound, or vocabulary word.
2. Your teacher calls out the letters, sounds, or vocabulary words one at a time.
3. Cross off the letter, sound, or word if you have it on your card.
4. The winner is the first student to cross off the squares in a row horizontally, vertically, or diagonally.

		FREE SPACE		

Business Letter

A business letter is short and has one or two points.

1. Use a colon after the greeting.
2. In the first paragraph, say why you are writing.
3. If necessary, add supporting information in a second paragraph.
4. In the last paragraph, write a polite conclusion.
5. Use a comma after the closing.
6. Proofread for spelling, grammar, capital letters, and proper business form.

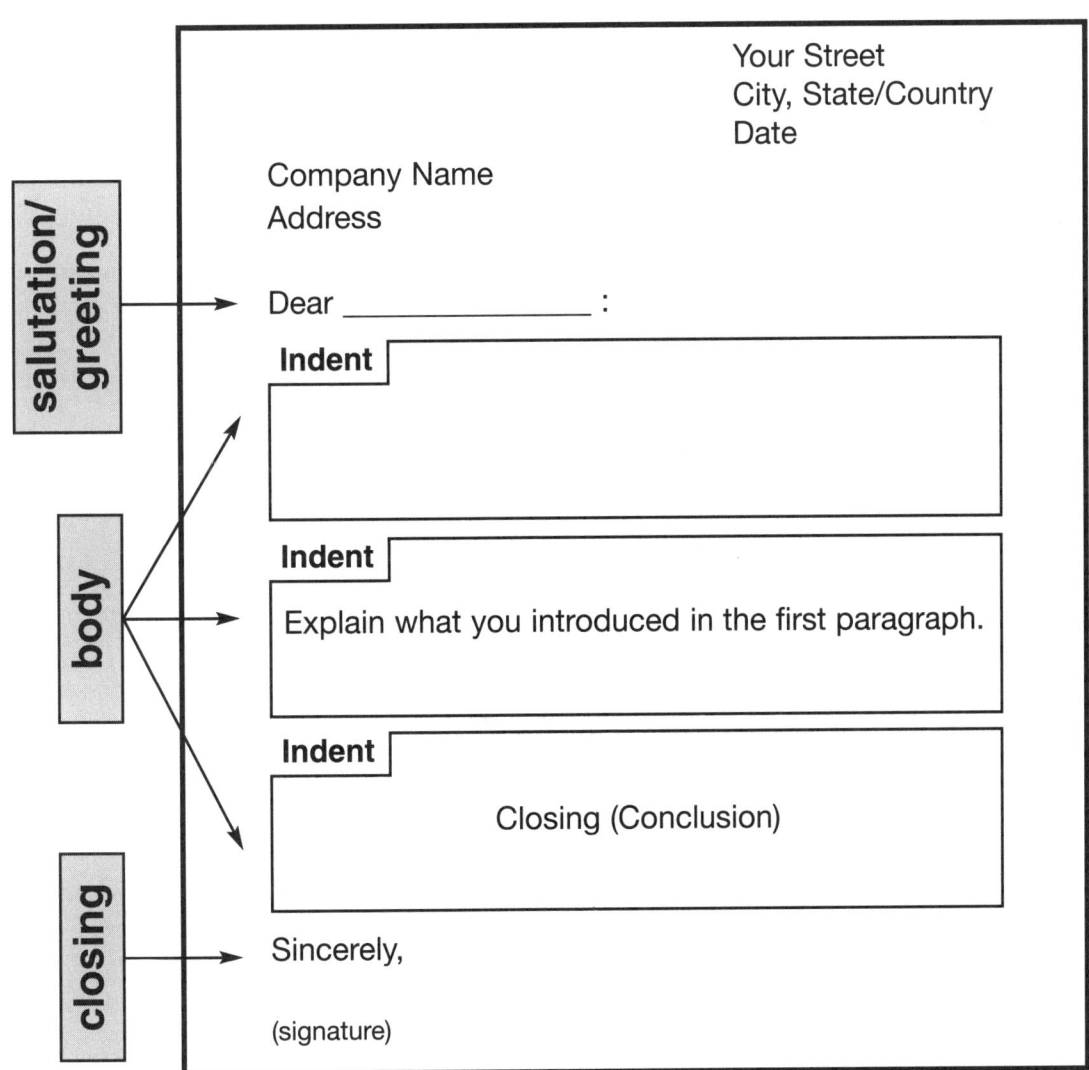

Name _____ Date _____

Cluster Map

Use a Cluster Map to help you organize your ideas.

1. Write the topic in the large circle in the middle.
2. Write the main ideas about the topic in the medium-sized circles.
3. Write details about the main ideas in the small circles.

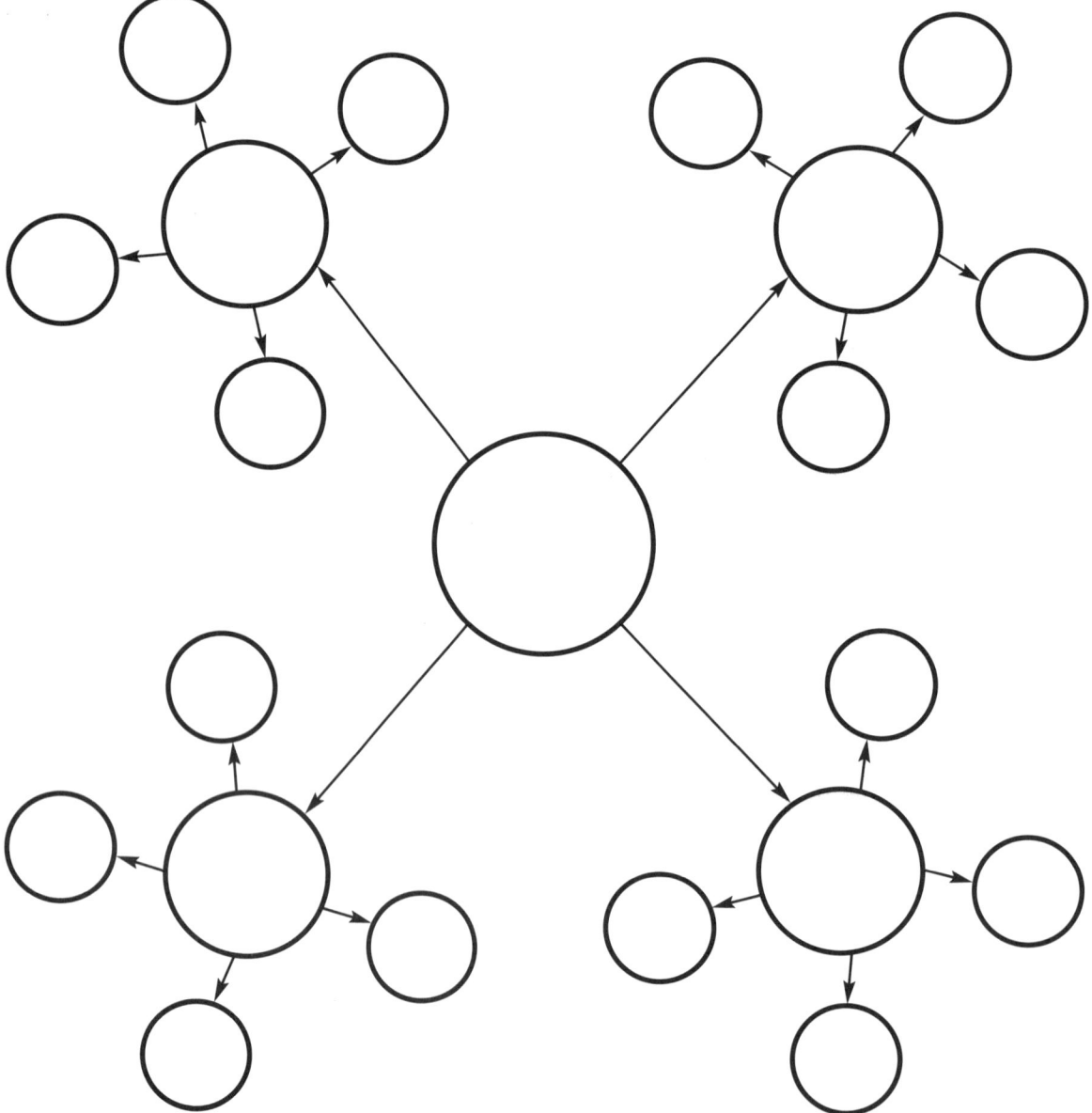

Name _____ Date _____

Cursive Alphabet (A–I)

1. Say the letter names.
2. Write the capital and lowercase letters.
3. Space the letters.

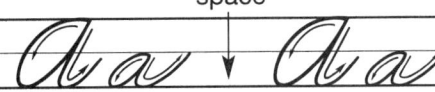
space

Name _____   Date _____

Cursive Alphabet (J–R)

1. Say the letter names.
2. Write the capital and lowercase letters.
3. Space the letters.

space

 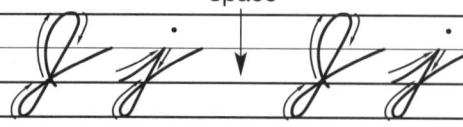

 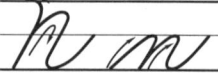

Cursive Alphabet (S–Z)

1. Say the letter names.
2. Write the capital and lowercase letters.
3. Space the letters.

Name _____ Date _____

Frequently-Used Sight Words 1

These are words you hear and read often in English. Copy each word twice. Spell the words aloud.

1. and _____ _____
2. of _____ _____
3. one _____ _____
4. was _____ _____

5. see _____ _____
6. after _____ _____
7. down _____ _____
8. you _____ _____

 Activities

A

1. Which word has two letters? _____
2. Which words have three letters?
_____ _____ _____ _____ _____
3. Which word has four letters? _____
4. Which word has five letters? _____
5. Which words include the vowel *a*?
_____ _____ _____
6. Which words include the vowel *o*?
_____ _____ _____ _____

B

1. The opposite of *before*: _____
2. The past tense of *is*: _____
3. The opposite of *up*: _____
4. You do this with your eyes: _____

82 TEACHER RESOURCE

Name _____ Date _____

Frequently-Used Sight Words 2

These are words you hear and read often in English. Copy each word twice. Spell the words aloud.

1. the _____ _____
2. we _____ _____
3. give _____ _____
4. will _____ _____

5. day _____ _____
6. his _____ _____
7. no _____ _____
8. out _____ _____

▶ **Activities**

A

1. Which words have two letters? _____ _____
2. Which words have three letters?
   _____ _____ _____ _____
3. Which words have four letters? _____ _____
4. Which words include the vowel *i*?
   _____ _____ _____
5. Which words include the consonant *w*?
   _____ _____

B

1. The opposite of *in:* _____
2. The opposite of *night:* _____
3. We use this word to talk about the future: _____
4. The opposite of *yes:* _____
5. You + me: _____

TEACHER RESOURCE 83

Name _____ Date _____

Frequently-Used Sight Words 3

These are words you hear and read often in English. Copy each word twice. Spell the words aloud.

1. they _____ _____
2. good _____ _____
3. his _____ _____
4. have _____ _____

5. come _____ _____
6. when _____ _____
7. little _____ _____
8. first _____ _____

➤ **Activities**

A

1. Which words have four letters?
_____ _____ _____ _____ _____

2. Which word has five letters? _____

3. Which word has six letters? _____

4. Which words include the consonant *t*?
_____ _____ _____

5. Which words include the vowel *e*?
_____ _____ _____ _____ _____

B

1. The opposite of *bad:* _____

2. Another word for *small:* _____

3. A question word that asks about time: _____

4. The opposite of *last:* _____

5. Possessive adjective for a boy or man: _____

Name _____ Date _____

Frequently-Used Sight Words 4

These are words you hear and read often in English. Copy each word twice. Spell the words aloud.

1. who _____ _____
2. up _____ _____
3. had _____ _____
4. out _____ _____

5. or _____ _____
6. he _____ _____
7. then _____ _____
8. two _____ _____

➤ **Activities**

A

1. Which words have two letters?
   _____ _____ _____

2. Which words have three letters?
   _____ _____ _____ _____

3. Which word has four letters? _____
4. Which words include the vowel *o*?
   _____ _____ _____

5. Which words include the consonant *h*?
   _____ _____ _____ _____

B

1. The past tense of *have:* _____
2. The opposite of *in:* _____
3. A word that gives a choice: _____
4. The opposite of *down:* _____
5. one + one: _____

TEACHER RESOURCE 85

Name _____ Date _____

Frequently-Used Sight Words 5

These are words you hear and read often in English. Copy each word twice. Spell the words aloud.

1. did _____ _____
2. not _____ _____
3. here _____ _____
4. in _____ _____

5. were _____ _____
6. my _____ _____
7. why _____ _____
8. before _____ _____

➤ **Activities**

A

1. Which words have two letters? _____ _____
2. Which words have three letters? _____ _____ _____
3. Which words have four letters? _____ _____
4. Which word has six letters? _____
5. Which words include the vowel e? _____ _____ _____

B

1. The past tense of *do:* _____
2. The opposite of *there:* _____
3. A negative word: _____
4. The opposite of *after:* _____
5. The opposite of *out:* _____

Name _____ Date _____

Friendly Letter

This format is used for writing a letter to a friend.

1. Begin your letter with a greeting.
   Use a comma after the greeting.
2. End your letter with a closing.
   Use a comma after the closing.
3. Use your best handwriting or use a computer.
4. Proofread your spelling and punctuation.

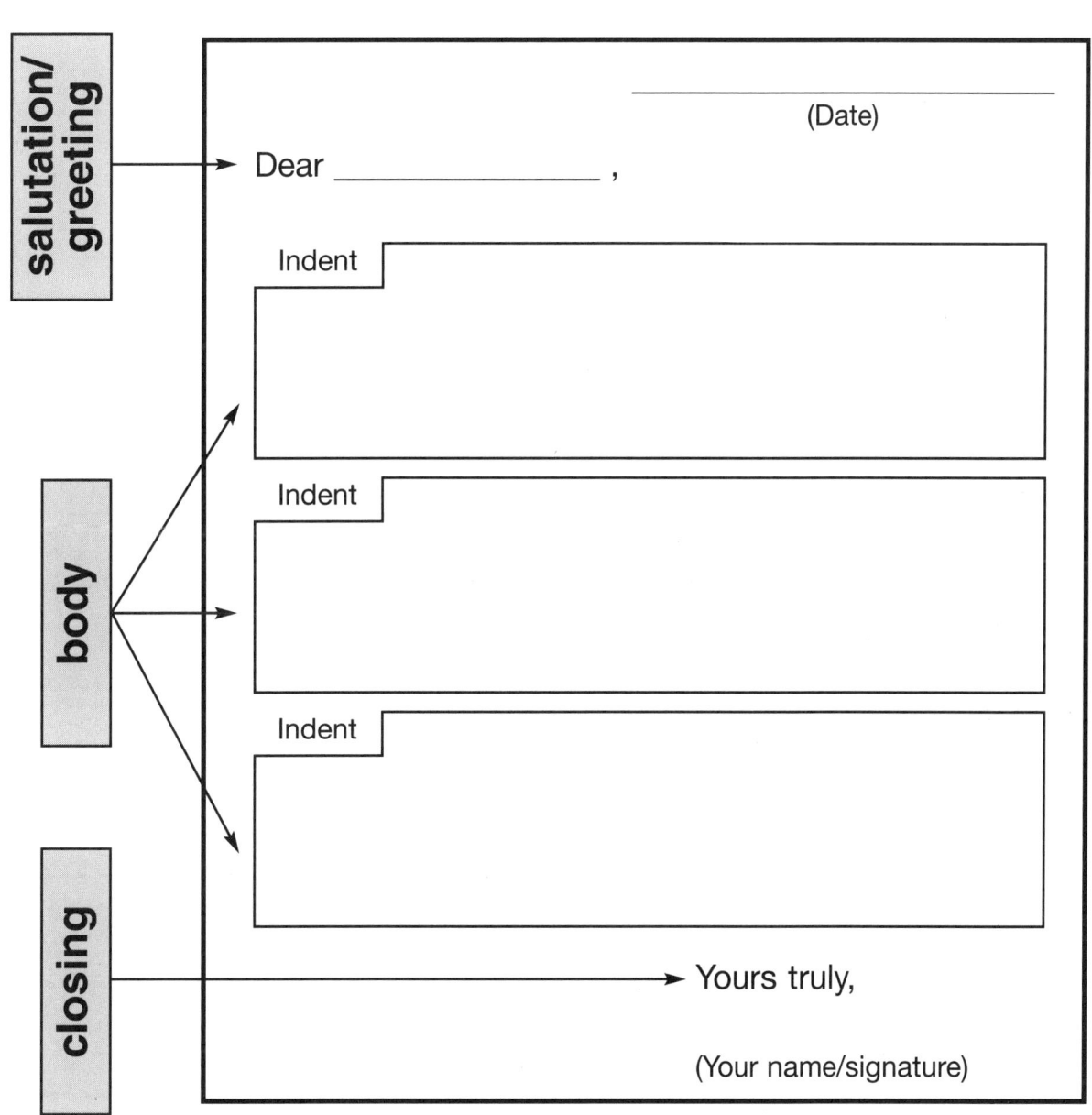

TEACHER RESOURCE 87

Name _____ Date _____

How-to (Step-by-Step) Instructions

Use this graphic organizer to explain the steps involved in doing something.

1. Fill in the chart with information.

2. Use the chart to plan a paragraph or an oral presentation.

Introduction What are you going to explain?

_____

_____

Steps What are the steps?

1. First, _____

_____

2. Then, _____

_____

3. Next, _____

_____

4. After, _____

_____

5. Finally, _____

_____

Conclusion

_____

_____

Name _____ Date _____

Interview

1. Write a list of questions.
2. Record the interviewee's answers.

Interview questions for
_____
(Name of interviewee)

1. Question:
_____?
   Answer:

2. Question:
_____?
   Answer:

3. Question:
_____?
   Answer:

4. Question:
_____?
   Answer:

Name _____   Date _____

Know/Want to Know/Learned Chart (KWL)

1. Write the topic in the top box.
2. Write things you **know** in the first column.
3. Write things you **want to know** in the second column.
4. Write things you **learned** in the third column.

Topic:		
Know What do I already know about the topic?	**Want to Know** What do I want to know about the topic?	**Learned** What did I learn about the topic?

Name _____ Date _____

Letter Tiles (Lowercase Letters a–m)

Use these letter tiles.

1. Spell and read words with short vowels, long vowels, r-controlled vowels, and consonant blends.
2. Create and state a series of rhyming words.
3. Change words by adding, deleting, or changing a target sound (*cow* to *how*).
4. Spell sight words and frequently used irregular words.
5. Arrange words in alphabetical order.

a	b	c	d	e
f	g	h	i	j
k	l	m		

Name _____ Date _____

Letter Tiles (Lowercase Letters n–z)

Use these letter tiles.

1. Spell and read words with short vowels, long vowels, r-controlled vowels, and consonant blends.
2. Create and state a series of rhyming words.
3. Change words by adding, deleting, or changing a target sound (*cow* to *how*).
4. Spell sight words and frequently used irregular words.
5. Arrange words in alphabetical order.

n	o	p	q	r
s	t	u	v	w
x	y	z		

Name _____ Date _____

Letter Tiles (Capital Letters A–M)

Use these capital letter tiles.

1. Spell and write words that use capital letters—people's names, titles, days, months, holidays, the pronoun *I*, geographical names, names of newspapers and magazines.

2. Create and write sentences with a capital letter at the beginning.

A	B	C	D	E
F	G	H	I	J
K	L	M		

TEACHER RESOURCE 93

Name _____ Date _____

Letter Tiles (Capital Letters N–Z)

Use these capital letter tiles.

1. Spell and write words that use capital letters—people's names, titles, days, months, holidays, the pronoun *I,* geographical names, names of newspapers and magazines.

2. Create and write sentences with a capital letter at the beginning.

N	O	P	Q	R
S	T	U	V	W
X	Y	Z		

Name _____ Date _____

Narrative

Brainstorming

Use this graphic organizer for writing narratives and for listening/speaking presentations.

Headings	Notes or drawings to help you plan your writing or presentation.
Title	
Setting (Where? When?)	
Characters (Who?)	
Events (Who? What? When? Where? Why? How?)	
Conflict/Problem and Solution	
Ending (Summary/Conclusion)	

TEACHER RESOURCE 95

Name _____ Date _____

Narrative

Draft

Use this graphic organizer when you write your first draft. Use transition words.

	Title
	Name
	Date

Beginning — Indent | **Introduction**

Middle — Indent | **Body**

End — Indent | **Conclusion or Resolution**

96 TEACHER RESOURCE

Name _____   Date _____

Note-Taking

Research Report

1. Use index cards.
2. Go to the library and locate a variety of sources for your research.
3. Take notes on index cards.
4. Record the sources you use.

Topic: _____

Paraphrase your source.

or

Summarize from your source.

or

"Quote" your source.

Source

Name _____ Date _____

Numerals 1–10

1. Write the numerals.
2. Write the words.

Numerals   **Words**

1   1   one

2   2

3   3

4   4

5   5

6   6

7   7

8   8

9   9

10 10

Name _____ Date _____

Numerals 11–20

1. Write the numerals.
2. Write the words.

	Numerals	**Words**
11		
12		
13		
14		
15		
16		
17		
18		
19		
20		

Name _____ Date _____

Outline

Expository Compositions, Narratives, and Information Reports

Use an outline to organize your notes and write a draft.

1. Keep it simple. Do not write complete sentences.
2. List major sections after a Roman numeral and a period.
3. List topics after a capital letter and a period.
4. List details, facts, and examples after a number and a period.

Title

I. Introduction: Main Idea

II. Body

   A. Topic A
      1. Detail
      2. Detail
      3. Detail

   B. Topic B
      1. Detail
      2. Detail
      3. Detail

III. Conclusion: Summary

Name _____ Date _____

Paragraph

All the sentences in a paragraph should be about the same subject.

1. Indent the first line of a paragraph.
2. Check for correct capitalization and punctuation.
3. Use a dictionary to check spelling and to find words.
4. Write a topic sentence, supporting details, and a closing sentence.

Title

Indent

(topic sentence with main idea)

(facts and details)

(closing sentence)

Name _____ Date _____

Personal Dictionary

1. Keep a list of new words you learn.
2. Use a dictionary to find the meanings.
3. Put the new words in alphabetical order.
4. Use each new word in a sentence or question.

Word	Definition	Your Sentence

Name _____ Date _____

Print Alphabet (A–I)

1. Say the letter names.
2. Print the capital and lowercase letters.
3. Space the letters.

Aa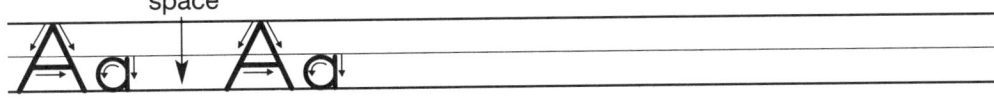

Bb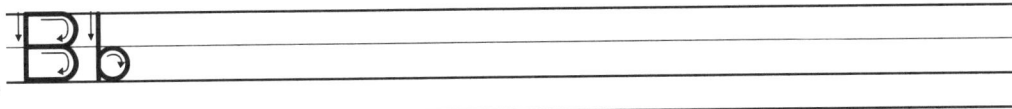

Cc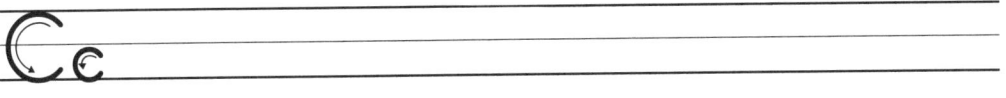

Dd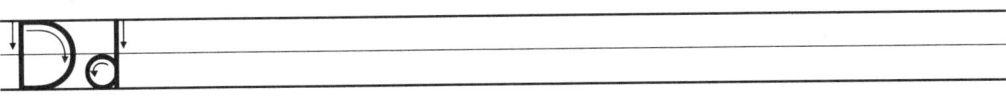

Ee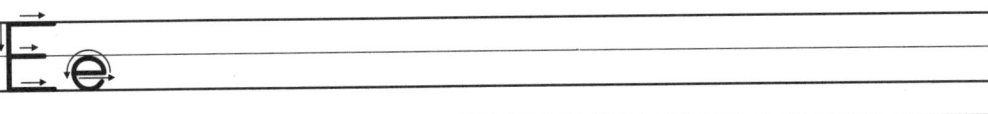

Ff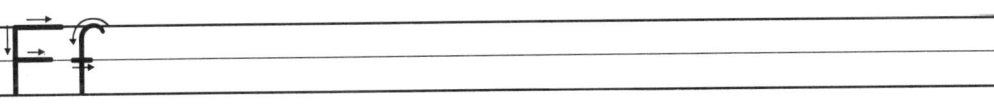

Gg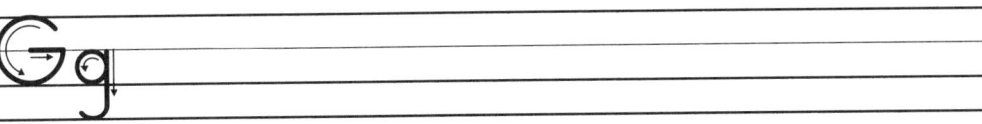

Hh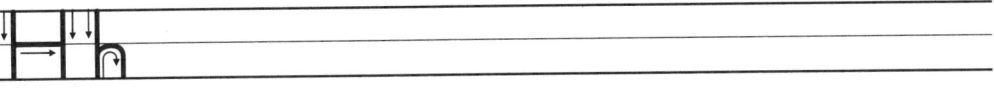

Ii

TEACHER RESOURCE 103

Name _____ Date _____

Print Alphabet (J–R)

1. Say the letter names.
2. Print the capital and lowercase letters.
3. Space the letters.

Jj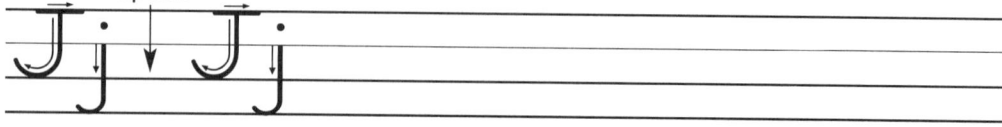

Kk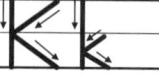

Ll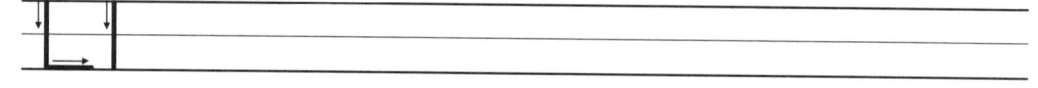

Mm

Nn

Oo

Pp

Qq

Rr

Name _____ Date _____

Print Alphabet (S–Z)

1. Say the letter names.
2. Print the capital and lowercase letters.
3. Space the letters.

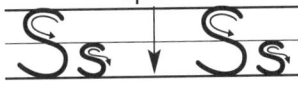

Ss

Tt

Uu

Vv

Ww

Xx

Yy

Zz

Reading Log

1. Keep a log of your classroom reading and independent reading.
2. Share your log with your classmates and talk about what you enjoyed.

Name _____ Date _____

Date	Title of Reading and Author	Reading Time	Pages Read	Comments
Sept. 2	Bread, Bread, Bread, by Ann Morris	20 minutes	pp. 10-15	Beautiful pictures. They make me hungry!

Name _____ Date _____

Sense Chart

1. Write the subject in the first box.
2. Write what the subject makes you see, hear, feel, taste, and smell in the boxes.

Subject	See	Hear	Feel	Taste	Smell

TEACHER RESOURCE 107

Name _____ Date _____

Sentence Builders

Unit A

Use these word boxes.

1. **Build sentences.**
2. **Recognize and use correct word order in sentences.**
3. **Write and speak in complete sentences (copy the sentences; read them aloud).**
4. **Distinguish between complete and incomplete sentences.**

.	?	!	,	s	
a	afternoon	am		an	boy
bye	girl	good	good-bye		hello
hi	I	I'm	is	later	man
Miss	morning		Mr.	Mrs.	Ms.
my	name	school		see	
student		teacher		this	what's
who's	woman	you	your		

108 TEACHER RESOURCE

Name _____ Date _____

Sentence Builders

Unit B

Use these word boxes.

1. Build sentences.
2. Recognize and use correct word order in sentences.
3. Write and speak in complete sentences (copy the sentences; read them aloud).
4. Distinguish between complete and incomplete sentences.

are	backpack	black	blue	board
book	brown	chair	classroom	clock
eighteen	close	computer		desk
door	eight	eleven	erase	eraser	fifteen
fifty	five	flag	forty	four	fourteen
from	go	green	he	how	I
I'm	marker	nine	nineteen	notebook	
old	one	open	orange	pen	pencil
pink	please	purple	red	seven	
seventeen	she	sit	six	sixteen
ten	thirteen	thirty	three	to
twelve	twenty	two	where	white
window	write	years	yellow	you

TEACHER RESOURCE 109

Name _____ Date _____

Sentence Builders

Unit C

Use these word boxes.

1. Build sentences.
2. Recognize and use correct word order in sentences.
3. Write and speak in complete sentences (copy the sentences; read them aloud).
4. Distinguish between complete and incomplete sentences.

a	are	arm	black	blond	blue
body	brown	cheek	chin	classmates	
color	down	ear	elbow	eye	face
fingers		foot	friends		gray
great	green	hair	hand	has	hat
head	her	I	is	jacket	
jeans	knee	left	leg	like	lips
mouth	my	neck	nose	pants	put
red	right	she	shirt	shoes	skirt
sneakers		stomach		sweater	
teeth	thank	thanks		that	touch
what	you	your			

Name _____ Date _____

Sentence Builders

Unit D

Use these word boxes.

1. Build sentences.
2. Recognize and use correct word order in sentences.
3. Write and speak in complete sentences (copy the sentences; read them aloud).
4. Distinguish between complete and incomplete sentences.

across	bathroom	between	
bookcase	bookshelf	bulletin board	
cafeteria	elevator	entrance	
excuse	first	floor	from	gym
hall	I	is	left	librarian
library	locker	main	me	
need	next	nurse's	office	
on	principal's	right	second	
stairs	the	to	want	where

TEACHER RESOURCE 111

Name _____ Date _____

Storyboard

Use a Storyboard to summarize and show sequence with words and pictures.

1. Write a sequence of the most important steps or events.
2. Put the events in the order they happen.
3. Draw a picture if you want.

1. First, _____ _____ _____	**2.** Second, _____ _____ _____
3. Third, _____ _____ _____	**4.** Fourth, _____ _____ _____
5. Fifth, _____ _____ _____	**6.** Finally, _____ _____ _____

Name _____ Date _____

Story Map

Take Notes and Organize Information in a Sequence

Use this graphic organizer for writing narratives and for listening/speaking presentations.

Beginning	Middle	End

Name _____ Date _____

Sunshine Organizer

Reporting

Use a Sunshine Organizer to help you answer questions about a topic or to write a report.

1. Write the topic on the line in the circle.

2. Write answers to the questions next to the triangles.

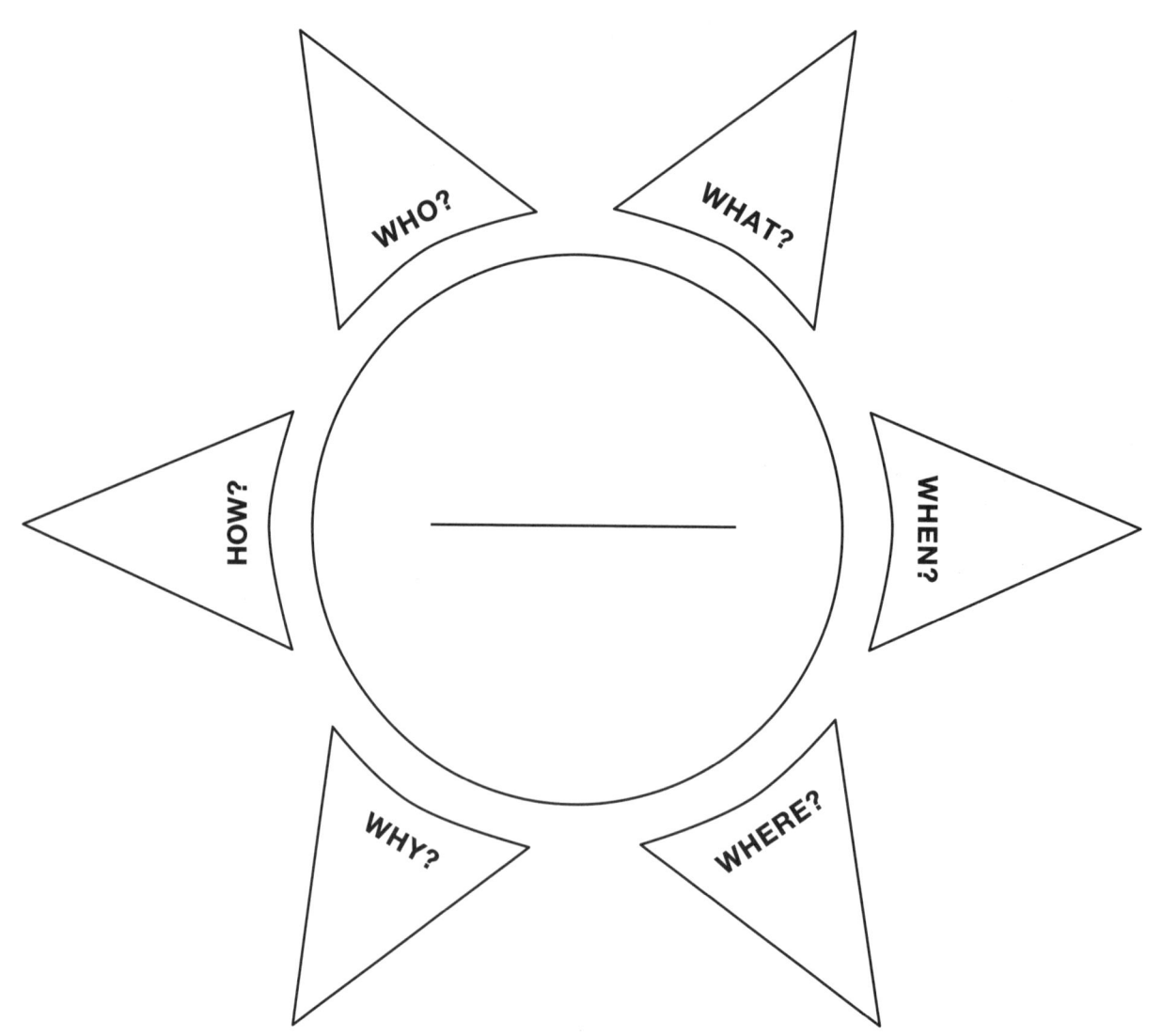

114 TEACHER RESOURCE

Name _____ Date _____

Syllabication Spelling Pattern: Closed Syllables

A **syllable** is a unit of pronunciation. A syllable contains only one vowel sound. A word can have one or more syllables. Dividing words into syllables helps you learn how to pronounce them.

Closed Syllables

- A closed syllable ends in a consonant.
- A closed syllable has one vowel.
- The vowel sound in a closed syllable is short.

Examples:
sat, run, nap/kin, **sub**/ject

➤ Activities

A The following words have two closed syllables. Can you find the closed syllables in each word? (Hint: Divide between two consonants.)

1. problem
2. sandwich
3. pencil
4. lesson
5. dentist
6. address
7. children
8. absent
9. object
10. husband
11. subtract
12. hundred
13. custom
14. subject
15. until

B Read the words in Activity A. Pause between each syllable.

TEACHER RESOURCE 115

Name _____ Date _____

Syllabication Spelling Pattern: Open Syllables

A **syllable** is a unit of pronunciation. A syllable contains only one vowel sound. A word can have one or more syllables. Dividing words into syllables helps you learn how to pronounce them.

Open Syllables

- An open syllable ends in a vowel.
- The vowel sound in an open syllable is usually long.

Examples:
me, no, she, mu/sic, **ta**/ble, **o**/pen

➤ Activities

A The first syllable of each of the following words is an open syllable. Can you find the open syllable in each word? (Hint: Divide between a vowel and a single consonant.)

1. paper
2. focus
3. baby
4. basic
5. favor
6. polite
7. final
8. future
9. human
10. label
11. local
12. photograph
13. program
14. total
15. prefix

B Read the words in Activity A. Pause between each syllable.

Name _____ Date _____

Syllabication Spelling Pattern: Final -e (VCe) Syllables

A **syllable** is a unit of pronunciation. A syllable contains only one vowel sound. A word can have one or more syllables. Dividing words into syllables helps you learn how to pronounce them.

Final -e (VCe) Syllables

- A final -e (VCe) syllable ends in a vowel, a consonant, and a final -e.
- The final -e is silent and makes the earlier vowel long.

Examples:
make, cute, hope, a/**lone**, in/**side**

➤ Activity

The last syllable of each of the following words is a final -e (VCe) syllable. Can you find the final -e (VCe) syllable in each word?

1. compare
2. invite
3. confuse
4. erase
5. describe
6. provide
7. debate
8. inside
9. combine
10. mistake
11. delete
12. prepare
13. excuse
14. translate
15. complete

TEACHER RESOURCE 117

Name _____ Date _____

Syllabication Spelling Pattern: Vowel Digraphs (Vowel Teams)

Sometimes two letters together create one vowel sound. Each syllable in a word has only one vowel sound. However, there may be two vowels that make up this one vowel sound. When two vowels work together to make one vowel sound, these vowels are not separated into two different syllables. They stay together in the same syllable. This syllable spelling pattern is called a **vowel digraph** (or a **vowel team**).

- A vowel digraph syllable always has a vowel pair (or team).
- The vowel sound in a vowel digraph syllable is long.

Examples:
boat, **meat**, ex/**plain**, re/**peat**, **sea**/son

▶ Activity

One syllable in each of the following words is a vowel digraph syllable. Can you find each vowel digraph syllable? Pronounce the words.

1. agree
2. coffee
3. explain
4. fingernail
5. teenager
6. afraid
7. contain
8. reason
9. classroom
10. meaning
11. detail
12. heater
13. complain
14. volunteer
15. piece

Name _____ Date _____

Syllabication Spelling Pattern: *r*-Controlled Vowels

One common syllable spelling pattern is ***r*-controlled vowels.** When the letter *r* follows a vowel, it affects the sound of the vowel. When dividing a word into syllables, the vowel and the *r* usually stay in the same syllable.

- *r*-controlled vowels contain a vowel followed by an *r*.
- The vowel sound is affected by the *r*.

Examples:
car, her, bird, but/**ter,** en/**ter, per**/son

➤ Activity

One syllable in each of the following words is a syllable with an *r*-controlled vowel. Can you find the syllable with the *r*-controlled vowel?

1. winter
2. letter
3. finger
4. order
5. number
6. partner
7. carpet
8. after
9. before
10. birthday
11. doctor
12. dollar
13. firefighter
14. forty
15. sister

Name _____ Date _____

Syllabication Spelling Pattern: Consonant + -*le*

One common syllable spelling pattern is **consonant + -*le*.** This letter combination usually forms the last syllable in a word.

- This syllable is made up of a consonant + -*le*.
- The *l* is silent.
- This syllable appears at the end of a word.

Examples:
fa/**ble**, cir/**cle**, ti/**tle**

➤ Activity

One syllable in each of the following words is a consonant + -*le* syllable. Can you find the consonant + -*le* syllable in each word?

1. table
2. able
3. single
4. dimple
5. apple
6. middle
7. purple
8. sample
9. simple
10. bicycle
11. uncle
12. bottle
13. little
14. double

Name _____   Date _____

Test-Taking Tips

Use these tips to help you improve your performance on tests.

BEFORE THE TEST

1. Complete all of your assignments on time.
2. Take notes in class as you go over your assignments.
3. Save and review your class notes, assignments, and quizzes.
4. Ask your teacher what topics will be covered on the test.
5. Ask your teacher what kind of test you will take. For example, will the questions be true/false, multiple choice, or essay?
6. Be organized. Make a study guide. Making note cards or rewriting information will help you review.
7. Study, and then get a good night's sleep before the test.
8. Eat a good, healthy breakfast on the day of the test.
9. Bring everything that you need to the test (pencils, erasers, pens, and so on).

DURING THE TEST

1. Pay close attention to the teacher's instructions. Ask questions if you do not understand.
2. Read the instructions on the test carefully.
3. Look at the test before you begin to see how long it is.
4. Don't spend too much time on any one section or question. Skip questions that you don't know. Return to them if you have time at the end.
5. Watch the time to make sure you finish the whole test.
6. Save time to look over the test before you turn it in. Don't worry if other students finish before you. Use all the time that you have.

AFTER THE TEST

1. When your test is returned to you, look at it carefully.
2. Look up the answers to any questions you left blank or got wrong.
3. Ask your teacher about any questions that you still don't understand. The same question might appear again on another test.

Name _____ Date _____

Three-Column Chart

Take Notes and Organize Information

Use this chart to take notes and organize information for speaking and writing. Also use it to take notes on characters, setting, and plot (events).

1. Write the topic or title in the top box.
2. Write the names of the three categories in the next row.
3. List words in the three categories as appropriate.

Name _____ Date _____

Three-Paragraph Composition

1. Write in a notebook or on the computer.
2. Write a topic sentence with your main idea.
3. Give reasons, details, and facts to support your main idea.
4. Use transition words.
5. Write a summary to conclude your composition.
6. Use a dictionary or computer software for help with words and spelling.

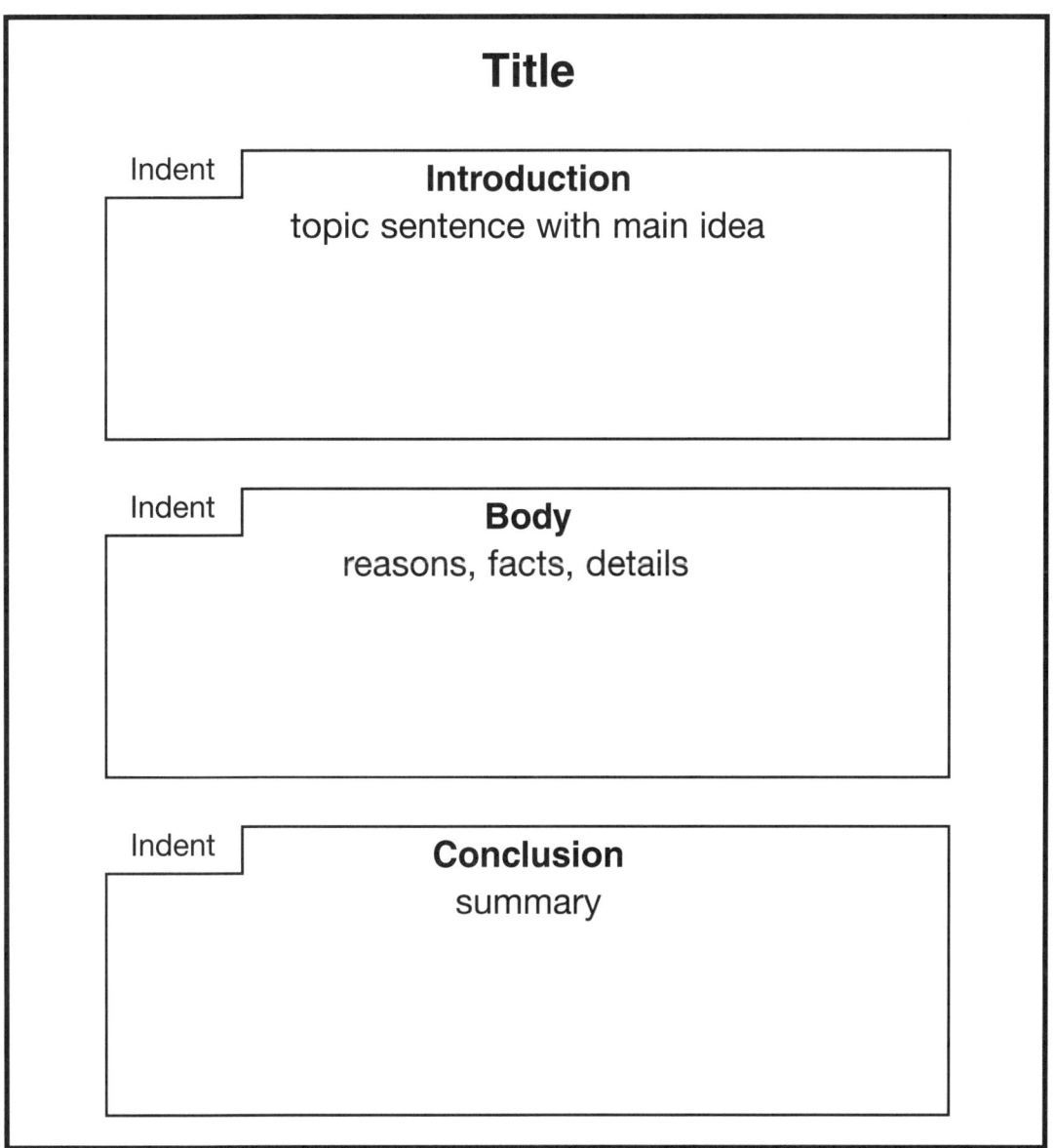

Name _____ Date _____

Two-Column Chart

Take Notes and Organize Information

Use this chart to take notes and organize information for speaking and writing assignments.

Also use it when you read and take notes on Main Idea/Details, Fact/Opinion, Cause/Effect, Problem/Solution, Words/Synonyms (or Antonyms), or Advantages/Disadvantages.

1. Write the topic or title in the top box.
2. In the left column of the first row, write the first word; for example: Main Idea.
3. In the right column of the first row, write the second word; for example: Details.

Name _____ Date _____

Venn Diagram

Use a Venn Diagram to compare and contrast.

1. Write the two things you are comparing on the lines in the two circles.
2. List ways the two things are different under the lines.
3. List ways the two things are alike in the space where the circles overlap.

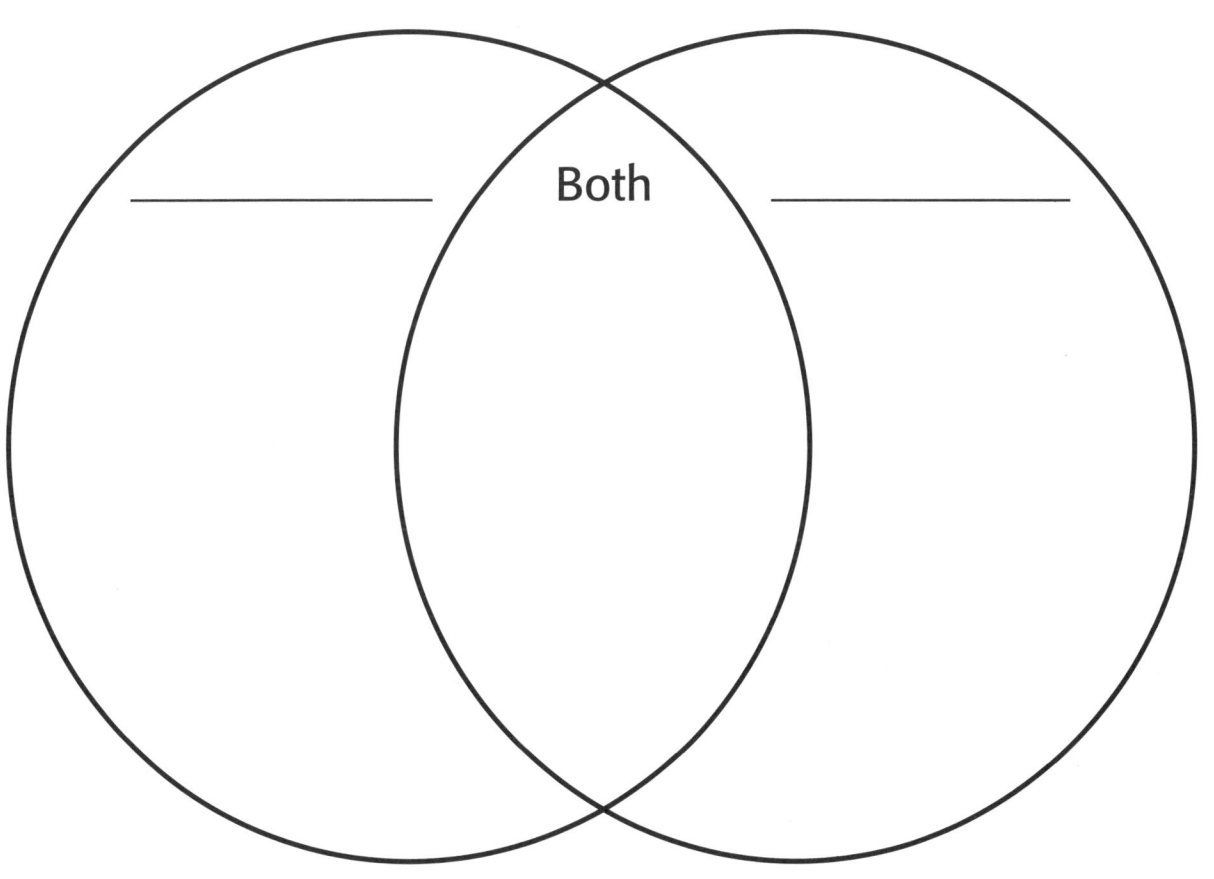

Web

Use a Web to build vocabulary or to identify the main idea and details.

1. Write the main idea or vocabulary word in the large oval in the middle.
2. Write related vocabulary words and details in the smaller ovals.
3. Add or delete ovals as needed.

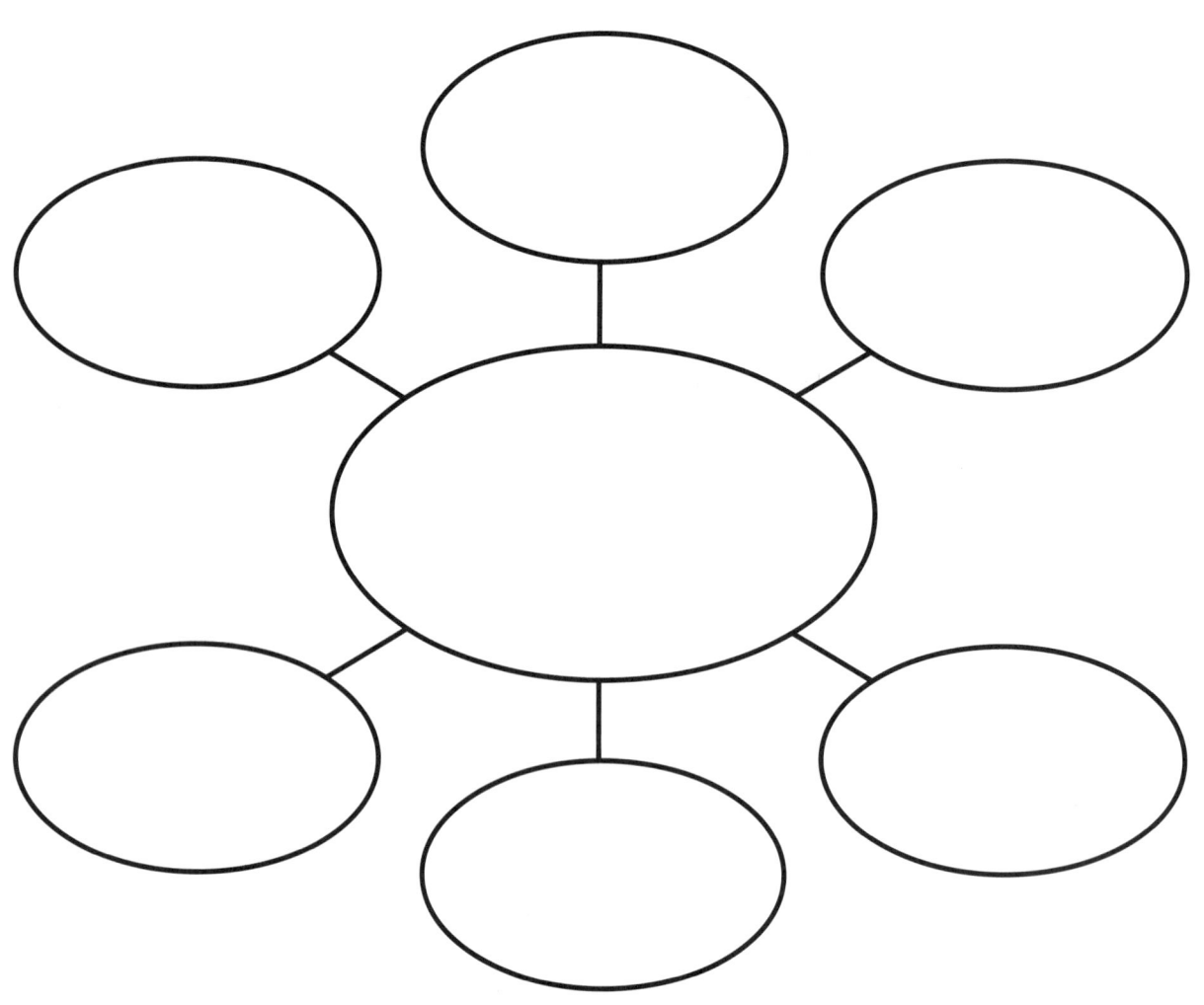

Name _____ Date _____

Word Squares

Use Word Squares to help you remember the meanings of new words.

1. Write a new word in the **Word** box.
2. Use a dictionary. Write the meaning of the word in the **Meaning** box.
3. Draw a symbol (picture) in the **Symbol** box.
4. Write a sentence with the word in the **Sentence** box.

Word	Symbol
Meaning	Sentence

Word	Symbol
Meaning	Sentence

Word	Symbol
Meaning	Sentence

Word	Symbol
Meaning	Sentence

Name _____ Date _____

Writing Lines

Use these writing lines to:

1. Print and write legibly.
2. Space letters, words, and sentences.

School-Home Connection
Sharing Visions

UNIT A   At School

Name _____

Date _____

Dear Family,

In class, we learned about people we meet at school. _____ *(student's name)* wants to share with you what we learned.

Language and Vocabulary. At school, we meet teachers and students. Some teachers are men. Some teachers are women. Some students are boys and some are girls. We learned how to say our names and to say hello and good-bye.

Letters, Sounds, Words. We learned to say and write some consonants. We practiced the sounds the letters make. We also learned short vowel sounds (*a, e, i, o, u*). We learned about words that rhyme. The words *cat* and *bat* rhyme.

Reading and Writing. We practiced reading words and sentences. We learned the alphabet, and we practiced writing print and cursive letters. We also wrote words and sentences.

We know you want to support your student's achievement in school. We would like you to participate in an activity to share with the class. Thank you for your support.

Sincerely,

_____ *(Teacher)*

Practice greetings and introductions with your family and friends.

1. **A:** Hi. My name is _____. What's your name?

   B: Hello, my name is _____.

   A: Nice to meet you.

   B: Nice to meet you, too!

2. **A:** Good morning, _____.

   B: Good morning, _____.

3. **A:** Good-bye, _____.

   B: Bye, _____. See you later, _____.

4. Read the alphabet.

   A B C D E F G H I J K L M N O P Q R S T U V W X Y Z

School-Home Connection
Sharing Visions

មេរៀនទី A នៅសាលារៀន

ឈ្មោះ _____

កាលបរិច្ឆេទ _____

ឪពុក ម្ដាយជាទីស្រឡាញ់

នៅក្នុងថ្នាក់រៀន យើងបានរៀនអំពីមនុស្សដែលយើងជួបនៅសាលារៀន ។ _____ (ឈ្មោះសិស្ស) ចង់ចែករំលែកនូវអ្វីដែលយើងបានរៀនជាមួយនឹងអ្នក ។

ភាសា និង វាក្យសព្ទ នៅសាលារៀន យើងជួបគ្រូបង្រៀន និង សិស្ស ។ គ្រូមួយចំនួនគឺបុរស ។ គ្រូ មួយចំនួនទៀតគឺស្ត្រី ។ សិស្សមួយចំនួនគឺប្រុស និង មួយចំនួនទៀតគឺស្រី ។ យើងបានរៀនពីរបៀប និយាយឈ្មោះរបស់យើង និង របៀបនិយាយសួស្ដី និង លាគ្នា ។

អក្សរ, សម្លេង, ពាក្យ យើងបានរៀននិយាយ និង សរសេរព្យញ្ជនៈមួយចំនួន ។ យើងបានហាត់ រៀនបញ្ចេញសម្លេងនៃអក្សរ ។ យើងក៏បានរៀនពីសម្លេងស្រៈខ្លី *(a, e, i, o, u)* ។ យើងបានរៀនអំពី ពាក្យដែលរណ្ដំ ។ ពាក្យ *cat* និង *bat* រណ្ដំគ្នា ។

ការអាន និង ការសរសេរ យើងបានហាត់អានពាក្យ និង ប្រយោគ ។ យើងបានរៀនក្រមអក្សរ ហើយយើងបានហាត់សរសេរអក្សរពុម្ព និង អក្សរសរសេរដៃបន្ដគ្នា ។ យើងក៏បានសរសេរពាក្យ និង ប្រយោគ ។

យើងដឹងថាអ្នកចង់គាំទ្រនូវការសម្រេចបានរបស់សិស្សអ្នកនៅសាលារៀន ។ យើងចង់ឱ្យអ្នកចូលរួម នៅក្នុងសកម្មភាពដែលចែករំលែកគ្នាជាមួយនឹងថ្នាក់រៀន ។ សូមអរគុណចំពោះការគាំទ្ររបស់អ្នក ។

ដោយក្ដីគោរពរាប់អាន

_____ (គ្រូបង្រៀន)

ហាត់រៀនសួស្ដី និង ការណែនាំជាមួយគ្រួសារ និង មិត្តភ័ក្ដិអ្នក ។

១. A: សួស្ដី! ខ្ញុំឈ្មោះ _____ ។ តើអ្នកឈ្មោះអ្វី?

   B: សួស្ដី! ខ្ញុំឈ្មោះ _____ ។

   A: រីករាយណាស់ដែលបានជួបអ្នក ។

   B: ខ្ញុំក៏រីករាយណាស់ដែរ ដែលបានជួបអ្នក!

២. A: អរុណ មុរនិងរួង _____ ។

   B: អរុណសួស្ដី _____ ។

៣. A: លាហើយ _____ ។

   B: លាហើយ _____ ។ ជួបគ្នាថ្ងៃក្រោយ _____ ។

៤. សូមអានក្រមអក្សរខាងក្រោម ។

A B C D E F G H I J K L M N O P Q R S T U V W X Y Z

School-Home Connection
Sharing Visions

姓名 _____

日期 _____

單元 A　在學校

親愛的家長：

我們在課堂上學了我們在學校遇到的人。_____（學生姓名）想和您們分享我們的上課內容。

語言和字彙　我們在學校會遇到老師和學生。有些老師是男性，有些老師是女性。有些學生是男生，有些學生是女生。我們學習如何說我們的名字，以及說你好和再見。

字母、發聲、詞彙　我們學習說和寫一些子音。我們練習一些字母的發聲。我們也學習發短母音（*a, e, i, o, u*），也學習哪些字押韻。*cat*（貓）和 *bat*（蝙蝠）押韻。

閱讀和寫作　我們練習閱讀字和句子，學習字母，並練習印刷體和草寫體的寫法。我們也寫下字和句子。

我們知道您們很樂意協助孩子學習。希望您們能參與以下活動，我們會在課堂分享結果。感謝您們的協助。

敬上

_____（老師）

與家人和朋友練習打招呼和自我介紹。

1. **A:** 你好，我的名字是 _____。你叫什麼名字？
   B: 你好，我的名字是 _____。
   A: 很高興認識你。
   B: 我也很高興認識你。

2. **A:** 早安，_____。
   B: 早安，_____。

3. **A:** 再見，_____。
   B: 再見，_____。待會見，_____。

4. 讀 26 個字母。

   A B C D E F G H I J K L M N O P Q R S T U V W X Y Z

School-Home Connection
Sharing Visions
SEKSYON A Nan Lekòl la

Non _____

Dat _____

Chè Fanmi,

  Nan klas la, nou aprann sou moun nou rankontre nan lekòl la. _____ *(non elèv la)* ta renmen pataje avèk ou sa nou aprann.

  Langaj ak Vokabilè. Nan lekòl la, nou rankontre pwofesè ak elèv. Kèk pwofesè se gason. Kèk pwofesè se fanm. Kèk elèv se gason e kèk se fi. Nou aprann ki jan pou nou di non nou e ki jan pou nou di bonjou ak orevwa.

  Lèt, Son, Mo. Nou aprann di ak ekri kèk konsonn. Nou repete son lèt yo fè. Nou aprann tou son vwayèl kout yo *(a, e, i, o, u)*. Nou aprann son mo ki rime. Mo *cat* ak *bat* rime.

  Li ak Ekri. Nou egzèse li mo ak fraz. Nou aprann alfabè, e nou egzèse ekri lèt enprime ak lèt awondi. Nou ekri tou mo ak fraz.

  Nou konnen ke ou vle ankouraje reyisit pitit ou nan lekòl la. Nou ta renmen ke ou patisipe nan yon aktivite pou pataje ak klas la. Mèsi pou sipò ou.

  Sensèman,

  _____ *(Pwofesè)*

Egsèse salitasyon ak entwodiksyon avèk fanmi w ak zanmi w.

1. **A:** Bonjou, mwen rele _____. Kijan ou rele?

   B: Bonjou, mwen rele _____.

   A: Mwen kontan rankontre w.

   B: Mwen menm tou!

2. **A:** Bonjou, _____.

   B: Bonjou, _____.

3. **A:** Orevwa, _____.

   B: Babay, _____. Na wè pita, _____.

4. Li alfabè a,

   A B C D E F G H I J K L M N O P Q R S T U V W X Y Z

School-Home Connection
Sharing Visions
SOB KAWM A Tom Tsev Kawm Ntawv

Npe _____

Hnub Tim _____

Nyob zoo txog Tsev Neeg,

Hauv chav kawm ntawv, peb kawm txog cov neeg uas peb ntsib tom tsev kawm ntawv. _____ *(tus menyuam kawm ntawv lub npe)* yuav xav qhia rau koj seb pab kawm txog dab tsi.

Hom lus thiab Ntsiab Lus. Tom tsev kawm ntawv, peb ntsib cov kws qhia ntawv thiab cov menyuam kawm ntawv. Ib co kws qhia ntawv yog txiv neej. Ib co kws qhia ntawv yog poj niam. Ib co menyuam kawm ntawv yog menyuam tub thiab ib co yog menyuam ntxhais. Peb kawm hais peb lub npe thiab hais nyob zoo thiab mus zoo.

Cov tsiaj ntawv, Cov suab, Cov Lus. Peb kawm hais thiab sau cov tsiaj ntawv. Peb xyaum hais lub suab ntawm cov tsiaj ntawv. Peb tseem kawm txog cov niam ntawv *(a, e, i, o, u)*. Peb kawm txog cov lus uas sib dhos. Cov lus *cat* thiab *bat* sib dhos.

Kev nyeem ntawv thiab Sau ntawv. Peb xyaum nyeej cov lus thiab cov sob lus. Peb kawm cov tsiaj ntawv, thiab peb xyaum sau cov ntawv thiab cov ntawv sib cab. Peb tseem cov lus thiab sau cov sob lus.

Peb paub tias koj xav txhawb koj tus menyuam kev kawm kom tau zoo hauv tsev kawm ntawv. Peb xav kom koj koom hauv ib qho kev ua uas coj los qhia rau hauv chav kawm. Ua tsaug rau koj txoj kev txhawb nqa.

Sau npe,

_____ *(Tus kws qhia ntawv)*

Xyaum kev txais tos thiab kev qhia nrog koj tsev neeg thiab cov phooj ywg.

1. **A:** Nyob zoo. Kuv lub npe hu ua ____. Koj lub npe hu li cas?
   B: Nyob zoo. Kuv lub npe hu ua ____.
   A: Zoo siab tau ntsib koj.
   B: Zoos siab tau ntsib koj thiab!

2. **A:** Nyob zoo sawv ntxov, ____.
   B: Nyob zoo sawv ntxov, ____.

3. **A:** Mus zoo koj, ____.
   B: Mus zoo koj, ____. Ntsib koj ib chim, ____.

4. Nyeem cov tsiaj ntawv.
   A B C D E F G H I J K L M N O P Q R S T U V W X Y Z

School-Home Connection
Sharing Visions

UNIDAD A   En la escuela

Nombre _____

Fecha _____

Querida Familia:

En clase, aprendimos sobre las personas que conocemos en la escuela. A _____ *(nombre del alumno)* le gustaría compartir con ustedes lo que hemos aprendido.

Lengua y Vocabulario. En la escuela, conocemos maestros, maestras y estudiantes. Hay maestros varones. Y hay maestras mujeres. Entre los alumnos hay niños y niñas. Aprendimos a decir nuestros nombres y a decir hola y adiós.

Letras, Sonidos, Palabras. Aprendimos a decir y escribir más consonantes. Aprendimos los sonidos que hacen las letras. También aprendimos los sonidos de las vocales cortas *(a, e, i, o, u)*. Aprendimos palabras que riman. Las palabras *cat* y *bat* riman.

Leer y Escribir. Practicamos la lectura de palabras y oraciones. Aprendimos el alfabeto y escribimos letras en imprenta y en cursiva. También escribimos palabras y oraciones.

Sabemos que ustedes quieren apoyar el esfuerzo que realiza su estudiante en la escuela. Nos gustaría que participen en alguna actividad para compartir con la clase. Gracias por su apoyo.

Atentamente,

_____ *(Maestro/a)*

Practica saludos y presentaciones con tu familia y amigos.

1. **A:** Hola. Mi nombre es _____. ¿Cómo te llamas?

   B: Hola, me llamo _____.

   A: Mucho gusto.

   B: El gusto es mío.

2. **A:** Buen día, _____.

   B: Buen día, _____.

3. **A:** Adiós, _____.

   B: Adiós, _____. Hasta luego, _____.

4. Lee el alfabeto.

   A B C D E F G H I J K L M N O P Q R S T U V W X Y Z

School-Home Connection
Sharing Visions

Bài A Ở Trường

Tên: _____

Ngày tháng năm: _____

Thưa Gia Đình,

Ở lớp, chúng đã đã học về những người ta gặp ở trường. _____ *(tên học sinh)* muốn chia sẻ với quý vị những gì chúng ta đã học.

Ngôn Ngữ và Từ Vựng. Ở trường, chúng ta gặp các giáo viên và học sinh. Một số giáo viên là nam giới. Một số giáo viên là phụ nữ. Một số học sinh là con trai và một số là con gái. Chúng ta đã học cách nói tên của mình và cách nói lời chào và tạm biệt.

Chữ Cái, Âm, Từ. Chúng ta học cách nói và viết một số phụ âm. Chúng ta thực tập các âm mà các chữ cái tạo nên. Chúng ta cũng học các âm do nguyên âm ngắn (*a, e, i, o, u*). Chúng ta học về các từ vần nhau. Các từ *cat* và *bat* là vần nhau.

Đọc và Viết. Chúng ta tập đọc các chữ và câu. Chúng ta học bảng chữ cái, và chúng ta tập viết các chữ cái in và thảo. Chúng ta cũng viết các chữ và câu.

Chúng tôi biết rằng quý vị muốn hỗ trợ thành tích học tập của con em mình ở trường. Chúng tôi muốn quý vị tham gia vào một hoạt động để chia sẻ với lớp. Xin cám ơn vì sự ủng hộ của quý vi.

Trân Trọng Kính Chào,

_____ *(Giáo Viên)*

Hãy luyện tập những lời chào và lời giới thiệu với gia đình và bạn bè.

1. **A:** Chào. Tên tôi là _____. Tên bạn là gì?

   B: Xin chào, tên tôi là _____.

   A: Rất vui được gặp bạn.

   B: Tôi cũng rất vui được gặp bạn!

2. **A:** Xin chào buổi sáng, _____.

   B: Xin chào buổi sáng, _____.

3. **A:** Tạm biệt, _____.

   B: Tạm biệt, _____. Hẹn gặp sau nhé, _____.

4. Hãy đọc bảng chữ cái.

   A B C D E F G H I J K L M N O P Q R S T U V W X Y Z

School-Home Connection
Sharing Visions
UNIT B   In the Classroom

Name _____

Date _____

Dear Family,

In class, we learned about things in the classroom. _____ (student's name) wants to share with you what we learned.

Language and Vocabulary. We learned to name things in the classroom. We also learned how to give and follow instructions. It is polite to use the word *please* when you ask someone to do something. We learned numbers and colors. We also learned to give our age, country, and nationality.

Sounds and Words. We learned how to say and write more consonants. We learned the sounds the consonants make. We also learned long vowel sounds.

Reading and Writing. We read about the American flag. We wrote information about ourselves.

We know you want to support your student's achievement in school. We would like you to participate in an activity to share with the class. Thank you for your support.

Sincerely,

_____ (Teacher)

Practice greetings and introductions with your family and friends.

1. A: What is your name?
   B: My name is _____.

2. A: How old are you?
   B: I am _____.

3. A: Where are you from?
   B: I'm from _____.

4. A: What color is the flag?
   B: The flag is _____.

5. A: What's your nationality?
   B: I'm _____.

School-Home Connection
Sharing Visions

មេរៀនទី B នៅក្នុងថ្នាក់រៀន

ឈ្មោះ _____

កាលបរិច្ឆេទ _____

ជូនចំពោះ គ្រួសារ

នៅក្នុងថ្នាក់រៀន យើងបានរៀនអំពីវត្ថុនៅក្នុងថ្នាក់រៀន ។ _____ (ឈ្មោះសិស្ស) ចង់ចែករំលែកនូវអ្វីដែលយើងបានរៀនជាមួយនឹងអ្នក ។

ភាសា និង វាក្យសព្ទ យើងបានរៀនដាក់ឈ្មោះឲ្យវត្ថុនៅក្នុងថ្នាក់រៀន ។ យើងក៏បានរៀនពីរបៀប ផ្ដល់ និង ធ្វើតាមការណែនាំ ។ វាជាការគួរសមដែលយើងប្រើពាក្យ *please* នៅពេលយើងសុំឲ្យ នរណាម្នាក់ធ្វើអ្វីមួយ ។ យើងបានរៀនពីលេខ និង ពណ៌ ។ យើងក៏បានរៀនប្រាប់ពីអាយុ ប្រទេស និង សញ្ជាតិរបស់យើង ។

សម្លេង និង ពាក្យ យើងបានរៀនរបៀបនិយាយ និង សរសេរព្យញ្ជនៈជាច្រើនទៀត ។ យើងបាន រៀនបញ្ចេញសម្លេងព្យញ្ជនៈ ។ យើងក៏បានរៀនពីសម្លេងស្រៈវែង ។

ការអាន និង ការសរសេរ យើងបានអំពីទង់ជាតិអាមេរិកាំង ។ យើងបានសរសេរព័ត៌មានអំពីខ្លួន យើងផ្ទាល់ ។

យើងដឹងថាអ្នកចង់គាំទ្រនូវការសម្រេចចានរបស់សិស្សអ្នកនៅសាលារៀន ។ យើងចង់ឲ្យអ្នកចូលរួម នៅក្នុងសកម្មភាពដែលចែករំលែកគ្នាជាមួយនឹងថ្នាក់រៀន ។ សូមអរគុណចំពោះការគាំទ្ររបស់អ្នក ។

ដោយក្ដីគោរពរាប់អាន

_____ (គ្រូបង្រៀន)

សូមសួរទៅសមាជិកគ្រួសារនូវសំណួរទាំងនេះ ។ សូមសរសេរចម្លើយ ។

១. **A:** តើអ្នកមានឈ្មោះអ្វី?
   B: ឈ្មោះរបស់ខ្ញុំគឺ _____ ។

២. **A:** តើអ្នកមានអាយុប៉ុន្មាន?
   B: ខ្ញុំមានអាយុ ។

៣. **A:** តើអ្នកមកពីណា?
   B: ខ្ញុំមកព _____ ។

៤. **A:** តើទង់ជាតិមានពណ៌អ្វី?
   B: ទង់ជាតិមានពណ៌ _____ ។

៥. **A:** តើអ្នកមានសញ្ជាតិអ្វី?
   B: ខ្ញុំមានសញ្ជាត _____ ។

School-Home Connection
Sharing Visions

單元 B　在教室裡

姓名 _____

日期 _____

親愛的家長：

　　我們在課堂上學習教室裡的擺設。_____（學生姓名）想和您們分享我們的上課內容。

　　語言和字彙　我們學習說出教室的擺設名稱，也學會如何給指示，以及遵照指示。若請求別人做事時，禮貌地使用「請」please 字。我們學習數字和顏色，也學習如何說我們的年紀、國家和國籍。

　　發音和詞彙　我們學習說和寫其他子音，練習子音和長母音的發聲。

　　閱讀和寫作　我們閱讀講解美國國旗的文章，也寫下自我介紹。

　　我們知道您們很樂意幫助孩子學習。希望您們能參與以下活動，我們將在課堂上分享。感謝您們的協助。

　　　　　　　　　　　　　　　　　敬上

　　　　　　　　　　_____（老師）

問一位家人以下問題。寫下答案。

1. **A:** 你叫什麼名字？

   B: 我的名字是 _____？

2. **A:** 你幾歲？

   B: 我_____。

3. **A:** 你來自哪裡？

   B: 我來自 _____。

4. **A:** 這面國旗是什麼顏色？

   B: 這面國旗是 _____。

5. **A:** 你是哪一國人？

   B: 我是 _____？

School-Home Connection
Sharing Visions
SEKSYON B Nan Saldeklas la

Non _____

Dat _____

Chè Fanmi,

Nan klas la, nou aprann sou bagay ki nan saldeklas la. _____ *(non elèv la)* ta renmen pataje avèk ou sa nou aprann.

Langaj ak Vokabilè. Nou aprann nonmen bagay ki nan saldeklas la. Nou aprann tou ki jan pou nou bay ak swiv enstriksyon. Se bon lizaj pou itilize *please* lè wap mande yon moun fè kichoy. Nou aprann chif ak koulè. Nou aprann tou bay laj nou, peyi nou, ak nasyonalite nou.

Son ak Mo. Nou aprann ki jan pou pwononse ak ekri plis konsonn. Nou aprann son konsonn yo fè. Nou aprann tou son vwayèl long yo.

Li ak Ekri. Nou li sou drapo Ameriken. Nou ekri enfòmasyon tou sou noumenm.

Nou konnen ke ou vle ankouraje reyisit pitit ou nan lekòl la. Nou ta renmen ke ou patisipe nan yon aktivite pou pataje ak klas la. Mèsi pou sipò ou.

Sensèman,

_____ *(Pwofesè)*

Poze yon manm fanmi w kesyon sa yo. Ekri repons yo.

1. **A:** Kijan ou rele?
   B: Mwen rele _____.
2. **A:** Ki laj ou?
   B: Mwen gen _____.
3. **A:** Ki kote ou soti?
   B: Mwen soti _____.
4. **A:** Ki koulè drapo a?
   B: Drapo a _____.
5. **A:** Ki nasyonalite ou?
   B: Mwen se _____.

School-Home Connection
Sharing Visions

SOB KAWM B Hauv Chav Kawm Ntawv

Npe _____

Hnub Tim _____

Nyob zoo txog Tsev Neeg,

Hauv chav kawm ntawv, peb kawm txog khoom nyob hauv chav kawm ntawv. _____ (*tus menyuam kawm ntawv lub npe*) yuav xav qhia rau koj seb pab kawm txog dab tsi.

Hom lus thiab Ntsiab Lus. Peb kawm hais cov khoom nyob hauv chav kawm ntawv. Peb tseem kawm qhia thiab ua raws li cov lus qhia ua. Nws yog ib qho coj cwj pwm zoo rau peb hais lo lus *please* thaum peb hais kom ib tus neeg twg ua ib yam dab tsi. Peb kawm hais cov kob cuj (numbers) thiab cov yeeb yuj (colors). Peb tseem kawm qhia seb peb muaj pes tsawg xyoo, peb lub teb chaws, thiab peb yog haiv neeg twg.

Cov Suab thiab Cov Lus. Peb kawm hais thiab sau cov tsiaj ntawv ntxiv. Peb kawm txog cov suab ntawm cov tsiaj ntawv. Peb kawm cov suab ntev.

Nyeem ntawv thiab Sau ntawv. Peb nyeem txog Mis Kas tus chij. Peb sau cov lus qhia txog peb tus kheej.

Peb paub tias koj xav txhawb koj tus menyuam kev kawm kom tau zoo hauv tsev kawm ntawv. Peb xav kom koj koom hauv ib qho kev ua uas coj los qhia rau hauv chav kawm. Ua tsaug rau koj txoj kev txhawb nqa.

Sau npe,

_____ (*Tus kws qhia ntawv*)

Nug ib tug neeg hauv tsev neeg cov nqe lus nug no. Sau cov lus teb.

1. **A:** Koj lub npe hu li cas?

   B: Kuv lub npe hu ua _____.

2. **A:** Koj muaj tsawg xyoo?

   B: Kuv muaj _____.

3. **A:** Koj tuaj qhov twg tuaj?

   B: Kuv tuaj _____.

4. **A:** Tus chij yog yeeb yuj (color) dab tsi?

   B: Tus chij yog _____.

5. **A:** Koj yog haiv neeg dab tsi?

   B: Kuv yog _____.

School-Home Connection
Sharing Visions

UNIDAD B En el salón de clase

Nombre _____

Fecha _____

Querida Familia:

En clase, aprendimos sobre los lugares que rodean la escuela. A _____ *(nombre del alumno)* le gustaría compartir con ustedes lo que hemos aprendido.

Lengua y Vocabulario. Aprendimos a nombrar las cosas del salón de clase. También aprendimos cómo dar y seguir instrucciones. Es buena educación decir *please* cuando le pedimos a alguien que haga algo. Aprendimos los números y los colores. También aprendimos a decir nuestra edad, país y nacionalidad.

Sonidos y Palabras. Aprendimos cómo decir y escribir más consonantes. Aprendimos los sonidos que hacen las consonantes. También aprendimos los sonidos de las vocales largas.

Leer y Escribir. Leímos sobre la bandera estadounidense. Escribimos información sobre nosotros.

Sabemos que ustedes quieren apoyar el esfuerzo que realiza su estudiante en la escuela. Nos gustaría que participen en alguna actividad para compartir con la clase. Gracias por su apoyo.

Atentamente,

_____ *(Maestro/a)*

Haz preguntas a un miembro de la familia. Escribe las respuestas.

1. **A:** ¿Cómo te llamas?
   B: Mi nombre es _____.

2. **A:** ¿Cuántos años tienes?
   B: Tengo _____.

3. **A:** ¿De dónde eres?
   B: Soy de _____.

4. **A:** ¿Qué color es la bandera?
   B: La bandera es _____.

5. **A:** ¿Cuál es tu nacionalidad?
   B: Soy _____.

School-Home Connection
Sharing Visions
Bài B Trong Phòng Học

Tên: _____

Ngày tháng năm: _____

Thưa Gia Đình,

Ở lớp, chúng đã đã học về những thứ trong phòng học. _____ *(tên học sinh)* muốn chia sẻ với quý vị những gì chúng ta đã học.

Ngôn Ngữ và Từ Vựng. Chúng ta đã học cách gọi tên các thứ trong phòng học. Chúng ta cũng học cách đưa ra và làm theo những chỉ dẫn. Khi nhờ ai đó làm việc gì đó thì ta dùng chữ *please* cho lịch sự. Chúng ta học các con số và màu sắc. Chúng ta cũng học cách nói tuổi, đất nước và quốc tịch của mình.

Các Âm và Từ. Chúng ta đã học cách nói và viết nhiều phụ âm nữa. Chúng ta học những âm mà các phụ âm tạo nên. Chúng ta còn học các âm tạo bởi nguyên âm dài.

Đọc và Viết. Chúng ta đọc về lá cờ Mỹ. Chúng ta viết những thông tin về chính mình.

Chúng tôi biết rằng quý vị muốn hỗ trợ thành tích học tập của con em mình ở trường. Chúng tôi muốn quý vị tham gia vào một hoạt động để chia sẻ với lớp. Xin cám ơn vì sự ủng hộ của quý vị.

Trân Trọng Kính Chào,

_____ *(Giáo Viên)*

Hãy đặt các câu hỏi cho một người trong gia đình và viết các câu trả lời ra.

1. **A:** Tên em là gì?

   B: Tên tôi là _____.

2. **A:** Em bao nhiêu tuổi?

   B: Tôi được _____.

3. **A:** Em từ đâu đến?

   B: Tôi từ _____.

4. **A:** Lá cờ có màu gì?

   B: Lá cờ có màu _____.

5. **A:** Quốc tịch của em là gì?

   B: Tôi là người _____.

School-Home Connection
Sharing Visions
UNIT C   Classmates

Name _____

Date _____

Dear Family,

In class, we learned about classmates. _____ *(student's name)* wants to share with you what we learned.

Language and Vocabulary. We learned words for clothes and for parts of the face and body. We learned how to give compliments and say thank you. We also learned how to give and follow directions.

Sounds, Words, Sentences. We learned how to say and write more consonants. We learned the sounds the consonants make. We also learned about consonant and vowel combinations and the sounds they make.

Reading and Writing. We read *Friends*. This is a reading about Jen and Tim. It describes their faces, their hair, and their clothes.

We know you want to support your student's achievement in school. We would like you to participate in an activity to share with the class. Thank you for your support.

Sincerely,

_____ (Teacher)

Describe a family member. Ask the person to help you complete the chart.

1. Name	
2. Age	
3. Hair color	
4. Eye color	
5. Clothes	

School-Home Connection
Sharing Visions

មេរៀនទី C មិត្តរួមថ្នាក់

ឈ្មោះ _____

កាលបរិច្ឆេទ _____

ជូនចំពោះ គ្រួសារ

នៅក្នុងថ្នាក់រៀន យើងបានរៀនអំពីមិត្តរួមថ្នាក់ ។ _____ (ឈ្មោះសិស្ស) ចង់ចែករំលែកនូវអ្វីដែលយើងបានរៀនជាមួយនឹងអ្នក ។

ភាសា និង វាក្យស័ព្ទ យើងបានរៀនពាក្យប្រើសម្រាប់សម្លៀកបំពាក់ និង ផ្នែកនៃមុខ និង រាង កាយ ។ យើងបានរៀនពីរបៀបនិយាយសរសើរ និង អរគុណ ។ យើងក៏បានរៀនពីរបៀបផ្ដល់ និង ធ្វើតាមការបញ្ជាក់ ។

សម្លេង, ពាក្យ និង ប្រយោគ យើងបានរៀនរបៀបនិយាយ និង សរសេរព្យញ្ជនៈជាច្រើនទៀត ។ យើងបានរៀនបញ្ចេញសម្លេងព្យញ្ជនៈ ។ យើងក៏បានរៀនអំពីការបញ្ចូលគ្នារវាងព្យញ្ជនៈ និង ស្រៈ និង សម្លេងរបស់វា ។

ការអាន និង ការសរសេរ យើងបានអានអត្ថបទ *Friends* ។ នេះគឺជាអត្ថបទអានអំពី ផ្ញី ន និង ទិម ។ វាពិណ៌នាអំពីមុខមាត់របស់ពូកគេ សក់របស់ពូកគេ និង សម្លៀកបំពាក់របស់ ពូកគេ ។

យើងដឹងថាអ្នកចង់តាំទ្រនូវការសម្រេចបានរបស់សិស្សអ្នកនៅសាលារៀន ។ យើងចង់ឲ្យអ្នកចូលរួម នៅក្នុងសកម្មភាពដែលចែករំលែកគ្នាជាមួយនឹងថ្នាក់រៀន ។ សូមអរគុណចំពោះការតាំទ្ររបស់អ្នក ។

ដោយក្តីគោរពរាប់អាន

_____ (គ្រូបង្រៀន)

ពិពណ៌នាអំពីសមាជិកគ្រួសារ ។ សូមឲ្យពាត់ជួយអ្នកបំពេញតារាងខាងក្រោម ។

១.	ឈ្មោះ
២.	អាយុ
៣.	ពណ៌សក់
៤.	ពណ៌ភ្នែក
៥.	សម្លៀកបំពាក់

School-Home Connection
Sharing Visions

單元 C　同學

姓名 _____

日期 _____

親愛的家長：

　　我們在課堂上學習同學。_____（學生姓名）想和您們分享我們的上課內容。

　　語言和字彙　我們學習描述衣服、臉部和身體部位的字。我們學會讚美和感謝，也學會如何指示方向，以及依照指示前進。

　　發聲、字、句子　我們學習寫和說其他子音，子音的發聲，以及子音和母音結合在一起的發聲。

　　閱讀和寫作　我們閱讀 *Friends*。這篇閱讀講的是珍和提姆，描述他們的長相、頭髮和衣服。

　　我們知道您們很樂意協助孩子學習。希望您們能參與以下活動，我們將在課堂分享結果。謝謝您們的協助。

　　　　　　　　　　　　　　　　　敬上

　　　　　　　　_____（老師）

描述一位家人請這位家人幫你填這份表格。

1. 姓名	
2. 年齡	
3. 髮色	
4. 眼珠顏色	
5. 衣服	

School-Home Connection
Sharing Visions
SEKSYON C Kanmarad Lekòl

Non _____

Dat _____

Chè Fanmi,

Nan klas la, nou aprann sou kanmarad lekòl. _____ (non elèv la) ta renmen pataje avèk ou sa nou aprann.

Langaj ak Vokabilè. Nou aprann mo pou rad ak sou pati figi ak kò nou. Nou aprann ki jan pou fè konpliman ak di mèsi. Nou aprann tou ki jan pou nou bay ak swiv direksyon.

Son, Mo, Fraz. Nou aprann ki jan pou pwononse ak ekri plis konsonn. Nou aprann son konsonn yo fè. Nou aprann tou sou konbinezon konsonn ak vwayèl e son yo fè.

Li ak Ekri. Nou li *Friends*. Se yon lekti sou Jen ak Tim. Li dekri figi, cheve, ak rad yo.

Nou konnen ke ou vle ankouraje reyisit pitit ou nan lekòl la. Nou ta renmen ke ou patisipe nan yon aktivite pou pataje ak klas la. Mèsi pou sipò ou.

Sensèman,

_____ (Pwofesè)

Dekri yon manm fanmi w. Mande moun sa a ede w konplete tablo a.

1. Non	
2. Laj	
3. Koulè cheve	
4. Koulè je	
5. Rad	

School-Home Connection
Sharing Visions

SOB KAWM C Cov menyuam kawm ntawv hauv chav kawm

Npe _____

Hnub Tim _____

Nyob zoo txog Tsev Neeg,

Hauv chav kawm ntawv, peb kawm txog cov menyuam kawm ntawv hauv chav kawm. _____ (tus menyuam kawm ntawv lub npe) yuav xav qhia rau koj seb pab kawm txog dab tsi.

Hom lus thiab Ntsiab Lus. Peb kawm txog cov lus rau khaub ncaws thiab rau lub ntsej muag thiab lub cev. Peb kawm txog seb yuav hais tej yam zoo thiab yuav hais ua tsaug li cas. Peb tseem kawm txog seb yuav hais thiab ua raws li cov kev qhia li cas.

Cov suab, Cov lus, Cov nqe lus. Peb kawm hais thiab sau cov tsiaj ntawv ntxiv. Peb kawm txog lub suab thiab cov tsiaj ntawv. Peb tseem kawm txog cov niam ntawv thiab lub suab uas lawv ua.

Kev nyeem ntawv thiab Sau ntawv. Peb nyeem *Friends*. Qhov no yog ib qho kev nyeem txog Jen thiab Tim. Nws qhia txog nkawv lub ntsej muag, nkawv cov plaub hau, thiab nkawv cov khaub ncaws.

Peb paub tias koj xav txhawb koj tus menyuam kev kawm kom tau zoo hauv tsev kawm ntawv. Peb xav kom koj koom hauv ib qho kev ua uas coj los qhia rau hauv chav kawm. Ua tsaug rau koj txoj kev txhawb nqa.

Sau npe,

_____ (Tus kws qhia ntawv)

Qhia txog ib tug neeg hauv tsev neeg. Nug kom tus neeg ntawv pab koj sau daim duab hauv qab no.

1.	Npe
2.	Muaj tsawg xyoo
3.	Yeeb yuj ntawm cov plaub hau
4.	Yeeb yuj ntawm qhov muag
5.	Khaub ncaws

School-Home Connection
Sharing Visions
UNIDAD C Compañeros de clase

Nombre _____

Fecha _____

Querida Familia:

En clase, aprendimos sobre los compañeros de clase. A _____ *(nombre del alumno)* le gustaría compartir con ustedes lo que hemos aprendido.

Lengua y Vocabulario. Aprendimos palabras para describir la ropa y las partes de la cara y el cuerpo. Aprendimos cómo hacer cumplidos y dar las gracias. También aprendimos cómo dar y seguir indicaciones para llegar a algún lado.

Sonidos, Palabras, Oraciones. Aprendimos cómo decir y escribir más consonantes. Aprendimos los sonidos que hacen las consonantes. También aprendimos combinaciones de consonantes y vocales y los sonidos que hacen al combinarse.

Leer y Escribir. Leímos *Friends*. Es una historia sobre Jen y Tim. La historia describe las caras, el cabello y la ropa de Jen y Tim.

Sabemos que ustedes quieren apoyar el esfuerzo que realiza su estudiante en la escuela. Nos gustaría que participen en alguna actividad para compartir con la clase. Gracias por su apoyo.

Atentamente,

_____ *(Maestro/a)*

Describe a un miembro de la familia. Pídele ayuda a esta persona para completar el cuadro.

1. Nombre	
2. Edad	
3. Color de cabello	
4. Color de ojos	
5. Ropa	

**School-Home Connection
Sharing Visions**

Bài C Các bạn cùng lớp

Tên: _____

Ngày tháng năm: _____

Thưa Gia Đình,

Ở lớp, chúng đã đã học về các bạn cùng lớp. _____ (tên học sinh) muốn chia sẻ với quý vị những gì chúng ta đã học.

Ngôn Ngữ và Tự Vựng. Chúng ta học các từ chỉ quần áo và chỉ các bộ phận của khuôn mặt và cơ thể. Chúng ta học cách đưa ra những lời khen và nói cám ơn. Chúng ta cũng học cách đưa ra và làm theo những lời chỉ dẫn.

Các Âm, Từ và Câu. Chúng ta học cách nói và viết nhiều phụ âm nữa. Chúng ta học những âm mà các phụ âm tạo nên. Chúng ta còn học những sự kết hợp giữa phụ âm và nguyên âm và các âm mà chúng tạo nên.

Đọc và Viết. Chúng ta đã đọc *Friends*. Đây là một bài đọc về Jen và Tim. Nó miêu tả khuôn mặt họ, tóc và quần áo của họ.

Chúng tôi biết rằng quý vị muốn hỗ trợ thành tích học tập của con em mình ở trường. Chúng tôi muốn quý vị tham gia vào một hoạt động để chia sẻ với lớp. Xin cám ơn vì sự ủng hộ của quý vị.

Trân Trọng Kính Chào,

_____ *(Giáo Viên)*

Hãy miêu tả một người trong gia đình. Nhờ người đó giúp bạn điền vào sơ đồ.

1.	Tên	
2.	Tuổi	
3.	Màu Tóc	
4.	Màu Mắt	
5.	Quần Áo	

School-Home Connection
Sharing Visions
UNIT D   Around the School

Name _____

Date _____

Dear Family,

In class, we learned about places around the school. _____ (*student's name*) would like to share with you what we learned.

Language and Vocabulary. We learned the names for places in the school. We learned how to ask for and give directions to the places. We also learned to say we need or want something.

Sounds, Words, Sentences. We practiced saying and spelling words that begin or end with two consonants. We also learned that when the letter **r** follows a vowel, the vowel sound usually changes. We learned about word parts, called syllables, and compound words. Compound words are big words made up of two smaller words, like *classroom*.

Reading and Writing. We read an article from a school newspaper. It tells where to find things at school. We wrote words and sentences about places in school and things we need or want.

We know you want to support your student's achievement in school. We would like you to participate in an activity to share with the class. Thank you for your support.

Sincerely,

_____ (Teacher)

Talk with a family member about your school. Ask and answer questions about the location of these places.

1. main office
2. nurse's office
3. cafeteria
4. principal's office
5. gym
6. library

Questions	Answers
1. Where is the main office?	*The main office is next to the entrance.*
2.	
3.	
4.	
5.	

School-Home Connection
Sharing Visions

មេរៀនទី **D** ជួរវិញសាលារៀន

ឈ្មោះ _____

កាលបរិច្ឆេទ _____

ជូនចំពោះ គ្រួសារ

នៅក្នុងថ្នាក់រៀន យើងបានរៀនអំពីទិកន្លែងជួរវិញសាលារៀន ។ _____ (ឈ្មោះសិស្ស) នឹងចែក វ៉ែលេកនូវអ្វីដែលយើងបានរៀនជាមួយនឹងអ្នក ។

ភាសា និង វាក្យសព្ទ យើងបានរៀនពីឈ្មោះកន្លែងនៅក្នុងសាលារៀន ។ យើងបានរៀនពីរបៀប សួរ និង ផ្តល់ទិសដៅទៅកន្លែងនោះ ។ យើងក៏បានរៀននិយាយពីអ្វីដែលយើងត្រូវការ និង ចង់បាន ។

សម្លេង, ពាក្យ និង ប្រយោគ យើងបានហាត់និយាយ និង ប្រកបពាក្យដែលចាប់ផ្តើម ឬ បញ្ចប់ ដោយព្យញ្ជនៈពីរ ។ យើងក៏បានរៀនធំដែរថានៅពេលដែលអក្សរ **r** នៅពីក្រោយស្រៈមួយ សម្លេងស្រៈនោះធម្មតានឹងផ្លាស់ប្តូរ ។ យើងបានរៀនអំពីផ្នែកនៃពាក្យ ដែលហៅថា ព្យាង្គ និង ពាក្យផ្សំ ។ ពាក្យផ្សំគឺជាពាក្យផ្សំដែលកើតឡើងដោយពាក្យតូច១ពីរ ដូចជា *classroom* ។

ការអាន និង ការសរសេរ យើងបានអានអត្ថបទកស្រង់ចេញពីសារព័ត៌មានរបស់សាលា ។ អត្ថបទនោះប្រាប់ពីកន្លែងដែលត្រូវស្វែងរកវត្តុនៅសាលារៀន ។ យើងបានសរសេរពាក្យ និង ប្រយោគអំពីកន្លែងនៅសាលា និង វត្តុដែលយើងត្រូវការ និង ចង់បាន ។

យើងដឹងថាអ្នកចង់តាំទ្រនូវការសម្រេចបានរបស់សិស្សអ្នកនៅសាលារៀន ។ យើងចង់ឱ្យអ្នកចូលរួម នៅក្នុងសកម្មភាពដែលចែករំលែកគ្នាជាមួយនឹងថ្នាក់រៀន ។ សូមអគុណចំពោះការតាំទ្ររបស់អ្នក ។

ដោយក្តីគោរពរាប់អាន

_____ (គ្រូបង្រៀន)

ជជែកជាមួយសមាជិកគ្រួសារអំពីសាលារៀនរបស់អ្នក ។ សួរ និង ឆ្លើយនូវសំណួរអំពីទិកន្លែងនៃកន្លែង ទាំងនេះ ។

១. ការិយាល័យធំ
២. ការិយាល័យគិលានុប្បដ្ឋាយិកា
៣. កន្លែងឥក់អាហារ
៤. ការិយាល័យនាយក
៥. កន្លែងហាត់ប្រាណ
៦. បណ្ណាល័យ

សំណួរ	ចម្លើយ
១. កន្លែងណាជាការិយាល័យធំ?	ការិយាល័យធំនៅជិតទ្វាចូល ។
២.	
៣.	
៤.	
៥.	

School-Home Connection
Sharing Visions

單元 D　校園

姓名 _____

日期 _____

親愛的家長：

　　我們在課堂上學習校園裡的地點。_____（學生姓名）想和您們分享我們的上課內容。

　　語言和字彙　我們學習校園裡的地點名稱，學習如何問方向，和指示方向。我們也學習表達我們的需要。

　　發聲、字、句子　我們練習說和拼以兩個子音開始和結尾的字我們也學到若字母 **r** 在母音後，發音通常會改變。我們學到字的音節，以及複合字。複合字是由兩個字拼成的字，如 *classroom*（教室）。

　　閱讀和寫作　我們閱讀校刊上的一篇文章，它說明校園每個地點提供的服務。我們寫下字和句子，來說明這些地點，與我們需要的服務。

　　我們知道您們很樂意協助孩子學習。希望您們能參與以下活動，我們將在課堂分享結果。感謝您們的協助。

　　　　　　　　　　　　　　　　　　敬上

　　　　　　　　　　　_____（老師）

與一位家人討論你的學校。詢問以下地點的位置，並回答。

1. 行政辦公室
2. 健康中心
3. 餐廳
4. 校長室
5. 體育館
6. 圖書館

問題	答案
1. 行政辦公室在哪裡？	行政辦公室在大門旁。
2.	
3.	
4.	
5.	

School-Home Connection
Sharing Visions
SEKSYON D Toupre Lekòl la

Non _____

Dat _____

Chè Fanmi,

Nan klas la, nou aprann sou kote ki toupre lekòl la. _____ *(non elèv la)* ta renmen pataje avèk ou sa nou aprann.

Langaj ak Vokabilè. Nou aprann non kote ki andedan lekòl la. Nou aprann ki jan pou mande ak bay enstriksyon pou al nan kote sa yo. Nou aprann tou ki jan pou nou di nou bezwen oswa nou vle kichoy.

Son, Mo, Fraz. Nou egzèse pwononse ak eple mo ki kòmanse oswa fini ak de (2) konsonn. Nou aprann tou ke lè lèt **r** swiv yon vwayèl, son vwayèl sa a abityèlman chanje. Nou aprann sou pati mo yo rele silab, ak mo konpoze. Mo konpoze se yon gwo mo ki fèt ak de mo pi piti, tankou *classroom*.

Li ak Ekri. Nou li yon atik sou jounal lekòl la. Li di ki bò pou jwenn bagay nan lekòl la. Nou ekri mo ak fraz sou kote nan lekòl la ak sou bagay nou bezwen oswa nou vle.

Nou konnen ke ou vle ankouraje reyisit pitit ou nan lekòl la. Nou ta renmen ke ou patisipe nan yon aktivite pou pataje ak klas la. Mèsi pou sipò ou.

Sensèman,

_____ *(Pwofesè)*

Pale ak yon manm fanmi w sou lekòl ou a. Poze e reponn kesyon sou ki bò kote sa yo ye.

1. biwo prensipal
2. biwo enfimyè a
3. kafeterya
4. biwo direktè a
5. jimnazyòm
6. bibliyotèk

Kesyon	Repons
1. *Ki kote biwo prensipal la ye?*	*Biwo prensipal la apre antre a.*
2.	
3.	
4.	
5.	

School-Home Connection
Sharing Visions

SOB KAWM D Ib Ncig Ntawm Tsev Kawm Ntawv

Npe _____

Hnub Tim _____

Nyob zoo txog Tsev Neeg,

Hauv chav kawm ntawv, peb kawm txog cov chaw nyob ib ncig ntawm tsev kawm ntawv. _____ *(tus menyuam kawm ntawv lub npe)* yuav xav qhia rau koj seb pab kawm txog dab tsi.

Hom lus thiab Ntsiab Lus. Peb kawm cov npe rau cov chaw hauv tsev kawm ntawv. Peb kawm nug kev thiab qhia kev rau cov chaw. Peb tseem kawm hais seb peb xav tau dab tsi.

Cov suab, Cov lus, Cov nqe lus. Peb xyaum hais thiab sau cov lus uas pib los sis xaus nrog ob tug niam ntawv. Peb tseem kawm tias thaum tus ntawv **r** lawv ib tug niam ntawv, lub suab feem ntau hloov. Peb kawm txog cov seem ntawm lo lus, hu ua cov suab (syllables), thiab cov lus uas muaj ob lo lus los ua ke. Cov lus ua muaj ob lo lus los ua ke yog cov lus ntev uas muab lo lus me los tso ua ke, *classroom*.

Kev nyeem ntawv thiab Sau ntawv. Peb nyeem ib sob lus hauv tsev kawm ntawv tsab xov xwm. Nws qhia seb yuav nrhiav cov khoom hauv tsev kawm ntawv li cas. Peb sau cov lus thiab cov sob lus txog cov chaw hauv tsev kawm ntawv thiab cov khoom uas peb yuav tsum muaj los sis xav tau.

Peb paub tias koj xav txhawb koj tus menyuam kev kawm kom tau zoo hauv tsev kawm ntawv. Peb xav kom koj koom hauv ib qho kev ua uas coj los qhia rau hauv chav kawm. Ua tsaug rau koj txoj kev txhawb nqa.

Sau npe,

_____ *(Tus kws qhia ntawv)*

Nrog ib tug neeg hauv tsev neeg tham txog koj lub tsev kawm ntawv. Nug thiab teb cov nqe lus nug txog seb cov chaw no nyob qhov twg.

1. qhov chaw ua hauj lwm
2. tus kws ntsuam mob lub chav fai
3. chaw noj mov
4. qhov chaw ua hauj lwm ntawm tus thawj coj
5. chaw dhia ua si
6. tsev saib ntawv

Cov Lus Nug	Cov Lus Teb
1. *Lub chav fai nyob qhov twg?*	*Lub chav fai nyob ib sab ntawm lub qhov rooj nkag.*
2.	
3.	
4.	
5.	

School-Home Connection
Sharing Visions

UNIDAD D Los alrededores de la escuela

Nombre _____

Fecha _____

Querida Familia:

En clase, aprendimos sobre los lugares que rodean la escuela. A _____ *(nombre del alumno)* le gustaría compartir con ustedes lo que hemos aprendido.

Lengua y Vocabulario. Aprendimos los nombres de los lugares de la escuela. Aprendimos cómo pedir y dar indicaciones para llegar a esos lugares. También aprendimos cómo decir que necesitamos o queremos algo.

Sonidos, Palabras, Oraciones. Practicamos decir y deletrear palabras que comienzan o terminan con dos consonantes. También aprendimos que cuando la letra **r** va seguida de vocal, la vocal usualmente cambia de sonido. Aprendimos las partes de las palabras, que se llaman sílabas, y las palabras compuestas. Las palabras compuestas son palabras más largas que están formadas por dos palabras más pequeñas, como *classroom*.

Leer y Escribir. Leímos un artículo de un periódico escolar. Dice dónde podemos encontrar cosas en la escuela. Escribimos palabras y oraciones sobre los lugares de la escuela y las cosas que necesitamos o queremos.

Sabemos que ustedes quieren apoyar el esfuerzo que realiza su estudiante en la escuela. Nos gustaría que participen en alguna actividad para compartir con la clase. Gracias por su apoyo.

Atentamente,

_____ *(Maestro/a)*

Habla con algún miembro de la familia sobre tu escuela. Haz y responde preguntas sobre la ubicación de estos lugares.

1. oficina principal
2. enfermería
3. cafetería
4. oficina del director
5. gimnasio
6. biblioteca

Preguntas	Respuestas
1. ¿Dónde está la oficina principal?	*La oficina principal está al lado de la entrada.*
2.	
3.	
4.	
5.	

School-Home Connection
Sharing Visions
Bài D Xung Quanh Trường Học

Tên: _____

Ngày tháng năm: _____

Thưa Gia Đình,

Ở lớp, chúng đã đã học về các nơi chốn xung quanh trường học. _____ *(tên học sinh)* muốn chia sẻ với quý vị những gì chúng ta đã học.

Ngôn Ngữ và Tự Vựng. Chúng ta đã học tên gọi các nơi trong trường. Chúng ta học cách nhờ và đưa ra lời chỉ dẫn đường tới các nơi đó. Chúng ta còn học cách nói rằng mình cần hoặc muốn cái gì đó.

Các Âm, Từ và Câu. Chúng ta đã luyện tập cách nói và đánh vần các từ bắt đầu hay kết thúc bằng hai phụ âm. Chúng ta cũng học được rằng khi chữ **r** theo sau một nguyên âm thì âm của nguyên âm đó thường thay đổi. Chúng ta học về các bộ phận của từ, gọi là các âm tiết, và các từ ghép. Từ ghép là các từ dài được tạo thành từ hai từ ngắn hơn, như *classroom* chẳng hạn.

Đọc và Viết. Chúng ta đọc một bài trong một tờ báo của trường. Nó chỉ cho biết chỗ tìm ra các thứ ở trường. Chúng ta đã viết ra các từ và câu về những nơi trong trường và những thứ chúng ta cần hoặc muốn.

Chúng tôi biết rằng quý vị muốn hỗ trợ thành tích học tập của con em mình ở trường. Chúng tôi muốn quý vị tham gia vào một hoạt động để chia sẻ với lớp. Xin cám ơn vì sự ủng hộ của quý vi.

Trân Trọng Kính Chào,

_____ *(Giáo Viên)*

Hãy nói chuyện với một người trong gia đình về trường học của bạn. Hãy đặt và trả lời các câu hỏi về vị trí của các nơi này.

1. văn phòng chính
2. phòng y tá
3. căn tin
4. văn phòng hiệu trưởng
5. phòng thể dục
6. thư viện

	Câu hỏi	Câu trả lời
1.	*Văn phòng chính ở đâu?*	*Văn phòng chính ở kế bên lối vào.*
2.		
3.		
4.		
5.		

School-Home Connection
Sharing Visions

UNIT 1   A Day at School

Name _____
Date _____

Dear Family,

In class, we learned about a day at school. _____ (student's name) would like to share with you what we learned.

Chapter 1. We learned to greet people and ask for help. We also learned the days of the week and the months of the year. We practiced saying the date. We learned about nouns and pronouns, too. Nouns are words that name people, places, and things. Pronouns take the place of nouns.

Chapter 2. We read some information forms. Forms ask for a person's name, address, date of birth, and telephone number. We practiced filling out a form.

Chapter 3. We read a chapter from a math textbook called *How to Solve a Word Problem.* It tells how to solve math problems with addition, subtraction, multiplication, and division.

We know you want to support your student's achievement in school. We would like you to participate in an activity to share with the class. Thank you for your support.

Sincerely,

_____ (Teacher)

Ask a family member these questions. Write the answers.

1. Question: What is today's day and date?
   Answer: Today is _____.

2. Question: When is your birthday?
   Answer: My birthday is _____.

3. Question: What is your address?
   Answer: My address is _____.

4. Question: What is your phone number?
   Answer: My phone number is _____.

School-Home Connection
Sharing Visions

មេរៀនទី ១ ថ្ងៃនៅសាលារៀន

ឈ្មោះ _____

កាលបរិច្ឆេទ _____

ជូនចំពោះ គ្រួសារ

នៅក្នុងថ្នាក់រៀន យើងបានរៀនអំពីថ្ងៃនៅសាលារៀន ។ _____ (ឈ្មោះសិស្ស) ចង់ចែករំលែកនូវអ្វីដែលយើងបានរៀនជាមួយនឹងអ្នក ។

ជំពូក ១ យើងបានរៀនជំរាបសួរមនុស្សដទៃ និង សុំជំនួយ ។ យើងក៏បានរៀនអំពីថ្ងៃនៅក្នុង សប្តាហ៍ និង ខែនៃឆ្នាំ ។ យើងបានហាត់និយាយអំពីថ្ងៃខែឆ្នាំ ។ យើងបានរៀនអំពី នាម និង សព្វនាម ផងដែរ ។ នាមគឺជាពាក្យដែលដាក់ឈ្មោះឱ្យមនុស្ស កន្លែង និង វត្ថុ ។ សព្វនាម គឺជាពាក្យដែល ជំនួសឱ្យនាម ។

ជំពូក ២ យើងបានអានទម្រង់បែបបទព័ត៌មាន ។ ទម្រង់បែបបទដែលស្នើសុំឈ្មោះ អាស័យដ្ឋាន ថ្ងៃខែឆ្នាំកំណើត និង លេខទូរស័ព្ទ របស់មនុស្ស ។ យើងបានហាត់រៀនបំពេញទម្រង់បែបបទនោះ ។

ជំពូក ៣ យើងបានអានមេរៀនមួយនៅក្នុងសៀវភៅគណិតវិទ្យាដែលមានឈ្មោះថា *How to Solve a Word Problem* ។ សៀវភៅនេះប្រាប់អំពីរបៀប ដោះស្រាយបញ្ហាគណិតវិទ្យាជាមួយនឹងការប្រើលេខបូក ដក គុណ និង ចែក ។

យើងដឹងថាអ្នកចង់តាំងទ្រនូវការសម្រេចចានរបស់សិស្សអ្នកនៅសាលារៀន ។ យើងចង់ឱ្យអ្នកចូលរួម នៅក្នុងសកម្មភាពដែលចែករំលែកគ្នាជាមួយនឹងថ្នាក់រៀន ។ សូមអគុណចំពោះការតាំងទ្រនៃរបស់អ្នក ។

ដោយក្តីគោរពរាប់អាន

_____ (គ្រូបង្រៀន)

សូមសួរទៅសមាជិកគ្រួសារនូវសំណួរទាំងនេះ ។ សូមសរសេរនូវចម្លើយ ។

១. **សំណួរ** តើថ្ងៃនេះជាថ្ងៃអ្វី ហើយថ្ងៃទីប៉ុន្មាន?
   ចម្លើយ ថ្ងៃនេះគឺ _____ ។

២. **សំណួរ** តើថ្ងៃខែឆ្នាំកំណើតរបស់អ្នកនៅពេលណា?
   ចម្លើយ ថ្ងៃខែឆ្នាំកំណើតរបស់ខ្ញុំគឺ _____ ។

៣. **សំណួរ** តើអ្នកមានអាស័យដ្ឋាននៅទីណា?
   ចម្លើយ អាស័យដ្ឋានរបស់ខ្ញុំគឺ _____ ។

៤. **សំណួរ** តើលេខទូរស័ព្ទរបស់អ្នកប៉ុន្មាន?
   ចម្លើយ លេខទូរស័ព្ទរបស់ខ្ញុំគឺ _____ ។

School-Home Connection
Sharing Visions

單元一　在學校的一天

姓名 _____

日期 _____

親愛的家長：

　　我們在課堂上學了在學校的一天。_____（學生姓名）想和您們分享我們的上課內容。

　　第一章　我們學打招呼與求助。我們也學會講星期一到星期日，以及一月到十二月。我們練習說日期，也學習什麼是名詞和代名詞。人、事、物是名詞。代名詞則代替名詞。

　　第二章　我們閱讀表格。這些表格問人的姓名、地址、生日和電話號碼。我們練習填表格。

　　第三章　我們閱讀數學課本的一章，章名叫 *How to Solve a Word Problem*，這一章指導學生用加法、減法、乘法和除法解決數學問題。

　　我們知道您們很樂意協助孩子學習。希望您們能參與以下活動，我們將在課堂分享結果。感謝您們的協助。

　　　　　　　　　　　　　　　敬上

　　　　　_____（老師）

問一位家人這些問題，寫下答案。

1. 問題：　今天是幾號？星期幾？
   答案：　今天是 _____ 。

2. 問題：　你的生日是幾號？
   答案：　我的生日是 _____ 。

3. 問題：　你的住址是？
   答案：　我的住址是 _____ 。

4. 問題：　你的電話號碼是？
   答案：　我的電話號碼是 _____ 。

School-Home Connection
Sharing Visions

SEKSYON 1 Yon jounen lekòl

Non _____

Dat _____

Chè Fanmi,

Nan klas la, nou aprann sou yon jounen lekòl. _____ *(non elèv la)* ta renmen pataje avèk ou sa nou aprann.

Chapit 1. Nou aprann resewa moun ak mande èd. Nou aprann tou jou nan semenn yo ak mwa nan ane yo. Nou fè egzèsis sou repete dat. Nou aprann sou non ak pwonon tou. Non yo se mo ki nonmen moun, anplasman ak bagay. Pwonon yo pran plas non yo.

Chapit 2. Nou li kèk fòm sou enfòmasyon. Fòm sa yo mande pou non moun, adrès, dat nesans, ak nimewo telefòn li. Nou fè egzèsis sou jan pou plen fòm sa yo.

Chapit 3. Nou li yon chapit ki soti nan yon liv matematik ki rele *How to Solve a Word Problem.* Li di ki jan pou solisyone pwoblèm matematik avèk adisyon, soustraksyon, miltiplikasyon ak divizyon.

Nou konnen ke ou vle ankouraje reyisit pitit ou nan lekòl la. Nou ta renmen ke ou patisipe nan yon aktivite pou pataje ak klas la. Mèsi pou sipò ou.

Sensèman,

_____ *(Pwofesè)*

Mande yon manm fanmi w kesyon sa yo. Ekri repons yo.

1. Kesyon: Ki jou ak ki dat jodi a?

   Repons: Jodi a se _____.

2. Kesyon: Ki lè ki dat fèt ou?

   Repons: Dat fèt mwen se _____.

3. Kesyon: Ki kote ou rete?

   Repons: Mwen rete nan _____.

4. Kesyon: Ki nimewo telefòn ou?

   Repons: Nimewo telefòn mwen se _____.

School-Home Connection
Sharing Visions

SOB KAWM 1 Ib Hnub tom Tsev Kawm Ntawv

Npe _____

Hnub Tim _____

Nyob zoo txog Tsev Neeg,

Hauv chav kawm ntawv, peb kawm txog ib hnub tom tsev kawm ntawv. _____ *(tus menyuam kawm ntawv lub npe)* yuav xav qhia rau koj seb pab kawm txog dab tsi.

Tshooj 1. Peb kawm txog kev hwm neeg thiab thov kev pab. Peb tseem kawm txog cov hnub ntawm lub plua (week) thiab cov hli ntawm lub xyoo. Peb xyaum hais cov hnub tim. Peb kawm txog cov lus txog ib yam dab tsi (nouns) thiab cov lus cim neeg (pronouns), thiab. Cov lus txog ib yam dab tsi (nouns) yog cov lus uas hais txog neeg, chaw, thiab khoom. Cov lus cim neeg (pronouns) yog los hloov cov lus txog ib yam dab tsi (nouns).

Tshooj 2. Peb nyeem ib cov lus qhia txog cov ntawv sau thov ib qho dab tsi. Cov ntawv sau thov ib qho dab tsi nug txog tus neeg lub npe, chaw nyob, hnub yug, thiab xov tooj. Peb xyaum sau ib daim ntawv thov ib qho dab tsi.

Tshooj 3. Peb nyeem ib tshooj hauv phau ntawv ua zauv hu ua *How to Solve a Word Problem.* Nws qhia txog seb yuav ua ib qho zauv nrog cov zauv sib ntxiv, sib rho, sib khoo, thiab sib faib li cas.

Peb paub tias koj xav txhawb koj tus menyuam kev kawm kom tau zoo hauv tsev kawm ntawv. Peb xav kom koj koom hauv ib qho kev ua uas coj los qhia rau hauv chav kawm. Ua tsaug rau koj txoj kev txhawb nqa.

Sau npe,

_____ *(Tus kws qhia ntawv)*

Nug ib tug neeg hauv tsev neeg cov lus nug no. Sau cov lus teb.

1. Lus nug: Hnub no yog hnub dab tsi thiab yog hnub tim dab tsi?

   Lus teb: Hnub no yog _____.

2. Lus nug: Koj lub hnub yug yog thaum twg?

   Lus teb: Kuv lub hnub yug yog _____.

3. Lus nug: Koj qhov chaw nyob yog li cas?

   Lus teb: Kuv qhov chaw nyob yog _____.

4. Lus nug: Koj tus xov tooj yog li cas?

   Lus teb: Kuv tus xov tooj yog _____.

School-Home Connection
Sharing Visions

UNIDAD 1 Un día en la escuela

Nombre _____

Fecha _____

Querida Familia:

En clase, aprendimos sobre un día en la escuela. A _____ *(nombre del alumno)* le gustaría compartir con ustedes lo que hemos aprendido.

Capítulo 1. Aprendimos a saludar a las personas y a pedir ayuda. También aprendimos los días de la semana y los meses del año. Practicamos cómo decir la fecha. También aprendimos sobre sustantivos y pronombres. Los sustantivos son palabras que nombran personas, lugares y cosas. Los pronombres toman el lugar de los sustantivos.

Capítulo 2. Leímos formularios de información. En los formularios hay que completar el nombre, el domicilio, la fecha de nacimiento y el número de teléfono de una persona. Practicamos cómo completar un formulario.

Capítulo 3. Leímos un capítulo de un manual de matemáticas llamado *How to Solve a Word Problem.* Dice cómo resolver problemas matemáticos con operaciones de suma, resta, multiplicación y división.

Sabemos que ustedes quieren apoyar el esfuerzo que realiza su estudiante en la escuela. Nos gustaría que participen en alguna actividad para compartir con la clase. Gracias por su apoyo.

Atentamente,

_____ *(Maestro/a)*

Haz estas preguntas a un miembro de la familia. Escribe las respuestas.

1. Pregunta: ¿Qué día y fecha es hoy?
   Respuesta: Hoy es _____.

2. Pregunta: ¿Cuándo es tu cumpleaños?
   Respuesta: Mi cumpleaños es _____.

3. Pregunta: ¿Cuál es tu domicilio?
   Respuesta: Mi domicilio es _____.

4. Pregunta: ¿Cuál es tu número de teléfono?
   Respuesta: Mi número de teléfono es _____.

School-Home Connection
Sharing Visions

Bài 1 Một Ngày ở Trường

Tên: _____

Ngày tháng năm: _____

Kính thưa Gia Đình,

Trong lớp, chúng ta đã học về một ngày ở trường. _____ *(tên học sinh)* muốn chia sẻ với quý vị những gì chúng ta đã học.

Chương 1. Chúng ta đã học cách chào mọi người và nhờ giúp đỡ. Chúng ta cũng còn học về các ngày trong tuần và các tháng trong năm. Chúng ta tập cách nói ngày tháng năm. Chúng ta cũng học về các danh từ và đại từ nữa. Danh từ là những từ chỉ tên người, nơi chốn và đồ vật. Đại từ thế chỗ cho danh từ.

Chương 2. Chúng ta đã học một số biểu mẫu thông tin. Các biểu mẫu hỏi về tên, địa chỉ, ngày tháng năm sinh và số điện thoại của một người. Chúng ta đã tập điền vào một mẫu đơn.

Chapter 3. Chúng ta đọc một chương trong một cuốn sách giáo khoa toán gọi là *How to Solve a Word Problem.* Nó cho biết cách giải các bài toán với các phép tính cộng, trừ, nhân và chia.

Chúng tôi biết rằng quý vị muốn hỗ trợ thành tích học tập của con em mình ở trường. Chúng tôi muốn quý vị tham gia vào một hoạt động để chia sẻ với lớp. Xin cám ơn vì sự ủng hộ của quý vị.

Trân Trọng Kính Chào,

_____ *(Giáo viên)*

Hãy đặt những câu hỏi này cho một thành viên gia đình và viết các câu trả lời ra.

1. Câu hỏi: Hôm nay thứ mấy ngày tháng năm mấy?

   Trả lời: _____.

2. Hỏi: Sinh nhật của em là khi nào?

   Trả lời: Sinh nhật của tôi là _____.

3. Hỏi: Địa chỉ của em là gì?

   Trả lời: Địa chỉ của tôi là _____.

4. Hỏi: Số điện thoại của em là gì?

   Trả lời: Số điện thoại của tôi là _____.

School-Home Connection
Sharing Visions

UNIT 2   Families

Name _____

Date _____

Dear Family,

In class, we learned about families. _____ *(student's name)* would like to share with you what we learned.

Chapter 1. Families can include a mother, a father, a sister, a brother, a cousin, an aunt, an uncle, a grandpa, and a grandma.

Chapter 2. We read two poems. ***Who is a Family?*** is a poem by John Mundahl. This poem names the people and pets in one family. ***Marianna Gomez*** is a poem by a fourteen-year-old girl. Her name is Marianna Gomez. Her poem tells about her life. She lives in California and she has a big, brown dog.

Chapter 3. We read an excerpt from a science textbook called ***Classifying Animals***. It tells us that scientists divide animals into four groups. The groups are fish, mammals, birds, and reptiles.

We know you want to support your student's achievement in school. We would like you to participate in an activity to share with the class. Thank you for your support.

Sincerely,

_____ *(Teacher)*

Talk with a family member about the four animal groups. Fill out the chart together.

What are the four animal groups?	Does this group lay eggs?	What are some animals in this group?
1.		
2.		
3.		
4.		

School-Home Connection
Sharing Visions

មេរៀនទី ២ គ្រួសារ

ឈ្មោះ _____

កាលបរិច្ឆេទ _____

ជូនចំពោះ គ្រួសារ

នៅក្នុងថ្នាក់រៀន យើងបានរៀនអំពីគ្រួសារ ។ _____ (ឈ្មោះសិស្ស) ចង់ចែករំលែកនូវរឿងអ្វីដែលយើងបានរៀនជាមួយនឹងអ្នក ។

ជំពូក ១ គ្រួសារអាចរួមមាន ម្តាយ ឪពុក បងប្អូនស្រី បងប្អូនប្រុស បងប្អូនជីដូនមួយ មីង ពូ ជីតា និង ជីដូន ។

ជំពូក ២ យើងបានអានកំណាព្យពីរ ។ *Who is a Family?* គឺជាកំណាព្យដែល និពន្ធឡើងដោយលោក John Mundahl ។ កំណាព្យនេះដាក់ឈ្មោះឱ្យមនុស្ស និង សត្វចិញ្ចឹមនៅក្នុង គ្រួសារមួយ ។ *Marianna Gomez* គឺជាកំណាព្យដែលនិពន្ធដោយក្មេងស្រីអាយុ ១៤ ឆ្នាំ ។ នាងមាន ឈ្មោះថា Marianna Gomez ។ កំណាព្យរបស់នាងប្រាប់អំពីជីវិតរបស់នាង ។ នាងរស់នៅក្នុងរដ្ឋ កាលីហ្វ័រញ៉ា ហើយ នាងមានផ្ទៃទីផ្ទាតធំមួយ ។

ជំពូក ៣ យើងបានអានសេចក្តីដកស្រង់ចេញពីសៀវភៅវិទ្យាសាស្ត្រមានឈ្មោះថា *Classifying Animals* ។ វាប្រាប់យើងថាអ្នកវិទ្យាសាស្ត្របានបែងចែកសត្វជា ៦ ក្រុម ។ ក្រុមទាំងនោះគឺ ពពួកសត្វត្រី សត្វចិញ្ចឹមកូនដោយទឹកដោះ សត្វល្មូន និង លូន ។

យើងដឹងថាអ្នកចង់គាំទ្រនូវការសម្រេចបានរបស់សិស្សអ្នកនៅសាលារៀន ។ យើងចង់ឱ្យអ្នកចូលរួម នៅក្នុងសកម្មភាពដែលចែករំលែកគ្នាជាមួយនឹងថ្នាក់រៀន ។ សូមអគុណចំពោះការគាំទ្ររបស់អ្នក ។

ដោយក្តីគោរពរាប់អាន

_____ (គ្រូបង្រៀន)

សូមជជែកជាមួយសមាជិកនៅក្នុងគ្រួសារអំពីក្រុមនៃសត្វទាំង៦ុន ។ សូមបំពេញនៅក្នុងតារាងខាងក្រោម ។

តើក្រុមនៃសត្វទាំង៦ុននោះមាន អ្វីខ្លះ?	តើក្រុមនេះមានសិតទេ?	តើមានសត្វអ្វីខ្លះនៅក្នុងក្រុមនេះ?
១.		
២.		
៣.		
៤.		

School-Home Connection
Sharing Visions

單元二　家庭

姓名 _____

日期 _____

親愛的家長：

　　我們在課堂上學習家庭。_____（學生姓名）想和您們分享我們的上課內容。

　　第一章　家庭包括母親、父親、姊妹、兄弟、堂表兄弟姊妹、姑姑阿姨、叔叔伯伯、祖父母和外祖父母。

　　第二章　我們讀了兩首詩。約翰馬道爾寫的 *Who is a Family*？這首詩列出一個家庭的成員和寵物的名字。*Marianna Gomez* 是十四歲的女孩寫的詩。她的名字是瑪莉安娜鞏梅茲。她以詩敘述自己的生活。她住在加州，有一隻棕色的大狗。

　　第三章　我們念自然課本裡的一篇短文 *Classifying Animals*。它解釋科學家將動物分為四類：魚類、哺乳類、鳥類和爬蟲類。

　　我們知道您們很樂意協助孩子學習。希望您們能參與以下的活動，我們將在課堂分享結果。感謝您們的協助。

　　　　　　　　　　　　　　　　　　　　　敬上

　　　　　　　　　　　　　　_____（老師）

與一位家人談論動物的四種分類，然後一起填表格。

動物有哪四類？	這類動物會下蛋嗎？	每一類的動物有哪些？
1.		
2.		
3.		
4.		

School-Home Connection
Sharing Visions
SEKSYON 2 Fanmi

Non _____
Dat _____

Chè Fanmi,

Nan klas la, nou aprann sou fanmi. _____ *(non elèv la)* ta renmen pataje avèk ou sa nou aprann.

Chapit 1. Yon fanmi ka gen yon manman, yon papa, yon sè, yon frè, yon kouzen, yon matant, yon tonton, yon granpè ak yon granmè.

Chapit 2. Nou li de (2) powèm. ***Who is a Family?*** ki se yon powèm John Mundahl ekri. Powèm sa a nonmen moun ak zannimo domestik ki nan yon fanmi. ***Marianna Gomez*** se yon powèm ke yon ti fi katòz an ekri. Li rele Marianna Gomez. Powèm li a rakonte vi li. Li rete Kalifòni e li gen yon gwo chen mawon.

Chapit 3. Nou li yon ekstrè de yon liv syans ki rele ***Classifying Animals.*** Li di nou ke syantis yo divize zannimo yo an kat gwoup. Gwoup sa yo se pwason, mamifè, zwazo ak reptil.

Nou konnen ke ou vle ankouraje reyisit pitit ou nan klas la. Nou ta renmen ke ou patisipe nan yon aktivite pou pataje ak klas la. Mèsi pou sipò ou.

Sensèman,

_____ *(Pwofesè)*

Pale ak yon manm fanmi w sou kat gwoup zannimo yo. Plen tablo sa a ansanm.

Ki non kat gwoup zannimo yo?	Èske gwoup sa a ponn ze?	Ki non kèk zannimo ki nan gwoup sa a?
1.		
2.		
3.		
4.		

School-Home Connection
Sharing Visions
SOB KAWM 2 Tsev Neeg

Npe _____

Hnub Tim _____

Nyob zoo txog Tsev Neeg,

   Hauv chav kawm ntawv, peb kawm txog tsev neeg. _____ *(tus menyuam kawm ntawv lub npe)* yuav xav qhia rau koj seb pab kawm txog dab tsi.

   Tshooj 1. Tsev neeg yuav muaj xws li niam, txiv, muam/viv ncaus, nus/kwv/tij, kwv tij, niam ntxawm/niam hlob, txiv ntxawm/txiv hlob, yawg/yawm txiv, thiab pog/niam tais.

   Tshooj 2. Peb nyeem ob txoj paj huam. *Who is a Family?* yog ib txoj paj huam sau los ntawm John Mundahl. Txoj paj huam no hais txog cov neeg thiab cov tsiaj tu hauv tsev hauv ib tse neeg. *Marianna Gomez* yog ib txoj paj huam sau los ntawm ib tug menyuam ntxhais muaj kaum plaub xyoos. Nws lub npe hu ua Marianna Gomez. Nws txoj paj huam qhia txog nws lub neej. Nws nyob hauv California thiab nws muaj ib tug aub uas loj thiab yeej yuj khas fes.

   Tshooj 3. Peb nyeem ib sob lus los ntawm phau ntawv kawm science hu ua *Classifying Animals.* Nws qhia rau peb tias cov scientists muab cov tsiaj cais ua plaub pawg. Cov pawg yog ntses, tsiaj loj, noog, thiab nab.

   Peb paub tias koj xav txhawb koj tus menyuam kev kawm kom tau zoo hauv tsev kawm ntawv. Peb xav kom koj koom hauv ib qho kev ua uas coj los qhia rau hauv chav kawm. Ua tsaug rau koj txoj kev txhawb nqa.

   Sau npe,

   _____ *(Tus kws qhia ntawv)*

Nrog ib tug neeg hauv tsev neeg tham txog plaub pawg tsiaj. Sau daim duab hauv qab ua ke.

Plaub pawg tsiaj yog dab tsi?	Pawg no puas ntiag qe?	Ib co tsiaj nyob hauv pawg no yog dab tsi?
1.		
2.		
3.		
4.		

School-Home Connection
Sharing Visions

UNIDAD 2 Familias

Nombre _____

Fecha _____

Querida Familia:

En clase, aprendimos sobre la familia. A _____ *(nombre del alumno)* le gustaría compartir con ustedes lo que hemos aprendido.

Capítulo 1. Las familias pueden tener madre, padre, hermana, hermano, primo, tía, tío, abuelo y abuela.

Capítulo 2. Leímos dos poemas. *Who is a Family?* es un poema de John Mundhal. Este poema menciona a las personas y las mascotas de una familia. *Marianna Gomez* es un poema de una niña de catorce años. Su nombre es Marianna Gomez. El poema habla de su vida. Marianna vive en California y tiene un perro marrón grande.

Capítulo 3. Leímos un pasaje de un manual de ciencias llamado *Classifying Animals*. Cuenta que los científicos dividen a los animales en cuatro grupos. Los grupos son peces, mamíferos, aves y reptiles.

Sabemos que ustedes quieren apoyar el esfuerzo que realiza su estudiante en la escuela. Nos gustaría que participen en alguna actividad para compartir con la clase. Gracias por su apoyo.

Atentamente,

_____ *(Maestro/a)*

Habla con algún miembro de la familia sobre los cuatro grupos de animales. Completen juntos el cuadro.

¿Cuáles son los cuatro grupos de animales?	¿Este grupo pone huevos?	Menciona algunos animales de este grupo.
1.		
2.		
3.		
4.		

**School-Home Connection
Sharing Visions**

Bài 2 Gia Đình

Tên: _____

Ngày tháng năm: _____

Thưa Gia Đình,

Ở lớp, chúng ta đã học về gia đình. _____ *(tên học sinh)* muốn chia sẻ với quý vị những gì chúng ta đã học.

Chương 1. Gia đình có thể bao gồm một người mẹ, một người cha, một chị, một em trai, một em họ, một người cô, một người chú, một người ông và một người bà.

Chương 2. Chúng ta đọc hai bài thơ. ***Who is a Family?*** là một bài thơ của John Mundahl. Bài thơ này kể tên mọi người và thú vật nuôi trong một gia đình. ***Marianna Gomez*** là một bài thơ của một cô bé mười bốn tuổi. Tên em là Marianna Gomez. Bài thơ của em kể về cuộc sống của em. Em sống ở California và em có một con chó to màu nâu.

Chương 3. Chúng ta đã đọc một đoạn trích từ một cuốn sách giáo khoa về khoa học gọi là ***Classifying Animals***. Nó cho chúng ta biết rằng các nhà khoa học chia các loài vật làm bốn nhóm. Các nhóm đó là cá, loài có vú, chim và bò sát.

Chúng tôi biết rằng quý vị muốn hỗ trợ thành tích học tập của con em mình ở trường. Chúng tôi muốn quý vị tham gia vào một hoạt động để chia sẻ với lớp. Xin cám ơn vì sự ủng hộ của quý vị.

Trân Trọng Kính Chào,

_____ *(Giáo viên)*

Hãy nói chuyện với một thành viên gia đình về bốn nhóm động vật. Hãy cùng nhau điền vào sơ đồ.

Bốn nhóm động vật là gì?	Nhóm này có đẻ trứng không?	Kể tên vài loài vật thuộc nhóm này?
1.		
2.		
3.		
4.		

School-Home Connection
Sharing Visions
UNIT 3 After School

Name _____

Date _____

Dear Family,

In class, we learned about after-school activities. _____ (student's name) would like to share with you what we learned.

Chapter 1. We talked about activities that students do after school. Students do homework, play baseball, go shopping, work, and meet friends. We learned how to tell time. We also learned to use the simple past tense to tell or write about actions in the past.

Chapter 2. We read the story *Tomás Cleans the Car*. Tomás's mother tells him to clean the car. But Tomás wants to play with his friends. His friends help him clean the car.

Chapter 3. We read *The First Amendment to the U.S. Constitution*. We learned about freedoms that people have in the United States. These freedoms are written in a document called the Constitution.

We know you want to support your student's achievement in school. We would like you to participate in an activity to share with the class. Thank you for your support.

Sincerely,

_____ (Teacher)

Talk with your family about the freedoms in the First Amendment to the U.S. Constitution. Ask a family member to help you complete the chart.

Freedoms in the First Amendment	What does this freedom mean for Americans?
1. Freedom of religion	
2. Freedom of speech	
3. Freedom of press	
4. Freedom of assembly	

School-Home Connection
Sharing Visions

មេរៀនទី ៣ បន្ទាប់ពីរៀននៅសាលា

ឈ្មោះ _____

កាលបរិច្ឆេទ _____

ជូនចំពោះ គ្រួសារ

នៅក្នុងថ្នាក់រៀន យើងបានរៀនអំពីសកម្មភាពបន្ទាប់ពីរៀននៅសាលា ។ _____ (ឈ្មោះសិស្ស) ចង់ចែករំលែកនូវអ្វីដែលយើងបានរៀនជាមួយនឹងអ្នក ។

ជំពូក ១ យើងបានជជែកគ្នាអំពីសកម្មភាពដែលសិស្សទាំងឡាយធ្វើបន្ទាប់ពីរៀននៅសាលា ។ សិស្សទាំងឡាយធ្វើកិច្ចការនៅផ្ទះ លេងកីឡាបេសបល (baseball) ទៅផ្សារ ធ្វើការ និង ជួបជុំ មិត្តភ័ក្រ្ត ។ យើងបានរៀនពីរបៀបមើលម៉ោង ។ យើងក៏បានរៀនប្រើប្រាស់អតីតកាលធម្មតាដើម្បី ប្រាប់ ឬ សរសេរអំពីសកម្មភាពដែលកើតឡើងនៅអតីតកាល ។

ជំពូក ២ យើងបានអានរឿង *Tomás Cleans the Car* ម្តាយរបស់ Tomás ប្រាប់គាត់ឱ្យសម្អាតឡាន ។ ប៉ុន្តែ Tomás ចង់លេងជាមួយមិត្តភ័ក្ត្ររបស់គាត់ ។ មិត្តភ័ក្ត្រ របស់គាត់ជួយគាត់សម្អាតឡាន ។

ជំពូក ៣ យើងបានអាន *The First Amendment to the U.S. Constitution* ។ យើងបានរៀនអំពីសេរីភាពដែលមនុស្សមាននៅក្នុង សហរដ្ឋអាមេរិក ។ សេរីភាពទាំងនេះគឺត្រូវបានសរសេរទុកនៅក្នុងឯកសារដែលហៅថារដ្ឋធម្មនុញ្ញ ។

យើងដឹងថាអ្នកចង់គាំទ្រនូវការសម្រេចបានរបស់សិស្សអ្នកនៅសាលារៀន ។ យើងចង់ឱ្យអ្នកចូលរួម នៅក្នុងសកម្មភាពដែលចែករំលែកគ្នាជាមួយនឹងថ្នាក់រៀន ។ សូមអរគុណចំពោះការគាំទ្ររបស់អ្នក ។

ដោយក្តីគោរពរាប់អាន

_____ (គ្រូបង្រៀន)

ជជែកជាមួយគ្រួសាររបស់អ្នកអំពីសេរីភាពនៅក្នុងវិសោធនកម្មទី១បូងលើរដ្ឋធម្មនុញ្ញសហរដ្ឋអាមេរិក ។
សូមសួរទៅសមាជិកគ្រួសារដើម្បីជួយអ្នកបំពេញតារាងខាងក្រោម ។

សេរីភាពនៅក្នុងវិសោធនកម្មទី១បូង	តើសេរីភាពនេះមានអត្ថន័យអ្វីខ្លះសម្រាប់ជនជាតិ អាមេរិកាំង?
១. សេរីភាពសាសនា	
២. សេរីភាពនៃការបញ្ចេញមតិ	
៣. សេរីភាពសារព័ត៌មាន	
៤. សេរីភាពនៃសភា	

School-Home Connection
Sharing Visions

單元三　下課後

姓名 _____

日期 _____

親愛的家長：

　　我們在課堂上學習下課後的活動。_____（學生姓名）想和您們分享我們的上課內容。

　　第一章　我們談論學生在下課後做的活動。他們做作業、玩棒球、購物、工作和朋友玩。我們學會看時間。我們也學會用簡單過去式，用說地和寫地描述在過去發生的行動。

　　第二章　我們讀了 *Tomás Cleans the Car* 的故事。湯瑪斯的媽媽叫他清車子，但是湯瑪斯想和朋友玩，所以他朋友幫他清理車子。

　　第三章　我們讀了 *The First Amendment to the U.S. Constitution*。我們學到美國人享有什麼自由。憲法明列這些自由。

　　我們知道您們很樂意協助孩子學習。希望您們參與以下活動，我們將在課堂分享結果。感謝您們的協助。

　　　　　　　　　　　　　　　　　　敬上

　　　　　　　　　_____（老師）

與家人討論美國憲法第一修正案，請一位家人幫忙你填以下表格。

憲法第一修正案保障的自由	這些自由對美國人的意義是什麼？
1. 宗教自由	
2. 言論自由	
3. 媒體自由	
4. 集會自由	

School-Home Connection
Sharing Visions
SEKSYON 3 Apre lekòl

Non _____

Dat _____

Chè Fanmi,

Nan klas la, nou aprann sou aktivite apre lekòl. _____ *(non elèv la)* ta renmen pataje avèk ou sa nou aprann.

Chapit 1. Nou pale sou aktivite elèv yo fè apre lekòl. Elèv yo fè devwa, jwe bezbòl, fè chòping, travay, ak rankontre zanmi. Nou aprann kouman pou nou di lè. Nou aprann tou itilize tan pase senp pou rakonte oswa ekri sou aksyon ki pase.

Chapit 2. Nou li istwa *Tomás Cleans the Car*. Manman Tomás di l pou li netwaye machin nan. Men Tomás vle jwe ak zanmi l yo. Zanmi l yo ede l netwaye machin nan.

Chapit 3. Nou li *The First Amendment to the U.S. Constitution*. Nou aprann libète moun genyen Ozetazini. Libète sa yo ekri nan yon dokiman ki rele Konstitisyon.

Nou konnen ke ou vle ankouraje reyisit pitit ou nan lekòl la. Nou ta renmen ke ou patisipe nan yon aktivite pou pataje ak klas la. Mèsi pou sipò ou.

Sensèman,

_____ *(Pwofesè)*

Pale ak yon manm fanmi w sou libète nan Premye Amannman Konstitisyon Etazini. Mande yon manm fanmi w ede w plen tablo sa a.

Libète nan Premye Amannman an	Ki sa libète sa a vle di pou Ameriken?
1. Libète Relijyon	
2. Libète Lapawòl	
3. Libète Laprès	
4. Libète Asanble	

School-Home Connection
Sharing Visions
SOB KAWM 3 Tom Qab Kawm Ntawv Tas

Npe _____

Hnub Tim _____

Nyob zoo txog Tsev Neeg,

Hauv chav kawm ntawv, peb kawm txog cov kev ua tom qab kawm ntawv tas. _____ *(tus menyuam kawm ntawv lub npe)* yuav xav qhia rau koj seb pab kawm txog dab tsi.

Tshooj 1. Peb tham txog cov kev ua uas cov menyuam kawm ntawv ua tom qab kawm ntawv tas. Cov menyuam mus saib ntawv, ntaus pob baseball, mus tom kh, mus ua hauj lwm, thiab mus ntsib phooj ywg. Peb tseem kawm txog kev siv cov lus uas qhia txog kev ua yav dhau los (simple past tense) los qhia los sis sau txog cov kev ua yav dhau los.

Tshooj 2. Peb nyeem txog zaj dab neeg *Tomás Cleans the Car.* Tomás niam qhia nws tu tsheb. Tiam sis Tomás xav ua si nrog nws cov phooj ywg. Nws cov phooj ywg pab nws tu tsheb.

Tshooj 3. Peb nyeem *The First Amendment to the U.S. Constitution.* Peb kawm txog cov kev ywj pheej uas neeg muaj hauv Teb Chaws Mis Kas. Cov kev ywj pheej no muaj sau rau hauv ib daim ntawv uas hu ua Tsab Cai Tswj Teb Chaws.

Peb paub tias koj xav txhawb koj tus menyuam kev kawm kom tau zoo hauv tsev kawm ntawv. Peb xav kom koj koom hauv ib qho kev ua uas coj los qhia rau hauv chav kawm. Ua tsaug rau koj txoj kev txhawb nqa.

Sau npe,

_____ *(Tus kws qhia ntawv)*

Nrog koj tsev neeg tham txog cov kev ywj pheej hauv Thawj Qhov Kev Kho hauv U.S. Tsab Cai Tswj Teb Chaws. Hais kom ib tug neeg hauv tsev neeg pab koj sau daim duab no.

Cov Kev Ywj Pheej hauv Thawj Qhov Kev Kho	Qhov no txhais tau li cas rau cov neeg Mis Kas?
1. Kev ywj pheej ntawm kev ntseeg ntuj	
2. Kev ywj pheej ntawm kev hais lus	
3. Kev ywj pheej ntawm kev tshaj xov xwm	
4. Kev ywj pheej ntawm kev sib sau ua ke	

School-Home Connection
Sharing Visions

UNIDAD 3 Después de la escuela

Nombre _____

Fecha _____

Querida Familia:

En clase, aprendimos sobre las actividades que hacemos después de la escuela. A _____ *(nombre del alumno)* le gustaría compartir con ustedes lo que hemos aprendido.

Capítulo 1. Hablamos sobre las actividades que los estudiantes hacen después de la escuela. Los estudiantes hacen la tarea, juegan al béisbol, van de compras, trabajan y se encuentran con amigos. Aprendimos cómo decir la hora. También aprendimos a usar el pasado simple para hablar o escribir sobre acciones en el pasado.

Capítulo 2. Leímos el cuento ***Tomás Cleans the Car.*** La madre de Tomás le pide que limpie el auto. Pero Tomás quiere jugar con sus amigos. Sus amigos le ayudan a limpiar el auto.

Capítulo 3. Leímos ***The First Amendment to the U.S. Constitution.*** Aprendimos sobre las libertades que tienen las personas en los Estados Unidos. Estas libertades están escritas en un documento llamado la Constitución.

Sabemos que ustedes quieren apoyar el esfuerzo que realiza su estudiante en la escuela. Nos gustaría que participen en alguna actividad para compartir con la clase. Gracias por su apoyo.

Atentamente,

_____ *(Maestro/a)*

Habla con tu familia sobre las libertades mencionadas en la Primera Enmienda de la Constitución de los Estados Unidos. Pídele ayuda a un miembro de la familia para completar el cuadro.

Libertades mencionadas en la Primera Enmienda.	¿Qué significa esta libertad para los estadounidenses?
1. Libertad de culto	
2. Libertad de expresión	
3. Libertad de prensa	
4. Libertad de reunión	

School-Home Connection
Sharing Visions
Bài 3 Sau Giờ Học

Tên: _____

Ngày tháng năm: _____

Thưa Gia Đình,

Ở lớp, chúng ta đã học về các hoạt động sau giờ học. _____ *(tên học sinh)* muốn chia sẻ với quý vị những gì chúng ta đã học.

Chương 1. Chúng ta đã nói về các hoạt động mà học sinh làm sau giờ học. Học sinh làm bài tập ở nhà, chơi bóng chày, đi mua sắm, làm việc và gặp gỡ bạn bè. Chúng ta học cách nói giờ. Chúng ta cũng còn học cách dùng thì quá khứ đơn để kể hoặc viết về các hành động trong quá khứ.

Chương 2. Chúng ta đã đọc câu chuyện *Tomás Cleans the Car.* Mẹ của Tomás bảo cậu ta lau chiếc xe hơi. Nhưng Tomás muốn chơi với các bạn. Các bạn cậu giúp cậu lau xe hơi.

Chương 3. Chúng ta đã đọc *The First Amendment to the U.S. Constitution.* Chúng ta học về các quyền tự do mà người dân có tại Hoa Kỳ. Các quyền này được việc trong một văn bản gọi là Hiến Pháp.

Chúng tôi biết rằng quý vị muốn hỗ trợ thành tích học tập của con em mình ở trường. Chúng tôi muốn quý vị tham gia vào một hoạt động để chia sẻ với lớp. Xin cám ơn vì sự ủng hộ của quý vi.

Trân Trọng Kính Chào,

_____ *(Giáo Viên)*

Hãy nói chuyện với gia đình quý vị về các quyền tự do trong Tu Chính Án Thứ Nhất cho bản Hiến Pháp Hoa Kỳ. Nhờ một thành viên gia đình giúp quý vị điền vào sơ đồ.

Các quyền tự do trong Tu Chính Án Thứ Nhất	Quyền tự do này có ý nghĩa gì với người Mỹ?
1. Tự do tôn giáo	
2. Tự do ngôn luận	
3. Tự do báo chí	
4. Tự do hội họp	

School-Home Connection
Sharing Visions
UNIT 4 Home

Name _____

Date _____

Dear Family,

In class, we learned about the homes that people live in. _____ (student's name) would like to share with you what we learned.

Chapter 1. We learned to describe rooms and furniture in houses and apartments. We also learned how to ask and answer questions.

Chapter 2. We read a story called *A House of My Own*. The author talks about a home that she wants.

Chapter 3. We read a chapter from a math textbook, called *Perimeter and Area*. It tells how to measure the outside edge of an object and the space inside an object.

We know you want to support your student's achievement in school. We would like you to participate in an activity to share with the class. Thank you for your support.

Sincerely,

_____ (Teacher)

Talk with your family about your home. Ask a family member to help you complete the chart.

Name of Room	Furniture	What We Do in the Room
1.		
2.		
3.		
4.		
5.		
6.		

School-Home Connection
Sharing Visions

មេរៀនទី ៤ ផ្ទះ

ឈ្មោះ _____

កាលបរិច្ឆេទ _____

ជូនចំពោះ គ្រួសារ

នៅក្នុងថ្នាក់រៀន យើងបានរៀនអំពីផ្ទះដែលមនុស្សរស់នៅ ។ _____ (ឈ្មោះសិស្ស) ចង់ចែករំលែកនូវអ្វីដែលយើងបានរៀនជាមួយនឹងអ្នក ។

ជំពូក ១ យើងបានរៀនពីពណ៌នាពីបន្ទប់ និង គ្រឿងសង្ហារិមនៅក្នុងផ្ទះ និង បន្ទប់ដួល ។ យើងក៏ បានរៀនអំពីរបៀបសួរ និង ឆ្លើយនូវរសំណួរ ។

ជំពូក ២ យើងបានអានរឿងមានចំណងជើងថា *A House of My Own* ។ អ្នក និពន្ធនិយាយអំពីផ្ទះដែលនាងចង់បាន ។

ជំពូក ៣ យើងបានអានមេរៀនពីសៀវភៅគណិតវិទ្យា ដែលមានឈ្មោះថា *Perimeter and Area.* សៀវភៅនេះប្រាប់ពីរបៀបវាស់ទំហំខាងក្រៅនៃវត្ថុមួយ និង ទំហំខាង ក្នុងនៃវត្ថុមួយ ។

យើងដឹងថាអ្នកចង់គាំទ្រនូវការសម្រេចបានរបស់សិស្សអ្នកនៅសាលារៀន ។ យើងចង់ឲ្យអ្នកចូលរួម នៅក្នុងសកម្មភាពដែលចែករំលែកគ្នាជាមួយនឹងថ្នាក់រៀន ។ សូមអរគុណចំពោះការគាំទ្ររបស់អ្នក ។

ដោយក្តីគោរពរាប់អាន

_____ (គ្រូបង្រៀន)

ជំដែកជាមួយគ្រួសាររបស់អ្នកអំពីផ្ទះរបស់អ្នក ។ សូមសួរទៅសមាជិកគ្រួសារដើម្បីជួយអ្នកបំពេញតារាង ខាងក្រោម ។

ឈ្មោះបន្ទប់	គ្រឿងសង្ហារិម	យើងធ្វើអ្វីខ្លះនៅក្នុងបន្ទប់នោះ
១.		
២.		
៣.		
៤.		
៥.		
៦.		

School-Home Connection
Sharing Visions

單元四　家

姓名 _____

日期 _____

親愛的家長：

我們在課堂上學習到我們生活的家園。_____（學生姓名）想和您們分享我們的上課內容。

第一章　我們學習描述家裡的房間和家具，也學會如何發問與回答。

第二章　我們讀了一篇叫 *A House of My Own* 的故事。作者談論她夢想中的家。

第三章　我們讀了數學課本中的一章，叫做 *Perimeter and Area*，教導學生如何測量物體的四周長度和物體內的空間。

我們知道您們很樂意協助孩子學習。希望您們能參與以下活動，我們將在課堂分享結果。感謝您們的協助。

敬上

_____（老師）

與家人談論你們的家請求一位家人幫助你完成以下表格。

房間名稱	家具	在這個房間做的活動
1.		
2.		
3.		
4.		
5.		
6.		

School-Home Connection
Sharing Visions
SEKSYON 4 Lakay

Non _____
Dat _____

Chè Fanmi,

Nan klas la, nou aprann sou kay moun yo rete ladan yo. _____ *(non elèv la)* ta renmen pataje avèk ou sa nou aprann.

Chapit 1. Nou aprann fè deskripsyon pyès ak mèb nan kay ak apatman. Nou aprann tou ki jan pou poze kesyon ak reponn kesyon.

Chapit 2. Nou li yon istwa ki rele *A House of My Own.* Otè a pale sou yon kay li ta renmen genyen.

Chapit 3. Nou li yon chapit nan yon liv matematik, ki rele, *Perimeter and Area.* Li esplike ki jan pou mezire arebò yon bagay ak espas andedan bagay la.

Nou konnen ke ou vle ankouraje reyisit pitit ou nan lekòl la. Nou ta renmen ke ou patisipe nan yon aktivite pou pataje ak klas la. Mèsi pou sipò ou.

Sensèman,

_____ *(Pwofesè)*

Pale ak fanmi w sou lakay ou. Mande yon manm fanmi w ede w konplete tablo a.

Non Pyès la	Mèb	Sa nou fè nan pyès la
1.		
2.		
3.		
4.		
5.		
6.		

School-Home Connection
Sharing Visions

SOB KAWM 4 Lub Tsev

Npe _____

Hnub Tim _____

Nyob zoo txog Tsev Neeg,

Hauv chav kawm ntawv, peb kawm txog cov tsev uas neeg nyob. _____ *(tus menyuam kawm ntawv lub npe)* yuav xav qhia rau koj seb pab kawm txog dab tsi.

Tshooj 1. Peb kawm txog kev qhia txog cov chav thiab cov roj tog hauv cov tsev thiab cov tsev loj. Peb tseem kawm txog seb yuav nug thiab teb cov lus nug li cas.

Tshooj 2. Peb nyeem ib zaj dab neeg hu ua *A House of My Own*. Tus neeg sau no tham txog ib lub tsev uas nws xav tau.

Tshooj 3. Peb nyeem ib tshooj hauv phau ntawv ua zauv, hu ua *Perimeter and Area*. Nws qhia seb yuav ntsuas cov ntug sab nraum ib qho khoom thiab qhov chaw sab hauv ib qho khoom li cas.

Peb paub tias koj xav txhawb koj tus menyuam kev kawm kom tau zoo hauv tsev kawm ntawv. Peb xav kom koj koom hauv ib qho kev ua uas coj los qhia rau hauv chav kawm. Ua tsaug rau koj txoj kev txhawb nqa.

Sau npe,

_____ *(Tus kws qhia ntawv)*

Nrog koj tsev neeg tham txog koj ub tsev. Nug ib tug neeg kom nws pab koj sau daim duab.

Lub Npe Ntawm Chav	Roj Tog	Peb Ua Dab Tsi Hauv Chav
1.		
2.		
3.		
4.		
5.		
6.		

School-Home Connection
Sharing Visions
UNIDAD 4 El hogar

Nombre _____

Fecha _____

Querida Familia:

En clase, aprendimos sobre los hogares donde viven las personas. A _____ *(nombre del alumno)* le gustaría compartir con ustedes lo que hemos aprendido.

Capítulo 1. Aprendimos a describir las habitaciones y los muebles en las casas y departamentos. También aprendimos cómo hacer y responder preguntas.

Capítulo 2. Leímos un cuento llamado *A House of My Own.* La autora habla de una casa que quiere.

Capítulo 3. Leímos un capítulo de un manual de matemáticas llamado *Perimeter and Area.* Habla de cómo medir el borde exterior de un objeto y el espacio dentro del objeto.

Sabemos que ustedes quieren apoyar el esfuerzo que realiza su estudiante en la escuela. Nos gustaría que participen en alguna actividad para compartir con la clase. Gracias por su apoyo.

Atentamente,

_____ *(Maestro/a)*

Habla con tu familia sobre tu hogar. Pídele ayuda a un miembro de la familia para completar el cuadro.

Nombre de la habitación	Muebles	Qué hacemos en esa habitación
1.		
2.		
3.		
4.		
5.		
6.		

School-Home Connection
Sharing Visions
Bài 4 Nhà

Tên: _____

Ngày tháng năm: _____

Thưa Gia Đình,

Ở lớp, chúng ta đã học về những căn nhà mà mọi người sống bên trong. _____ *(tên học sinh)* muốn chia sẻ với quý vị những gì chúng ta đã học.

Chương 1. Chúng ta học cách miêu tả các phòng và đồ đạc trong nhà và căn hộ. Chúng ta cũng học cách hỏi và trả lời các câu hỏi.

Chương 2. Chúng ta đọc một câu chuyện gọi là *A House of My Own.* Tác giả nói về một căn nhà mà bà ta muốn có.

Chương 3. Chúng ta đọc một chương trong một cuốn sách giáo khoa toán, gọi là *Perimeter and Area.* Nó chỉ cách đo cạnh bên ngoài của một vật và khoảng không bên trong một vật.

Chúng tôi biết rằng quý vị muốn hỗ trợ thành tích học tập của con em mình ở trường. Chúng tôi muốn quý vị tham gia vào một hoạt động để chia sẻ với lớp. Xin cám ơn vì sự ủng hộ của quý vị.

Trân Trọng Kính Chào,

_____ *(Giáo Viên)*

Hãy nói chuyện với gia đình bạn về ngôi nhà của mình. Nhờ một thành viên gia đình giúp bạn điền vào sơ đồ.

Tên Phòng	Đồ Đạc	Chúng Ta Làm Gì trong Phòng
1.		
2.		
3.		
4.		
5.		
6.		

School-Home Connection
Sharing Visions
UNIT 5   The Community

Name _____

Date _____

Dear Family,

In class, we learned about places in the community. _____ (student's name) would like to share with you what we learned.

Chapter 1. We talked about places in the community, such as the post office, supermarket, fire station, police station, and hospital. We learned about transportation and signs to help us get to the places. We also learned to talk about actions happening right now and to give directions and orders.

Chapter 2. We read news articles and letters to the editor in the newspaper *East City Community News*. A news article gives facts and information. A letter to the editor gives the opinion of someone in the community.

Chapter 3. We read *Resources in the United States*, an excerpt from a social studies textbook. It tells us about raw materials, manufacturing, and agriculture in the United States.

We know you want to support your student's achievement in school. We would like you to participate in an activity to share with the class. Thank you for your support.

Sincerely,

_____ *(Teacher)*

Talk with your family about four places in your community. Ask a family member to help you complete the chart.

Place in the Community	Transportation to Get There	Directions to Get There
1.		
2.		
3.		
4.		

School-Home Connection
Sharing Visions

មេរៀនទី ៥ សហគម

ឈ្មោះ _____

កាលបរិច្ឆេទ _____

ជូនចំពោះ ក្រុសារ

នៅក្នុងថ្នាក់រៀន យើងបានរៀនអំពីកន្លែងនៅក្នុងសហគម ។ _____ (ឈ្មោះសិស្ស) ចង់ចែករំលែកនូវអ្វីដែលយើងបានរៀនជាមួយនឹងអ្នក ។

ជំពូក ១ យើងបានដែកអំពីទីកន្លែងនៅក្នុងសហគម ដូចជាការិយាល័យប្រៃសណីយ៍ ផ្សារទំនើប ស្ថានីយពន្លត់អគ្គីភ័យ ស្ថានីយនគរបាល និង មន្ទីរពេទ្យ ។ យើងបានរៀនអំពីការធ្វើដំណើរ និង សញ្ញា ដើម្បីជួយយើងទៅដល់កន្លែងមួយ ។ យើងក៏បានរៀនដែកអំពីសកម្មភាពដែលកើតឡើងឥឡូវ ភ្លាម១ និង ផ្តល់ទិស និង ការបញ្ជា ។

ជំពូក ២ យើងបានអានអត្ថបទសារព័ត៌មាន និង លិខិតផ្ញើទៅកាន់អ្នកបោះពុម្ពផ្សាយនៅក្នុង កាសែត *East City Community News* ។ អត្ថបទ សារព័ត៌មានផ្តល់នូវវិការពិត និង ព័ត៌មាន ។ លិខិតផ្ញើទៅកាន់អ្នកបោះពុម្ពផ្សាយផ្តល់នូវវត៌និតរបស់ នណាម្នាក់នៅក្នុងសហគម ។

ជំពូក ៣ យើងបានអានអត្ថបទ *Resources in the United States* ដែលដកស្រង់ចេញពីសៀវភៅសិក្សាសង្គម ។ អត្ថបទនេះប្រាប់យើងអំពីវិត្ថុធាតុដើម ការផលិត និង កសិកម្មនៅសហរដ្ឋអាមេរិក ។

យើងដឹងថាអ្នកចង់គាំទ្រនូវការសម្រេចបានរបស់សិស្សអ្នកនៅសាលារៀន ។ យើងចង់ឱ្យអ្នកចូលរួម នៅក្នុងសកម្មភាពដែលចែករំលែកគ្នាជាមួយនឹងថ្នាក់រៀន ។ សូមអគុណចំពោះការគាំទ្ររបស់អ្នក ។

ដោយក្តីគោរពរាប់អាន

_____ (គ្រូបង្រៀន)

ជដែកជាមួយគ្រួសាររបស់អ្នកអំពីកន្លែងនៅក្នុងសហគមរបស់អ្នក ។ សូមសួរទៅសមាជិកគ្រួសារដើម្បីជួយ អ្នកបំពេញតារាងខាងក្រោម ។

កន្លែងនៅក្នុងសហគម	មធ្យោបាយធ្វើដំណើរទៅកាន់ទីនោះ	ទិសដៅទៅកាន់ទីនោះ
១.		
២.		
៣.		
៤.		

School-Home Connection
Sharing Visions

單元五　社區

姓名 _____

日期 _____

親愛的家長：

　　我們在課堂上學習社區裡的地點。_____ (學生姓名) 想和您們分享我們的上課內容。

　　第一章　我們談論社區裡的地點，如郵局、超市、消防隊、警察局和醫院。我們學習帶領我們到這些地點的運輸工具和路牌，也學會如何談論現在正在發生的事件，以及如何做指示和下命令。

　　第二章　我們閱讀 *East City Community News* 的新聞以及給編輯的信。新聞提供事實和資訊。給編輯的信則評論社區內的一位人士。

　　第三章　我們閱讀社會課本教科書的短文 *Resources in the United States*，本文說明美國的原物料業、製造業和農業。

　　我們知道您們樂意協助孩子學習。我們希望您們參與以下活動，我們會在課堂討論結果。謝謝您們的協助。

　　　　　　　　　　　　　　　　　　　敬上

　　　　　　　　　　_____ (老師)

與家人討論你住的社區的四個地點。請求一位家人幫忙你填以下表格。

社區裡的地點	到達這些地點的交通工具	如何到這些地點的方向指示
1.		
2.		
3.		
4.		

School-Home Connection
Sharing Visions
SEKSYON 5 Kominote a

Non _____

Dat _____

Chè Fanmi,

Nan klas la, nou aprann sou kote ki genyen nan kominote a. _____ *(non elèv la)* ta renmen pataje avèk ou sa nou aprann.

Chapit 1. Nou pale sou kote ki genyen nan kominote a, tankou biwo lapòs, makèt, estasyon ponpye, pòs polis, ak lopital. Nou aprann sou transpò ak siy pou ede nou ale kote sa yo. Nou aprann tou pou nou pale sou aksyon kap pase koulye a e bay enstriksyon ak lòd tou.

Chapit 2. Nou li atik sou nouvèl ak lèt yo ekri editè a nan jounal *East City Community News.* Yon atik sou nouvèl bay fè ak enfòmasyon. Yon lèt yo ekri editè a bay opinyon yon moun nan kominote a.

Chapit 3. Nou li *Resources in the United States,* yon ekstrè ki soti nan yon liv sou etid sosyal. Li pale nou sou matyè premyè, fabrikasyon, ak agrikilti Ozetazini.

Nou konnen ke ou vle ankouraje reyisit pitit ou nan lekòl la. Nou ta renmen ke ou patisipe nan yon aktivite pou pataje ak klas la. Mèsi pou sipò ou.

Sensèman,

_____ *(Pwofesè)*

Pale ak fanmi w sou kat kote ki genyen nan kominote w la. Mande yon manm fanmi w ede w konplete tablo a.

Kote nan kominote a	Transpò pou rive la	Enstriksyon pou rive la
1.		
2.		
3.		
4.		

School-Home Connection
Sharing Visions
SOB KAWM 5 Lub Zej Zos

Npe _____

Hnub Tim _____

Nyob zoo txog Tsev Neeg,

Hauv chav kawm ntawv, peb kawm txog cov chaw hauv lub zej zos. _____ *(tus menyuam kawm ntawv lub npe)* yuav xav qhia rau koj seb pab kawm txog dab tsi.

Tshooj 1. Peb tham txog cov chaw hauv lub zej zos, xws li chaw xa ntawv, khw muag khoom noj, tsev tua hluav taws xob, tsev tub ceev xwm, thiab tsev kho mob. Peb kawm txog tsheb thiab cov yuaj (signs) los pab peb mus rau cov chaws. Peb tseem kawm tham txog cov kev ua uas tshwm sim tam sim no thiab qhia kev thiab hais kom ua.

Tshooj 2. Peb nyeem cov ntawv xov xwm thiab cov ntawv sau rau tus sau ntawv hauv daim ntawv xov xwm *East City Community News.* Ib daim ntawv xov qhia tej yam muaj tseeb thiab qhia lus. Ib daim ntawv sau rau tus sau ntawv muab cov kev xav ntawm ib tug neeg hauv zej zos.

Tshooj 3. Peb nyeem *Resources in the United States,* ib sob lus los hauv phau ntawv kawm txog neeg. Nws qhia rau peb txog cov khom uas tsis tau muab ua dab tsi, kev ua khoom, thiab kev ua liaj ua teb hauv Teb Chaws Mis Kas.

Peb paub tias koj xav txhawb koj tus menyuam kev kawm kom tau zoo hauv tsev kawm ntawv. Peb xav kom koj koom hauv ib qho kev ua uas coj los qhia rau hauv chav kawm. Ua tsaug rau koj txoj kev txhawb nqa.

Sau npe,

_____ *(Tus kws qhia ntawv)*

Nrog koj tsev neeg tham txog plaub qhov chaws hauv koj lub zej zos. Kom ib tug neeg hauv koj tsev neeg pab koj sau daim duab.

Qhov Chaw Hauv Zej Zos	Tsheb Thauj Mus Rau Tov	Kev Qhia Mus Rau Tov
1.		
2.		
3.		
4.		

School-Home Connection
Sharing Visions

UNIDAD 5 La comunidad

Nombre _____

Fecha _____

Querida Familia:

En clase, aprendimos sobre los lugares de la comunidad. A _____ *(nombre del alumno)* le gustaría compartir con ustedes lo que hemos aprendido.

Capítulo 1. Hablamos sobre lugares de la comunidad, como la oficina de correo, el supermercado, la estación de bomberos, la estación de policía y el hospital. Aprendimos sobre el transporte y las señales que nos ayudan a llegar a los lugares. También aprendimos a describir las acciones que suceden en este mismo momento y a dar órdenes e instrucciones.

Capítulo 2. Leímos artículos periodísticos y cartas al editor en el periódico *East City Community News*. Una artículo periodístico da hechos e información. Una carta al editor da la opinión de una persona de la comunidad.

Capítulo 3. Leímos *Resources in the United States,* un pasaje de un manual de ciencias sociales. Habla de las materias primas, la producción y la agricultura en los Estados Unidos.

Sabemos que ustedes quieren apoyar el esfuerzo que realiza su estudiante en la escuela. Nos gustaría que participen en alguna actividad para compartir con la clase. Gracias por su apoyo.

Atentamente,

_____ *(Maestro/a)*

Habla con tu familia sobre cuatro lugares de tu comunidad. Pídele ayuda a un miembro de la familia para completar el cuadro.

Lugar de la comunidad	Transporte para llegar al lugar	Indicaciones para llegar al lugar
1.		
2.		
3.		
4.		

School-Home Connection
Sharing Visions
Bài 5 Cộng Đồng

Tên: _____

Ngày tháng năm: _____

Thưa Gia Đình,

Ở lớp, chúng ta đã học về những nơi chốn trong cộng đồng. _____ *(tên học sinh)* muốn chia sẻ với quý vị những gì chúng ta đã học.

Chương 1. Chúng ta đã nói về các nơi chốn trong cộng đồng, chẳng hạn bưu điện, siêu thị, trạm cứu hỏa, đồn cảnh sát và bệnh viện. Chúng ta học về phương tiện đi lại và các biển hiệu để giúp ta đến được các nơi đó. Chúng ta còn học cách nói về các hành động xảy ra ngay bây giờ và cách đưa ra các lời hướng dẫn và mệnh lệnh.

Chương 2. Chúng ta đọc các bài tin tức và thư từ gửi cho tổng biên tập tại tờ báo *East City Community News.* Một bài tin đưa ra những sự việc thật và những thông tin. Một bức thư gửi tổng biên tập nêu ý kiến của một người trong cộng đồng.

Chương 3. Chúng ta đọc *Resources in the United States,* một đoạn trích từ một cuốn sách giáo khoa về xã hội học. Nó cho ta biết về các nguồn nguyên liệu thô, ngành chế tạo và nông nghiệp tại Hoa Kỳ.

Chúng tôi biết rằng quý vị muốn hỗ trợ thành tích học tập của con em mình ở trường. Chúng tôi muốn quý vị tham gia vào một hoạt động để chia sẻ với lớp. Xin cám ơn vì sự ủng hộ của quý vị.

Trân Trọng Kính Chào,

_____ *(Giáo Viên)*

Hãy nói chuyện với gia đình bạn về bốn nơi trong cộng đồng của bạn. Nhờ một người trong gia đình giúp bạn điền vào sơ đồ.

Nơi trong Cộng Đồng	Phương Tiện Di Chuyển Đến Đó	Các Hướng để Đến Đó
1.		
2.		
3.		
4.		

School-Home Connection
Sharing Visions

UNIT 6   Food

Name _____

Date _____

Dear Family,

In class, we learned about food. _____ (student's name) would like to share with you what we learned.

Chapter 1. We learned about food and drinks we have for breakfast, lunch, and dinner. We talked about foods we like and foods we do not like. We learned how to ask for food politely.

Chapter 2. We read the poem, *How to Eat a Poem,* by Eve Merriam. This poem uses words that help you see a picture in your mind. We learned about repetition and rhythm in poems.

Chapter 3. We read a science text called *The Food Guide Pyramid.* It gives information about a healthy diet. It includes a diagram that shows the six food groups.

We know you want to support your student's achievement in school. We would like you to participate in an activity to share with the class. Thank you for your support.

Sincerely,

_____ (Teacher)

Ask a family member this question: What did you eat today? Have the family member help you fill out the chart.

Fats, Oils, & Sweets	Milk, Yogurt, & Cheese	Vegetables	Meat, Poultry, Fish, Dry Beans, Eggs, & Nuts	Fruit	Bread, Cereal, Rice, & Pasta

School-Home Connection
Sharing Visions

មេរៀនទី ៦ ចំណីអាហារ

ឈ្មោះ： _____

កាលបរិច្ឆេទ _____

ជូនចំពោះ ក្រុសារ

នៅក្នុងថ្នាក់រៀន យើងបានរៀនអំពីចំណីអាហារ ។ _____ (ឈ្មោះសិស្ស)
ចង់ចែករំលែកនូវអ្វីដែលយើងបានរៀនជាមួយនឹងអ្នក ។

ជំពូក ១ យើងបានរៀនអំពីចំណីអាហារ និង ភេជ្ជៈដែលយើងបរិភោគនៅពេលព្រឹក ពេលថ្ងៃ និង ពេលល្ងាច ។
យើងបានជជែកអំពីចំណីអាហារដែលយើងចូលចិត្ត និង ចំណីអាហារដែលយើងមិនចូល ចិត្ត ។
យើងបានរៀនពីរបៀបសុំចំណីអាហារដោយចេះគួរសម ។

ជំពូក ២ យើងបានអានកំណាព្យ *How to Eat a Poem* និពន្ធដោយ Eve Merriam ។
កំណាព្យនេះប្រើពាក្យដែលជួយអ្នកមើលឃើញរូបភាពនៅក្នុងគំនិតរបស់អ្នក ។ យើង បានរៀនអំពីពាក្យជួន និង
រណ្តំនៅក្នុងកំណាព្យ ។

ជំពូក ៣ យើងបានអានសៀវភៅវិទ្យាសាស្ត្រមានចំណងជើងថា ពីរ៉ាមីតចំណេះដំអំពីចំណីអាហារ *The Food Guide Pyramid* ។ សៀវភៅនេះផ្តល់ព័ត៌មានអំពីរបបអាហារដែលមានសុខភាព ។
វារួមមានដ្យាក្រាមដែលបង្ហាញពីក្រុមចំណីអាហារទាំង ៦ ។

យើងដឹងថាអ្នកចង់គាំទ្រនូវការសម្រេចបានរបស់សិស្សអ្នកនៅសាលារៀន ។ យើងចង់ជំរុញអ្នកចូលរួម
នៅក្នុងសកម្មភាពដែលចែករំលែកគ្នាជាមួយនឹងថ្នាក់រៀន ។ សូមអរគុណចំពោះការគាំទ្ររបស់អ្នក ។

ដោយក្តីគោរពរាប់អាន

_____ (គ្រូបង្រៀន)

សូមស្ទួរទៅសមាជិកគ្រួសារនូវសំណួរនេះ តើអ្នកបានបរិភោគអ្វីនៅថ្ងៃនេះ? សូមឱ្យសមាជិកគ្រួសារជួយ អ្នកបំពេញតារាងខាងក្រោម ។

កាកខ្លាញ់, ប្រេង និង ស្ករ	ទឹកដោះគោ, ទឹកដោះគោជូរ និង ឈីស	បន្លែ	សាច់, សាច់បក្សី, ត្រី, សណ្តែកសៀង, ស៊ុត និង គ្រាប់ធញ្ញជាតិ	ផ្លែឈើ	នំបុ័ង, ធញ្ញជាតិ, បាយ និង នំប៉័ស

School-Home Connection
Sharing Visions

單元六　食物

姓名 _____
日期 _____

親愛的家長：

我們在課堂上學習食物。_____（學生姓名）想和您們分享我們的上課內容。

第一章　我們學到在早餐、午餐和晚餐吃的食物和喝的飲料，討論我們喜歡和不喜歡的食物。我們學會如何禮貌地要求別人遞食物。

第二章　我們閱讀伊芙瑪莉安的詩：*How to Eat a Poem*。這首詩的詞彙描繪出一個生動的圖像。我們學到詩中的節奏和重複的音韻。

第三章　我們閱讀自然課本的一篇文章，叫做 *The Food Guide Pyramid*，教導我們如何健康飲食，包括六大食物群的圖表。

我們知道您們很樂意協助孩子學習。希望您們能參與以下活動，我們將在課堂分享結果。感謝您們的協助。

敬上

_____（老師）

問一位家人：你今天吃了什麼。請家人幫你完成此表格。

脂肪、油和醣類	牛奶、優格和乳酪	蔬菜	肉類、家禽、魚類、豆類、蛋類、和堅果類	水果	麵包、麥片、米類和義大利麵

School-Home Connection
Sharing Visions
SEKSYON 6 Manje

Non _____
Dat _____

Chè Fanmi,

Nan klas la, nou aprann sou manje. _____ *(non elèv la)* ta renmen pataje avèk ou sa nou aprann.

Chapit 1. Nou aprann sou manje ak bwason nou genyen pou dejne, goute, ak dine. Nou pale sou manje nou renmen ak manje nou pa renmen. Nou aprann ki jan pou nou mande manje ak bon lizaj.

Chapit 2. Nou li powèm, ***How to Eat a Poem,*** yon powèm Eve Merriam ekri. Powèm sa a itilize mo ki ede w wè yon imaj nan lespri w. Nou aprann sou repetisyon ak kadans nan powèm.

Chapit 3. Nou li yon tèks syans ki rele ***The Food Guide Pyramid.*** Li bay enfòmasyon sou yon rejim alimantè pou lasante. Li gen yon dyagram ki montre sis gwoup manje ladan li.

Nou konnen ke ou vle ankouraje reyisit pitit ou nan lekòl la. Nou ta renmen ke ou patisipe nan yon aktivite pou pataje ak klas la. Mèsi pou sipò ou.

Sensèman,

_____ *(Pwofesè)*

Poze yon manm fanmi w kesyon sa a: Ki sa ou manje jodi a? Mande manm fanmi w la ede w plen tablo a.

Grès, Lwil, Bagay dous	Lèt, Yogout, ak Fwomaj	Legim	Bèt volay, Pwason, Pwa chèch Ze ak Nwa	Fwi	Pen, Sereyal, Diri ak Pat Alimantè

School-Home Connection
Sharing Visions
SOB KAWM 6 Khoom Noj

Npe _____

Hnub Tim _____

Nyob zoo txog Tsev Neeg,

Hauv chav kawm ntawv, peb kawm txog khoom noj. _____ *(tus menyuam kawm ntawv lub npe)* yuav xav qhia rau koj seb pab kawm txog dab tsi.

Tshooj 1. Peb kawm txog khoom noj thiab dej haus uas peb noj ua tshais, ua su, thiab ua hmo. Peb tham txog cov khoom noj uas peb nyiam thiab tsis nyiam. Peb kawm nug kom muab khoom noj yam paub cais.

Tshooj 2. Peb nyeem zaj paj huam, *How to Eat a Poem,* los ntawm Eve Merriam. Zaj paj huam no siv cov lus uas pab kom koj pom ib daim duab hauv koj lub hlwb. Peb kawm txog qhov uas hais tas li thiab cov lus sib dhos hauv cov paj huam.

Tshooj 3. Peb nyeem ib sob lus hauv science hu ua *The Food Guide Pyramid.* Nws qhia lus txog kev noj kom muaj kev kaj huv ntawm cev. Nws muaj ib daim duab uas qhia txog rau pawg khoom noj.

Peb paub tias koj xav txhawb koj tus menyuam kev kawm kom tau zoo hauv tsev kawm ntawv. Peb xav kom koj koom hauv ib qho kev ua uas coj los qhia rau hauv chav kawm. Ua tsaug rau koj txoj kev txhawb nqa.

Sau npe,

_____ *(Tus kws qhia ntawv)*

Nug ib tug neeg hauv tsev neeg sob lus nug no: Hnub no koj noj dab tsi? Kom ib tug neeg hauv tsev neeg pab koj sau daim duab no.

Khoom Muaj Rog, Roj & Qab Zib	Mis Nyuj, Yogurt, & Cheese	Zaub	Nqaij, Poultry, Ntses, Taum Qhuav, Qe & Txiv Luam Huab Xeeb	Txiv Hmab Txiv Ntoo	Nplev, Cereal, Mov, & Pasta

School-Home Connection
Sharing Visions
UNIDAD 6 Los alimentos

Nombre _____

Fecha _____

Querida Familia:

En clase, aprendimos sobre los alimentos. A _____ *(nombre del alumno)* le gustaría compartir con ustedes lo que hemos aprendido.

Capítulo 1. Aprendimos sobre los alimentos y las bebidas del desayuno, el almuerzo y la cena. Hablamos de los alimentos que nos gustan y que no nos gustan. Aprendimos cómo pedir la comida educadamente.

Capítulo 2. Leímos un poema, *How to Eat a Poem,* de Eve Merriam. Este poema usa palabras que nos ayudan a formar una imagen mental. Aprendimos sobre la repetición y la rima en los poemas.

Capítulo 3. Leímos un libro de ciencias llamado *The Food Guide Pyramid.* Tiene información sobre una dieta saludable. También tiene un diagrama que muestra los seis grupos de alimentos.

Sabemos que ustedes quieren apoyar el esfuerzo que realiza su estudiante en la escuela. Nos gustaría que participen en alguna actividad para compartir con la clase. Gracias por su apoyo.

Atentamente,

_____ *(Maestro/a)*

Haz esta pregunta a un miembro de la familia: ¿Qué comiste hoy? Pídele ayuda para completar el cuadro.

Grasas, aceites y dulces	Leche, yogur y queso	Verduras	Carne, aves, pescado, frijoles secos, huevos y nueces	Frutas	Pan, cereales, arroz y pasta

School-Home Connection
Sharing Visions
Bài 6 Thức Ăn

Tên: _____

Ngày tháng năm: _____

Thưa Gia Đình,

Ở lớp, chúng ta đã học về thức ăn. _____ *(tên học sinh)* muốn chia sẻ với quý vị những gì chúng ta đã học.

Chương 1. Chúng ta đã học về thức ăn và các đồ uống mà ta dùng cho bữa sáng, trưa và tối. Chúng ta nói về các loại thức ăn chúng ta thích và không thích. Chúng ta học cách xin được ăn thứ gì đó một cách lịch sự.

Chương 2. Chúng ta đã đọc bài thơ, *How to Eat a Poem,* của tác giả. Bài thơ này dùng những từ ngữ giúp quý vị nhìn thấy một bức tranh trong đầu mình. Chúng ta học về phép láy lại và vần điệu trong các bài thơ.

Chương 3. Chúng ta đọc một bài viết khoa học gọi là *The Food Guide Pyramid.* Nó cung cấp thông tin về một chế độ ăn lành mạnh. Nó có một biểu đồ thể hiện sáu nhóm thức ăn.

Chúng tôi biết rằng quý vị muốn hỗ trợ thành tích học tập của con em mình ở trường. Chúng tôi muốn quý vị tham gia vào một hoạt động để chia sẻ với lớp. Xin cám ơn vì sự ủng hộ của quý vị.

Trân Trọng Kính Chào,

_____ *(Giáo Viên)*

Hãy đặt câu hỏi này với một người trong gia đình: Hôm nay em đã ăn gì? Nhờ người nhà giúp bạn điền vào sơ đồ.

Các Chất Béo, Dầu, & Đồ Ngọt	Sữa, Sữa Chua, & Phô Mai	Các loại Rau	Thịt, Gia Cầm, Cá, Đậu Khô, Trứng, & Quả Hạch	Trái Cây	Bánh Mì, Ngũ Cốc, Gạo, & Mì Sợi

School-Home Connection
Sharing Visions

UNIT 7 Money

Name _____

Date _____

Dear Family,

In class, we learned about money and budgets. _____ (student's name) would like to share with you what we learned.

Chapter 1. We talked about clothes and prices. We can pay for clothes with cash, a check, or a credit card. We learned to describe and compare clothes and other objects. We also learned the future tense. The future tense describes events in the future.

Chapter 2. Myths are very old stories. They teach a lesson called a moral. We read the Greek myth *The Midas Touch*. It is about King Midas. Everything the king touches turns to gold. As we read, we predicted, or made guesses about, what would happen next.

Chapter 3. We read a magazine article called *Making a Budget*. This article teaches you how to make a budget. A budget is a plan for spending and saving your money.

We know you want to support your student's achievement in school. We would like you to participate in an activity to share with the class. Thank you for your support.

Sincerely,

_____ (Teacher)

Talk with a family member about his or her monthly budget. Ask the person to help you complete the chart.

Budget Item	How much do you spend?	Do you pay by cash, check, or credit card?
1. Clothes		
2. Food		
3. Entertainment		
4. Transportation		
5. Savings		

School-Home Connection
Sharing Visions

មេរៀនទី ៧ លុយ

ឈ្មោះ _____

កាលបរិច្ឆេទ _____

ជូនចំពោះ ក្រុសារ

នៅក្នុងថ្នាក់រៀន យើងបានរៀនអំពីលុយ និង ថវិការ ។ _____ (ឈ្មោះសិស្ស)
ចង់ចែករំលែកនូវរឿងអ្វីដែលយើងបានរៀនជាមួយនឹងអ្នក ។

ជំពូក ១ យើងបានដែកអំពីសម្លៀកបំពាក់ និង ថ្លៃ ។ យើងអាចទិញសម្លៀកបំពាក់ដោយប្រើ លុយសុទ្ធ មូលប្បទានប័ត្រ ឬ ប័ណ្ណឥណទាន ។ យើងបានរៀនពិតណិនា និង ប្រៀបធៀបសម្លៀក បំពាក់ និង វត្ថុផ្សេងទៀត ។ យើងក៏បានរៀនអំពីអនាគតកាល ។ អនាគតកាលពិតណិនាពី ព្រឹត្តិការណ៍នៅពេលអនាគត ។

ជំពូក ២ ទេវកថាគឺជារឿងព្រេងពីយូងង់មកហើយ ។ រឿងនេះបង្រៀននូវមេរៀនដែលហៅថា សីលធម៌ ។ យើងបានអានទេវកថារបស់ក្រិច *The Midas Touch* ។ រឿងនេះគឺនិយាយអំពីស្តេច Midas ។ អ្វីទាំងឡាយដែលស្តេចនេះប៉ះនឹងក្លាយទៅជាមាស ។ នៅពេលដែលយើងបានអាន យើងបានស្មាន ឬ ទាយពីអ្វីដែលកើតឡើងបន្ទាប់ ។

ជំពូក ៣ យើងបានអានអត្ថបទទស្សនាវដ្ដីមានចំណងជើងថា *Making a Budget*។ អត្ថបទនេះបង្រៀនអ្នកពីរបៀបធ្វើថវិការ ។ ថវិការគឺជាតម្រោងសម្រាប់ការចំណាយ និង សន្សំ លើប្រាក់របស់អ្នក ។

យើងដឹងថាអ្នកចង់គាំទ្រនូវការសម្រេចបានរបស់សិស្សអ្នកនៅសាលារៀន ។ យើងធន់ឱ្យអ្នកចូលរួម នៅក្នុងសកម្មភាពដែលចែករំលែកគ្នាជាមួយនឹងថ្នាក់រៀន ។ សូមអគុណចំពោះការគាំទ្ររបស់អ្នក ។

ដោយក្តីគោរពរាប់អាន

_____ (គ្រូបង្រៀន)

ជំដែកជាមួយសមាជិកក្រុសារអំពីថវិការប្រចាំខែរបស់គាត់ ។ សូមឱ្យគាត់ជួយអ្នកបំពេញតារាងខាងក្រោម ។

ធាតុថវិការ	តើអ្នកចំណាយប៉ុន្មាន?	តើអ្នកចំណាយដោយប្រើលុយសុទ្ធ មូលប្បទានប័ត្រ ឬ ប័ណ្ណឥណទាន?
១. សម្លៀកបំពាក់		
២. ចំណីអាហារ		
៣. ការកំសាន្ត		
៤. ការធ្វើដំណើរ		
៥. ការសន្សំ		

School-Home Connection
Sharing Visions

單元七　金錢

姓名 _____
日期 _____

親愛的家長：

我們在課堂上學習金錢和預算。_____（學生姓名）想和您們分享我們的上課內容。

第一章　我們談論衣服和價格。我們能用現金、支票或信用卡付衣服的錢。我們學習描述和比較衣服等其他物品。我們也學習未來式。未來式描述在未來發生的事件。

第二章　神話是很久很久以前的故事。它們含有寓意。我們讀一個希臘神話叫 **The Midas Touch** 有個國王叫米達斯。只要他碰過的東西就會變成金子。我們一邊閱讀這個故事，一邊猜接著會發生什麼事。

第三章　我們閱讀一篇雜誌文章，叫做 *Making a Budget*。這篇文章教我們如何規劃預算。預算是如何花錢和存錢的計畫。

我們知道您們很樂意協助孩子學習。希望您們能參與以下活動，我們將在課堂分享結果。感謝您們的協助。

敬上

_____（老師）

與一位家人討論他或她的每月預算。請這位家人幫你填這個表格。

預算項目	所花金額？	用現金、支票還是信用卡支付？
1. 衣服		
2. 食物		
3. 娛樂		
4. 交通		
5. 存款		

School-Home Connection
Sharing Visions
SEKSYON 7 Lajan

Non _____
Dat _____

Chè Fanmi,

Nan klas la, nou aprann sou lajan ak bidjè. _____ *(non elèv la)* ta renmen pataje avèk ou sa nou aprann.

Chapit 1. Nou pale sou rad ak pri yo. Nou ka peye pou rad ak kach, chèk, oswa kat kredi. Nou aprann ekri ak konpare rad ak lòt bagay. Nou aprann tan fiti tou. Tan fiti dekri evennman ki pral rive pi devan.

Chapit 2. Mitoloji se istwa ki ansyen. Yo anseye yon leson ki rele *moral*. Nou li mitoloji Grèk *The Midas Touch*. Se yon istwa sou Wa Midas. Tou sa wa a manyen tounen lò. Pandan nou tap li, nou fè prediksyon, oswa devine sou sa ki pral rive apre.

Chapit 3. Nou li yon atik magazin ki rele *Making a Budget*. Atik sa a montre w ki jan pou fè yon bidjè. Yon bidjè se yon plan pou depanse ak ekonomize lajan.

Nou konnen ke ou vle ankouraje reyisit pitit ou nan lekòl la. Nou ta renmen ke ou patisipe nan yon aktivite pou pataje ak klas la. Mèsi pou sipò ou.

Sensèman,

_____ *(Pwofesè)*

Pale ak yon manm fanmi w sou bidjè li fè chak mwa. Mande moun sa a ede w konplete tablo a.

Atik pou Bidjè	Konbyen kòb ou depanse?	Èske ou peye kach, ak chèk, ou ak kat kredi?
1. rad		
2. manje		
3. amizman		
4. transpò		
5. ekonomi		

School-Home Connection
Sharing Visions
SOB KAWM 7 Nyiaj Txiag

Npe _____

Hnub Tim _____

Nyob zoo txog Tsev Neeg,

Hauv chav kawm ntawv, peb kawm txog nyiaj txiag thiab kev siv nyiaj. _____ *(tus menyuam kawm ntawv lub npe)* yuav xav qhia rau koj seb pab kawm txog dab tsi.

Tshooj 1. Peb tham txog khaub ncaws thiab cov nqi. Peb muab nyiaj ntsuab, tshev, los sis daim credit card los them rau cov khaub ncaws los tau. Peb kawm los qhia txog thiab muab cov khaub ncaws thiab lwm yam khoom los sib piv. Peb tseem kawm txog cov lus hais txog kev ua yav pem suab (future tense). Cov lus hais txog kev ua yav pem suab (future tense) hais txog tej yam uas yuav ua rau yav pem suab.

Tshooj 2. Cov dab neeg uas tej zaum yuav muaj los sis tsis muaj tseeb yog ib co dab neeg uas qub qub puag thaum ub. Lawv qhia txog ib qho kev kawm uas hu ua *kev qhia ib yam dab tsi zoo*. Peb nyem ib zaj dab neeg Greek uas tej zaum yuav muaj los sis tsis muaj tseeb uas hu ua **The Midas Touch**. Nws yog hais txog ib tug Huab Tais Midas. Txhua yam tus huab tais kov tig mus ua kub tag. Thaum uas peb nyeem, peb xav seb, yuav ua li cas txuas ntxiv.

Tshooj 3. Peb nyeem ib qho hauv phau ntawv hu ua **Making a Budget**. Daim ntawv no qhia rau koj seb yuav ua ib lub hom phiaj txog kev siv nyiaj thiab kev txuag nyiaj li cas. Ib lub hom phiaj no yog rau kev siv nyiaj thiab kev txuag koj cov nyiaj.

Peb paub tias koj xav txhawb koj tus menyuam kev kawm kom tau zoo hauv tsev kawm ntawv. Peb xav kom koj koom hauv ib qho kev ua uas coj los qhia rau hauv chav kawm. Ua tsaug rau koj txoj kev txhawb nqa.

Sau npe,

_____ *(Tus kws qhia ntawv)*

Nrog ib tug neeg hauv tsev neeg tham txog nws qhov uas nws siv nyiaj thiab txuag nyiaj txhua hli. Nug kom tus neeg ntawv pab koj ua daim duab hauv qab.

Cov Khoom Qhov Kev Siv Nyiaj	Koj siv pes tsawg?	Koj xuas nyiaj ntsuab, tshev, los sis credit card them?
1. khaub ncaws		
2. khoom noj		
3. kev lom zem		
4. tsheb		
5. tseg nyiaj		

School-Home Connection
Sharing Visions
UNIDAD 7 El dinero

Nombre _____

Fecha _____

Querida Familia:

En clase, aprendimos sobre el dinero y los presupuestos. A _____ *(nombre del alumno)* le gustaría compartir con ustedes lo que hemos aprendido.

Capítulo 1. Hablamos sobre la ropa y los precios. Podemos pagar la ropa con dinero en efectivo, cheque o tarjeta de crédito. Aprendimos a describir y comparar ropa y otros objetos. También aprendimos el tiempo verbal futuro. El tiempo futuro describe eventos en el futuro.

Capítulo 2. Los mitos son historias muy antiguas. Enseñan una lección llamada *"moraleja"*. Leímos un mito griego llamado **The Midas Touch.** Es sobre el Rey Midas. Todo lo que toca el rey se convierte en oro. Mientras leíamos el cuento, hacíamos predicciones o suposiciones de lo podía pasar después.

Capítulo 3. Leímos un artículo de una revista llamado **Making a Budget.** El artículo enseña cómo hacer un presupuesto. Un presupuesto es un plan para saber cómo gastar y ahorrar dinero.

Sabemos que ustedes quieren apoyar el esfuerzo que realiza su estudiante en la escuela. Nos gustaría que participen en alguna actividad para compartir con la clase. Gracias por su apoyo.

Atentamente,

_____ *(Maestro/a)*

Habla con un miembro de la familia sobre su presupuesto mensual. Pídele ayuda a esta persona para completar el cuadro.

Detalle del presupuesto	¿Cuánto gastas?	¿Pagas en efectivo, con cheque o tarjeta de crédito?
1. ropa		
2. alimentos		
3. diversión		
4. transporte		
5. ahorro		

School-Home Connection
Sharing Visions
Bài 7 Tiền Bạc

Tên: _____

Ngày tháng năm: _____

Thưa Gia Đình,

Ở lớp, chúng ta đã học về tiền bạc và ngân sách. _____ *(tên học sinh)* muốn chia sẻ với quý vị những gì chúng ta đã học.

Chương 1. Chúng ta đã nói về quần áo và giá cả. Chúng ta có thể trả tiền mặt, ngân phiếu hoặc thẻ tín dụng khi mua quần áo. Chúng ta đã học cách miêu tả và so sánh quần áo và các vật khác. Chúng ta cũng học thì tương lai. Thì tương lai miêu tả các sự kiện trong tương lai.

Chương 2. Thần thoại là những câu chuyện rất xưa. Chúng dạy một bài học gọi là *đạo đức*. Chúng ta đã đọc truyện thần thoại Hy Lạp **The Midas Touch.** Truyện kể về Vua King Midas. Mọi thứ nhà vua sờ vào đều biến thành vàng. Trong khi đọc, chúng ta dự báo, hoặc tiên đoán, về những gì sẽ xảy ra tiếp theo.

Chương 3. Chúng ta đọc một bài viết trên tạp chí gọi là **Making a Budget.** Bài viết này dạy quý vị cách lên một ngân sách. Ngân sách là một kế hoạch chi tiêu và để dành tiền.

Chúng tôi biết rằng quý vị muốn hỗ trợ thành tích học tập của con em mình ở trường. Chúng tôi muốn quý vị tham gia vào một hoạt động để chia sẻ với lớp. Xin cám ơn vì sự ủng hộ của quý vị.

Trân Trọng Kính Chào,

_____ *(Giáo Viên)*

Hãy nói chuyện với một người trong gia đình về ngân sách hàng tháng của người đó. Nhờ người đó giúp bạn điền vào sơ đồ.

Khoản trong ngân sách	Em tiêu xài bao nhiêu?	Em trả bằng tiền mặt, ngân phiếu hay thẻ tín dụng?
1. quần áo		
2. thức ăn		
3. giải trí		
4. phương tiện đi lại		
5. tiết kiệm		

School-Home Connection
Sharing Visions
UNIT 8   Jobs and Careers

Name _____

Date _____

Dear Family,

In class, we learned about jobs and careers. _____ *(student's name)* would like to share with you what we learned.

Chapter 1. We talked about jobs and careers, such as cashier, chef, firefighter, and doctor. We also talked about tools and equipment these people use. We described the skills and experience necessary for different jobs.

Chapter 2. A biography is a true story about a person's life. We read biographies about three scientists—a biologist, a chemist, and an astronaut. We took notes and wrote our own biographies about scientists.

Chapter 3. We read *Research on the Internet*. It is an excerpt from a technical manual. It teaches you how to find information on the Internet. We followed the steps we learned to write a research report.

We know you want to support your student's achievement in school. We would like you to participate in an activity to share with the class. Thank you for your support.

Sincerely,

_____ *(Teacher)*

Talk with your family about a family member's job or career. Complete the chart together.

Job or career	
Description	
Special tools and equipment	

School-Home Connection
Sharing Visions

មេរៀនទី ៨ ការងារ និង អាជីព

ឈ្មោះ _____

កាលបរិច្ឆេទ _____

ជូនចំពោះ គ្រួសារ

នៅក្នុងថ្នាក់រៀន យើងបានរៀនអំពីការងារ និង អាជីព ។ _____ (ឈ្មោះសិស្ស)
ចង់ចែករំលែកនូវអ្វីដែលយើងបានរៀនជាមួយនឹងអ្នក ។

ជំពូក ១ យើងបានជជែកអំពីការងារ និង អាជីព ដូចជា បេឡា, ចុងភៅ, អ្នកពន្លត់អគ្គីភ័យ និង វេជ្ជបណ្ឌិត ។
យើក៏បានជជែកអំពីឧបករណ៍ និង បរិក្ខាដែលអ្នកទាំងនោះប្រើប្រាស់ ។ យើងបាន ពិពណ៌នាពីជំនាញ និង
បទពិសោធន៍ដែលចាំបាច់សម្រាប់ការងារផ្សេងៗ ។

ជំពូក ២ ជីវប្រវត្តិគឺជារឿងពិតអំពីជីវិតរបស់មនុស្សម្នាក់ ។ យើងបានអានជីវប្រវត្តិរបស់អ្នក វិទ្យាសាស្ត្របីរូបគឺ ជីវសាស្ត្រវិទូ
គីមីវិទូ និង អវកាសវិទូ ។ យើងបានធ្វើកំណត់ចំណាំ និង បាន
សរសេរពីជីវប្រវត្តិផ្ទាល់ខ្លួនរបស់អ្នកវិទ្យាសាស្ត្រទាំងនោះដោយខ្លួនឯង ។

ជំពូក ៣ យើងបានអាន *Research on the Internet* ។ អត្ថបទ ដកស្រង់ចេញពីសៀវភៅក្បួនបច្ចេកទេស ។
វាបង្រៀនអ្នកពីរបៀបបំបែងរកព័ត៌មានលើអ៊ីនធឺណិត ។
យើងបានធ្វើតាមជំហានដែលយើងបានរៀនដើម្បីសរសេររបាយការណ៍ស្រាវជ្រាវ ។

យើងដឹងថាអ្នកចង់គាំទ្រនូវការសម្រេចបានរបស់សិស្សអ្នកនៅសាលារៀន ។ យើងចង់ឱ្យអ្នកចូលរួម
នៅក្នុងសកម្មភាពដែលចែករំលែកគ្នាជាមួយនឹងថ្នាក់រៀន ។ សូមអរគុណចំពោះការគាំទ្ររបស់អ្នក ។

ដោយក្តីគោរពរាប់អាន

_____ (គ្រូបង្រៀន)

ជជែកជាមួយគ្រួសាររបស់អ្នកអំពីការងារ ឬ អាជីពរបស់សមាជិកគ្រួសារ ។ បំពេញតារាងខាងក្រោម ទាំងអស់ ។

ការងារ ឬ អាជីព	
ការពិពណ៌នា	
ឧបករណ៍ និង បរិក្ខាពិសេស	

School-Home Connection
Sharing Visions
單元八　工作和事業

姓名 _____

日期 _____

親愛的家長：

　　我們在課堂上學習工作和事業。_____（學生姓名）想和您們分享我們的上課內容。

　　第一章　我們討論工作和事業，如收銀員、廚師、消防員和醫生。我們也討論這些人使用的工具和器材。以及各種工具需要的技巧和經驗。

　　第二章　自傳是人一生的真實故事。我們閱讀三位科學家（生物學家、化學家和太空人）的傳記。我們寫下筆記，再自己寫這些科學家的傳記。

　　第三章　我們閱讀 *Research on the Internet*。這是在一本技術手冊上的短文，它教導我們怎麼在網路上尋找資訊。我們依照學到的方式寫研究報告。

　　我們知道您們很樂意協助孩子學習。希望您們能參與這個活動，我們會在課堂討論結果。謝謝您們的協助。

　　　　　　　　　　　　　　　　　　敬上

　　　　　　　　　　　　_____（老師）

與家人討論一位家人的工作或事業，然後一起填寫這個表格。

工作或事業	
描述	
特殊工具和器材	

School-Home Connection
Sharing Visions

SEKSYON 8 Travay ak Karyè

Non _____

Dat _____

Chè Fanmi,

Nan klas la, nou aprann sou travay ak karyè. _____ *(non elèv la)* ta renmen pataje avèk ou sa nou aprann.

Chapit 1. Nou pale sou travay ak karyè, tankou kesye, chèf, ponpye, ak doktè. Nou pale tou sou zouti ak ekipman moun sa yo itilize. Nou dekri ladrès ak esperyans ki nesesè pou diferan travay sa yo.

Chapit 2. Yon byografi se yon istwa vre sou vi yon moun. Nou li byografi sou twa syantis – yon byolojis, yon chimis, ak yon astwonòt. Nou pran nòt e nou ekri pwòp byografi pa nou sou syantis yo.

Chapit 3. Nou li *Research on the Internet*. Se yon ekstrè ki soti nan yon liv teknik. Li anseye w ki jan pou jwenn enfòmasyon sou Entènèt. Nou swiv etap nou aprann yo pou nou ekri yon rapò rechèch.

Nou konnen ke ou vle ankouraje reyisit pitit ou nan lekòl la. Nou ta renmen ke ou patisipe nan yon aktivite pou pataje ak klas la. Mèsi pou sipò ou.

Sensèman,

_____ *(Pwofesè)*

Pale ak fanmi w sou travay oswa karyè yon manm fanmi an. Konplete tablo a ansanm.

Travay oswa karyè	
Deskripsyon	
Zouti espesyal ak ekipman	

School-Home Connection
Sharing Visions

SOB KAWM 8 Cov Hauj Lwm thiab Yam Hauj Lwm

Npe _____

Hnub Tim _____

Nyob zoo txog Tsev Neeg,

Hauv chav kawm ntawv, peb kawm txog hauj lwm thiab yam hauj lwm. _____ *(tus menyuam kawm ntawv lub npe)* yuav xav qhia rau koj seb pab kawm txog dab tsi.

Tshooj 1. Peb tham txog cov hauj lwm thiab yam hauj lwm, xws li ib tug neeg ntaus khoom, ib tug neeg ua khoom noj, ib tug neeg tua hluav taws xob thiab ib tug kws kho mob. Peb tseem tham txog cov twj thiab khoom uas cov neeg no siv. Peb piav txog cov txuj ci thiab cov kev sim ua kom paub uas tsim nyob rau cov hauj lwm.

Tshooj 2. Ib zaj dab neeg sau txog ib tug neeg yog ib zaj dab neeg uas muaj tseeb txog ib tug neeg lub neej. Peb nyeem cov dab neeg txog peb tug scientists —ib tug kws kawm txog tej yam muaj sia, ib tug kws tov tshuaj, thiab ib tug neeg uas mus saum ntuj (astronaut). Peb sau lus cia thiab sau txog peb zaj dab neeg txog cov scientists.

Tshooj 3. Peb nyeem *Research on the Internet.* Nws yog ib qho me me los ntawm ib phau ntawv sau txog tej yam nyuaj nyuaj. Nws qhia rau koj txog seb yuav nrhiav cov lus qhia hauv Internet li cas. Peb ua raws cov nqe lus uas peb kawm txog kev sau ib daim ntawv tshawb nrhiav.

Peb paub tias koj xav txhawb koj tus menyuam kev kawm kom tau zoo hauv tsev kawm ntawv. Peb xav kom koj koom hauv ib qho kev ua uas coj los qhia rau hauv chav kawm. Ua tsaug rau koj txoj kev txhawb nqa.

Sau npe,

_____ *(Tus kws qhia ntawv)*

Nrog koj tsev neeg tham txog ib tus neeg hauv tsev neeg txoj hauj lwm los sis yam hauj lwm. Sau daim duab hauv qab ua ke.

Txoj hauj lwm los sis yam hauj lwm	
Piav seb ua dab tsi	
Cov twj thiab khoom tshwj xeeb uas siv	

School-Home Connection
Sharing Visions

UNIDAD 8 Trabajos y profesiones

Nombre _____

Fecha _____

Querida Familia:

En clase, aprendimos sobre los trabajos y las profesiones. A _____ *(nombre del alumno)* le gustaría compartir con ustedes lo que hemos aprendido.

Capítulo 1. Hablamos sobre los trabajos y las profesiones, como cajero, chef, bombero y médico. También hablamos sobre las herramientas y los equipos que usan estas personas. Describimos las habilidades y la experiencia necesarias para los distintos trabajos.

Capítulo 2. Una biografía es una historia verdadera sobre la vida de una persona. Leímos biografías sobre tres científicos: un biólogo, un químico y un astronauta. Tomamos notas y escribimos nuestras propias biografías de los científicos.

Capítulo 3. Leímos *Research on the Internet.* Es un pasaje de un manual técnico. Enseña cómo encontrar información en Internet. Seguimos los pasos aprendidos para escribir un informe de investigación.

Sabemos que ustedes quieren apoyar el esfuerzo que realiza su estudiante en la escuela. Nos gustaría que participen en alguna actividad para compartir con la clase. Gracias por su apoyo.

Atentamente,

_____ *(Maestro/a)*

Habla con tu familia sobre el trabajo o profesión de un miembro de la familia. Completen juntos el cuadro.

Trabajo o profesión	
Descripción	
Herramientas y equipos especiales	

School-Home Connection
Sharing Visions
Bài 8 Việc Làm và Nghề nghiệp

Tên: _____

Ngày tháng năm: _____

Thưa Gia Đình,

Ở lớp, chúng đã đã học về việc làm và nghề nghiệp. _____ *(tên học sinh)* muốn chia sẻ với quý vị những gì chúng ta đã học.

Chương 1. Chúng ta đã nói chuyện về việc làm và nghề nghiệp, chẳng hạn thu ngân, đầu bếp, nhân viên cứu hỏa và bác sĩ. Chúng ta còn nói về các công cụ và trang thiết bị mà những người này sử dụng. Chúng ta miêu tả những kỹ năng và kinh nghiệm cần thiết cho các công việc khác nhau.

Chương 2. Tiểu sử là một câu chuyện thật về cuộc đời một con người. Chúng ta đã đọc các tiểu sử của ba nhà khoa học—một nhà sinh vật học, một nhà hóa học, và một phi hành gia. Chúng ta ghi chép và tự mình viết tiểu sử về các nhà khoa học.

Chương 3. Chúng ta đọc *Research on the Internet.* Đó là một đoạn trích từ một sổ tay hướng dẫn kỹ thuật. Nó dạy quý vị cách tìm ra thông tin trên mạng Internet. Chúng ta đã làm theo các bước đã học được để viết một bản tường trình về khảo cứu.

Chúng tôi biết rằng quý vị muốn hỗ trợ thành tích học tập của con em mình ở trường. Chúng tôi muốn quý vị tham gia vào một hoạt động để chia sẻ với lớp. Xin cám ơn vì sự ủng hộ của quý vị.

Trân Trọng Kính Chào,

_____ *(Giáo Viên)*

Hãy nói chuyện với gia đình bạn về việc làm hay nghề nghiệp của một người trong gia đình. Hãy cùng nhau điền vào sơ đồ.

Việc làm hay nghề nghiệp	
Đặc điểm	
Các công cụ và trang thiết bị đặc biệt	

Pre-Literacy Activities

page 1
1. 2314
2. 4213
3. 4231
4. 2134

page 2
Line should be traced from top to bottom.

page 3
L row: Three Ls should be circled.
I row: Three Is should be circled.
E row: Two Es should be circled.
N row: Two Ns should be circled.
M row: Three Ms should be circled.
B row: Two Bs should be circled.
S row: Two Ss should be circled.
C row: Two Cs should be circled.

Activity Book Answer Key

UNIT A

page 4
A.
1. teacher
2. student
3. Good-bye
4. See you later

B.
1. c.
2. d.
3. a.
4. b.

page 5
1. Good
2. name
3. This
4. Hi
5. Sam

page 6
A.
1. c   3. m   5. f   7. g
2. b   4. p   6. s   8. t
B. Students should print uppercase and lowercase letters.

page 7
A.
1. f   3. m   5. s   7. g
2. p   4. b   6. t   8. t
B. Students should print uppercase and lowercase letters.

page 8
A. Students should circle the following pictures:
1. gum   3. cat
2. bat   4. tack
B.
1. map   3. gum
2. bus   4. bat

page 9
A.
1. bat
2. pet
3. ten
4. tag
5. elk

B.
1. e
2. e
3. a

page 10
A.
1. u; bus
2. o; mop
3. i; pig
4. o; top
5. u; gum
6. i; bib
7. o; pot

B.
1. cup
2. sip

3. pig
4. cub

page 11
A.
1. top
2. bat
3. but
4. pet
5. sip

B.
1. gum
2. map
3. pot
4. bib
5. pet

page 12
A.
1. c.
2. d.
3. a.
4. e.
5. f.
6. b.

B.
1. bag
2. bat
3. map
4. cap

page 13
A.
1. b B
2. T t
3. G g
4. w W

B.
1. a
2. P
3. M
4. f
5. s
6. E

C.
1. boy
2. cat
3. leaf
4. bus
5. pan
6. saw

page 14
Students should practice printing letters Aa–Ii.

page 15
Students should practice printing letters Jj–Rr.

page 16
Students should practice printing letters Ss–Zz.

page 17
1.–10. Students should print the words shown legibly.

page 18
Students should practice writing cursive letters Aa–Ii.

page 19
Students should practice writing cursive letters Jj–Rr.

page 20
A. Students should practice writing cursive letters Ss–Zz.
B. 1.–6. Students should circle the matching print and cursive letters.

UNIT B

page 24
A.
1. desk
2. pen
3. window
4. clock
5. backpack
6. pencil
7. flag
8. computer
9. notebook
10. chair
B.
1. door
2. open
3. Write
4. go to
5. close

page 25
A.
1. e. five
2. i. 12
3. l. 20
4. a. nine
5. j. 3
6. g. thirteen
7. b. 1
8. c. fifty
9. f. seven
10. d. 2
11. h. 18
12. k. ten

B.
1. blue
2. yellow
3. brown
4. purple
5. red, white, blue

6. red
7. green
8. pink
9. orange

page 26
Students should practice writing numerals 1–10.

page 27
Students should practice writing numerals 11–20.

page 28
A.
1. He
2. She
3. I
4. you
5. He's
B.
1. A. Hi. My name is Irina. What's your name?
   B. I'm Tran. Where are you from?
   A. I'm from Russia.
2. A. I'm Oscar. I'm from Columbia. Where are you from?
   B. My name is Ana. I'm from Mexico.
   A. Hi, Ana.

page 29
A.
1. d   3. l   5. d
2. j   4. l   6. j
B.
1. den   2. dig   3. doll
C.
1. leg   2. lot   3. left
D.
1. job   2. jet   3. jeans

page 30
A.
1. ring   3. vest
2. nose   4. rake
B.
1. rat   3. vet
2. nut   4. rug

page 31
A.
1. r   3. n   5. d
2. l   4. x   6. r
B.
1. sun   4. car
2. hand   5. pencil
3. six   6. pen

page 32
A.
1. c. cape   3. d. dime
2. b. five   4. a. tape
B.
1. gate   3. cake
2. rake   4. game
C.
1. dime   3. time
2. lime   4. file

page 33
A.
1. e; robe   4. e; tube
2. e; code   5. e; cute
3. e; cube   6. e; note
B.
1. b. cute   3. c. nose
2. d. rope   4. a. mule

page 34
A.
```
V H W S D F L A G J Z Q
X T H I R T E E N W X H
L S R S Q Z T K R C A V
S T R I P E S N Q F A Q
A D U H L F H M K H R J
S T Z C G Y Q L U U H F
Y N C Q A M E R I C A N
H K H K F R H Z H Y K G
G F I F T Y P Q F E T K K
J B E V R J X G W T R
L D O B L U E H K J M X
M R Z J V J L K U R E D
P Z W Q B I H P H K R F
W A C O L O R S Q X W D
W H I T E B S T A R S
```
B.
1. The American Flag
2. blue
3. star
4. white stripe
5. red stripe

page 35
A. Answers will vary.
B. Answers will vary.

UNIT C

page 40
A.
```
A V E S K I R T N H A T
U Q J E G I C M O B E A
N S W E A T E R S M A Z
E L R O S F R I E N D S
H C X I T S O J V A W Q
S N E A K E R S N B I Y
R E V I S J A C K E T Q
A K H I Y E H C S H Q
M N U E A R T S I B L I
U B C L A S S M A T E S
D E S I U S T P O W A R
N I T C P O B S H O E S
S H I R T E P O W S H U
E R I J E A N S P L S C
```
B. Answers will vary.

page 41
1. head   6. hand
2. neck   7. fingers
3. stomach   8. leg
4. elbow   9. knee
5. arm   10. foot

page 42
A.
1. eye   4. lips   7. cheek
2. ear   5. hair   8. mouth
3. teeth 6. nose   9. chin
B.
1. Answers will vary.
2. Answers will vary.
3. I have two eyes.
4. I have ten fingers.
C. Answers will vary.

page 43
A.
1. h   3. q   5. h
2. k   4. q   6. k
B.
1. kite
2. horn
3. quarter

page 44
Across
1. yawn
3. zipper
4. yam

Down
1. yarn
2. window
3. zebra

page 45
A.
1. sh
2. th
3. ng
4. ch
5. ch
6. sh
7. ng
8. th

B.
1. d.
2. c.
3. a.
4. b.

page 46
A.
1. cot
2. ran
3. let
4. top
5. men
6. hat

B.
1. oa, boat
2. ee, tree
3. ai, nail
4. ay, tray
5. ea, seal
6. oa, road

page 47
A.
1. Roy
2. boy
3. coin
4. toy
5. house
6. down
7. shout
8. how

B.
1. d. 3. e. 5. h. 7. f.
2. a. 4. b. 6. g. 8. c.

page 48
A.
1. hair; Her
2. is; His; are
3. is
4. and
5. and
6. and
7. and; are

B.
1. and
2. are
3. hair
4. her
5. his
6. is

page 49
A. 1.–6. Answers will vary.

B.
1. is
2. his
3. hair
4. are
5. and
6. her

UNIT D • CHAPTER 1

page 54
1. library
2. hamburger
3. nurse's office
4. gym
5. cafeteria
6. wash my hands
7. to study
8. principal
9. bathroom
10. locker

page 55
1. main office; next to
2. elevator; next to OR across from
3. cafeteria; across from
4. the right
5. between
6. nurse's office; the left

page 56
A.
1. 3, 1, 2
Excuse me. Where is the gym?
It's on the left. It's next to Room 102.
Thanks.

2. 1, 3, 2
Is the cafeteria on the second floor?
No. It's on the first floor, across from the bathrooms.
Thanks.

3. 3, 2, 1
Excuse me. Is the nurse's office on the second floor?
Yes. It's across from the library.
Thanks.

B.
1. gym; first; left; next to
2. nurse; second; across from

UNIT D • CHAPTER 2

page 57
A.
1. E   6. C   11. K
2. H   7. A   12. F
3. O   8. N   13. M
4. G   9. I   14. D
5. J   10. B 15. L

B.
1. glass
2. drum
3. clown
4. brown
5. slot
6. trip

page 58
A.
1. snore
2. skate
3. swing

B.
R E S N A K K
K S I T K
A S W D F E
T A I P H O
E N Q C I Z
S W I M S T A R

page 59
A.
1. nd
2. nk
3. st
4. nt
5. nk
6. nd

B.
1. nt
2. nk
3. nd
4. st
5. st
6. st
7. nd
8. nk; st
9. nk
10. nt

page 60
A.
1. park
2. burn
3. shirt
4. card
5. spark
6. dirt

B.
1. card
2. nurse
3. yard
4. arm
5. twirl
6. harp

page 61
Compound Words
1. coat; raincoat
2. box; mailbox
3. fish; starfish
4. brush; hairbrush
5. phones; headphones
6. tub; bathtub
7. pack; backpack

Syllables
1. 2   3. 1   5. 2
2. 2   4. 2   6. 1

page 62
A. 7, 1, 4, 2, 6, 5, 3
1. do
2. from
3. need
4. on
5. she
6. want
7. where

B.
1. The school is a mess.
2. Answers will vary, but should define "mess" or show examples of messiness from the newspaper article.
3. classrooms

page 63
A.
1. It is time for gym class.
2. Do you know where it is?
3. The gym is across from the cafeteria.
4. I will follow you there.

B. 1.–4. Sentences will vary but all should relate to the photo. Two should be statements and two should be questions.

UNIT 1 • CHAPTER 1

page 68
A.
1. Tomorrow is November fifth.
2. Today is Friday, January tenth.
3. My birthday is June third.
4. Today is Tuesday, May fourteenth.

B.
1. c.   6. b.
2. d.   7. h.
3. e.   8. j.
4. i.   9. g.
5. a.   10. f.

C.
1. birthday
2. fifteenth
3. tomorrow
4. When

page 69
A.
1. noun
2. pronoun
3. noun
4. noun
5. pronoun
6. pronoun

B.
1. Subject: We; Verb: are
2. Subject: Alex; Verb: is
3. Subject: You; Verb: are
4. Subject: stapler; Verb: is
5. Subject: It; Verb: is

C.
1. is   4. is
2. are 5. are
3. am   6. am

page 70
1. I   5. C   9. I
2. C   6. I   10. I
3. C   7. I   11. C
4. I   8. C   12. I

page 71
A.
1. her
2. his
3. your
4. their
5. our
6. my
7. his
8. its

B.
1. His sister is in my class.
2. Their friends go to my school.
3. Their dogs run fast.
4. His birthday is in June.
5. We sit in the fourth row.

page 72
A.
1. cat
2. fish
3. bug
4. dog
5. hen
6. pig
7. rat
8. frog

B.
1. Possible answer: cat or rat
2. hen
3. Possible answer: fish or pig
4. Possible answer: dog or frog
5. bug

page 73
A.
1. b
2. c
3. a

B.
1. Friday is Nov. tenth.
2. Ms. Alvarez is here today.
3. Today is Feb. 3.
4. Thurs. is my birthday.
5. Our teacher is Mr. John Clarkson.

page 74–75
A.
1. They are in Room 24.
2. Answers will vary. Possible answer: Her birthday is May 2.
3. Answers will vary. Possible answer: The pencil is on the desk.
4. Answers will vary. Possible answer: She is in Room 8.
5. Answers will vary. Possible answer: This is his stapler.
6. Answers will vary. Possible answer: They are in Room 13.
7. Answers will vary. Possible answer: He is the teacher.
8. Answers will vary. Possible answer: Today is Wednesday, December 11.

UNIT 1 • CHAPTER 2

page 76
A.
1. Student's Name
2. Emergency Contact
3. Relationship
4. Telephone Number

B. 1–3: Answers will vary.

page 77
A.
1. Monday, Wednesday, and Friday, fifth period
2. seventh period
3. seventh period
4. no
5. Mrs. Ramos

B. Mr. Santos

page 78
For Library Card Form circle (any order): date of birth, address, city, state, zip code, emergency contact name, emergency contact telephone number

For overlap of circles (any order): name, telephone number, e-mail address, signature

For Computer Sign-up Form circle (any order): grade, homeroom, I need a computer for:, I need a computer on: day, time

page 79
A.
1. b   3. a   5. c
2. b   4. c

B.
1. 234 Bell Tower Street, Apt. 4J
2. Madison, WI 53705
3. 10/24/07
4. November 30, 2007
5. 16 Caroline Street, Unit 12
6. Los Angeles, CA 90043

page 80
Answers will vary.

page 81
A.
Student's Name: Domingo Santos
Date of Birth: April 2, 1993
Grade: 8
School: Madison School
Address: 1168 West 11th Street, Apt. 12C
City, State, Zip Code: New York, New York 10019
Telephone Number: 212-555-5050
E-mail: dsantos@visionsintro.esl
Parent or Guardian: Juanita Santos or Hector Santos
Address: 1168 West 11th Street, Apt. 12C, New York, New York 10019
Telephone: 212-555-5050

B. c

UNIT 1 • CHAPTER 3
page 82
A.
1. c   3. a.
2. b.   4. d.

B.
1. minus sign
2. equals sign
3. division sign
4. addition sign
5. multiplication sign
6. minus sign

C.
1. How many?
2. What is?
3. How much?
4. What are?
5. How much?
6. How many?

page 83
1. a.   2. b.   3. b.

page 84
1. b.   3. d.   5. a.
2. e.   4. c.

page 85
A.
1–3. In any order: Word problems have question words. *Sum* and *total* are synonyms. Fifteen less six is nine.
4–6. In any order: How much is four times six? What is 36 ÷ 9? How many students are in class?

B.
1. How many hours did John work?
2. This jug holds two gallons of juice.
3. Who are the winners?
4. There are six red and four yellow packages.
5. How many are left?
6. What is the sum of 24 and 56?

page 86
Answers will vary.

page 87
A. Answers will vary.

B.
1. a.   2. c.   3. a.

UNIT 2 • CHAPTER 1
page 88
A.
1. black   3. short
2. curly   4. thin

B.
1. e.   4. f.
2. c.   5. b.
3. d.   6. a.

page 89
A.
1. I am   4. It is
2. He is   5. They are
3. We are   6. You are

B.
1. He's not neat. He isn't neat.
2. They're not beautiful. They aren't beautiful.
3. We're not young. We aren't young.
4. She's not late. She isn't late.
5. It's not boring. It isn't boring.
6. You're not messy. You aren't messy.

page 90
A.
1. has; It doesn't have brown eyes.
2. has; She doesn't have a big dog.
3. have; We don't have straight hair.
4. have; I don't have a white cat.
5. have; You don't have medium length hair.

B.
1. b.   2. c.   3. b.

page 91
A.
1. loves   4. drinks
2. live   5. walks
3. want   6. cook

B.
1. eats   4. like
2. take   5. has
3. visits

C.
1. doesn't   4. doesn't
2. doesn't   5. don't
3. don't

page 92
A.
1. a; long *a*
2. a; long *i*
3. b; long *u*
4. b; long *o*

B.
I am in a play. I put on a brown robe and hide by a big gray rock. A nice girl sits on the rock. Her name is June. She takes a rose from her book and smells it with her nose. She uses a pen to write a note.
Long *a*: (in any order) play, gray, name, takes
Long *i*: (in any order) I, hide, nice, write
Long *o*: (in any order) robe, rose, nose, note
Long *u*: (in any order) June, uses

page 93
A.
1. birds   4. house
2. pets   5. sisters
3. brother   6. cats

B.
1. a.   4. b.
2. b.   5. b.
3. a.

page 94: Answers will vary.
page 95: Answers will vary.

UNIT 2 • CHAPTER 2
page 96
A.
1. daughter   4. uncle
2. aunt   5. mother
3. husband   6. cousin

B. Answers will vary.

page 97
A.
1. A Name for My Mother
2. Barbara Donovan
3. Answers will vary. Possible answer: names for a mother
4. big
5. Answers will vary. Possible answer: The boy or girl wants to choose a name for his or her mother.
6. Answers will vary. Possible answer: The boy or girl likes the name "Mom."

page 98
A.
1. 1, 2, 3, 5   4. 10 and 12
2. 4 and 6   5. care, there
3. 7, 8, 9, 11

B.
1. here   4. brown
2. wall   5. hat
3. blue

page 99
A.
1. b.   4. c.
2. c.   5. b.
3. b.

B.
1. families   4. classes
2. lunches   5. brushes
3. boxes

page 100: Answers will vary.

page 101
A. Answers will vary.

B.
1. a.   2. b.   3. a.

UNIT 2 • CHAPTER 3
page 102
A.
Word search with: FUR, FEATHER, REPTILE, HATCH, SCALES

B.
1. b.   3. b.   5. a.
2. a.   4. b.   6. b.

page 103
1. main idea   4. detail
2. detail   5. main idea
3. main idea   6. detail

page 104
A.
1. b.   3. b.   5. c.
2. a.   4. c.   6. d.

B.
1. title   2. label   3. data

page 105
Across
1. women
4. men
6. mice
9. babies
10. feathers
11. secretaries

Down
2. mammals
3. addresses
5. classes
7. cities
8. children
10. fish

page 106: Answers will vary.

page 107
A. Answers will vary.

B.
1. b
2. a

UNIT 3 • CHAPTER 1
page 108
A.
1. sing   4. dance
2. write   5. swim
3. paint   6. exercise

B.
1. It's on Monday at three thirty. (Or: It's at three thirty on Monday.)
2. It's on Saturday at noon. (Or: It's at noon on Saturday.)
3. It's on Thursday at four fifteen. (Or: It's at four fifteen on Thursday.)
4. on Monday at six forty-five (Or: at six forty-five on Monday)

page 109
A.
1. b.   3. a.   5. c.
2. c.   4. a.   6. b.

B.
1. spoke   4. smiled
2. said   5. made
3. walked

C.
1. met   4. stood
2. went   5. gave
3. swam

page 110
1. Kim didn't go to band practice last week.
2. I didn't talk to her about it.
3. She didn't say she was sick.
4. Pedro didn't get the information form.
5. They didn't run after school yesterday.
6. We didn't ride to school on Monday.
7. Rita didn't make a speech at ten o'clock.
8. I didn't walk with Dom and Stan.
9. They didn't sing on stage.
10. He didn't read that book last week.

page 111
1. Incorrect; Emilio was in the drama club last year.
2. Correct
3. Correct
4. Incorrect; She wasn't afraid to be on the stage.
5. Incorrect; All the student actors were good in their parts.
6. Correct
7. Incorrect; On Friday I was at the art club meeting.
8. Incorrect; You were a good painter.
9. Correct
10. Incorrect; They weren't at the baseball practice at four o'clock.

page 112
A.
1. c.
2. a.
3. b.
4. a.
5. c.

B.
1. This meal looks good.
2. Answers will vary but should include the word *wheel*.
3. Answers will vary but should include the word *seat*.
4. Answers will vary but should include the word *feet*.

page 113
A.
Across
1. multiplied
4. studied
6. applied

Down
2. tried
3. dried
5. carried

B.
1. dried
2. carried
3. tried
4. studied

page 114
Answers will vary.

page 115
1. b.
2. a.
3. b.
4. c.
5. a.
6. b.
7. b.
8. c.
9. c.
10. b.

page 116
A.
1. small, little
2. pretty, beautiful
3. large, big
4. neat, wonderful
5. clean, wash

B.
1. wash
2. clean
3. little
4. big
5. happy
6. large
7. small
8. glad

page 117
1. 7
2. 11
3. 3
4. 8
5. 5
6. 10
7. 1
8. 4
9. 9
10. 6
11. 2

page 118
Timeline events and times should appear in the following order:
3:15: Ramón found out that his mother was sick.
3:30: Possible answers: Paulina came home. Ramón gave Paulina a snack. Ramón sent Paulina out to play in the yard.
4:00: Possible answers: Ramón's mother called to him. Ramón's mother asked him to go to the store. Ramón's mother gave him money.
4:30: Ramón and Paulina returned from the store.
5:00: Ramón finished his homework and his father came home.

page 119
A.
1. Marco said, "Hi, Sue. I hear you have a new job." Or: "Hi, Sue. I hear you have a new job," Marco said.
2. Sue said, "Yes. I work at the video store," Or: "Yes. I work at the video store," Sue said.
3. Marco said, "When do you work there?" Or: "When do you work there?" Marco said.
4. Sue said, "On Wednesdays, Fridays, and Saturdays. I start at 4:00." Or: "On Wednesdays, Fridays, and Saturdays. I start at 4:00," Sue said.

B. Answers will vary.

page 120
Answers will vary.

page 121
A. Answers will vary.
B.
1. a.
2. b.
3. a.

page 122
A.
1. change
2. permission to do something
3. a set of legal rights protected by the government

B.
1. amendment
2. Freedom
3. right
4. religion

page 123
1. The people of the United States have rules and rights.
2. Answers will vary. Possible answers: The Constitution contains the laws of the United States. Or: Laws are the rules for the people who live here. Or: The Bill of Rights contains the rights of the people.
3. Answers will vary. Possible answer: My family has rules.
4. Answers will vary. Possible answers: There is a rule about homework. Or: There is a rule about housework. Or: There is a rule about money.
5. Answers will vary. Possible answer: My family has rights.
6. Answers will vary. Possible answers: One right is like freedom of speech. Or: We have the right to say what we think. Or: We can disagree with a rule. Or: We have the right to give our opinion.

page 124
1. pages 34, 36, 38
2. pages 102–108
3. the Supreme Court
4. pages 20–21 and page 24
5. pages 36–40
6. slavery
7. Benjamin Franklin and Thomas Jefferson
8. Congress, the United States Constitution, and James Madison

page 125
A.
1. c.
2. a.
3. b.
4. c.

B.
1. We are reading about the Constitution, the Bill of Rights, and the Amendments.
2. Freedom of religion includes freedom of belief, freedom of worship, and freedom from persecution.
3. We have the right to say, sing, or publish what we think.

page 126
Answers will vary.

page 127
A. Answers will vary.
B.
1. b.
2. b.
3. c.

UNIT 4 • CHAPTER 1

page 128
A.
1. bed; a.
2. sofa; c.
3. bookcase; e.
4. sink; b.
5. refrigerator; d.

B.
1. There are
2. There is
3. There are
4. There are
5. There is
6. There are
7. There are

C.
1. c.
2. a.
3. b.
4. d.

page 129
A.
1. Is
2. Are
3. Is
4. Are
5. Are

B.
1. Possible answers: Yes, he was. / No, he wasn't.
2. Possible answers: Yes, they were. / No, they weren't.
3. Possible answers: Yes, they were. / No, they weren't.
4. Possible answers: Yes, she was. / No, she wasn't.
5. Possible answers: Yes, they were. / No, they weren't.

page 130
A.
1. Does
2. Do
3. Does
4. Do
5. Does
6. Does
7. Do

B.
1. I did
2. we didn't
3. it did
4. she didn't
5. they did
6. he did

page 131
1. Is the window open?
2. Yes, the oven does feel hot.
3. Do you have a bookcase?
4. Are the chairs by the table?
5. No, the mirrors aren't dirty.
6. Does the bathroom have a shower?
7. Yes, my apartment is on the fifth floor.
8. Does he study in the living room?
9. Is the living room next to the bedroom?
10. Do you cook in the kitchen?

page 132
A.
1. d.
2. a.
3. e.
4. b.
5. c.

B.
1. sofabed
2. dishwasher
3. birdhouse
4. armchair
5. mailbox
6. housework

page 133
A.
1. Roger's
2. dogs'
3. May's
4. cousins'
5. rooms'

B.
1. John's party was fun.
2. His guests' names were Lee, Luis, and Mark.
3. They drove in John's mom's car to get pizza.
4. Lee's pizza was too hot to eat.
5. The boys' drinks had ice in them.

C.
1. Sam's bedroom is big.
2. The students' computer is new.
3. The dog's leash is red.
4. Clay's desk is small.

page 134
1. Answers will vary but should include *books* and *desk*.
2. Answers will vary but should describe the items in the room or the messiness of the room.
3. Answers will vary but should include *refrigerator*. Might also include *kitchen*.
4. Answers will vary but should include *sofabed*.
5. Answers will vary but should describe the table or the many items on the table.
6. Answers will vary but should include *bathtub*. Might also include *bathroom*.

page 135
Answers will vary.

UNIT 4 • CHAPTER 2

page 136
A.
1. b.
2. b.
3. a.
4. b.
5. a.

B.
1. b.
2. a.
3. b.
4. b.

page 137
1. Answers will vary.
2. a. Possible answer: The story is about someone in an apartment building. The person has a bike. The bike gets a flat tire.
   b. Answers will vary.
3. a. Flat
   b. Possible answers: a tire with no air; an apartment; a shoe with a low heel
4. Answers will vary.

page 138
1. She, fish
2. cake, rock
3. I, baby
4. sofa, pillow
5. water, glass
6. Jean, wind
7. Sak, mouse
8. hair, night
9. Marta, bird
10. face, tomato

page 139
A.
1. They're
2. its
3. two
4. It's
5. Their
6. to
7. It's
8. too
9. two
10. There

B.
1. b.
2. d.
3. c.
4. f.
5. e.
6. a.
7. g.

page 140
Answers will vary.

page 141
A. Answers will vary.

B.
1. b.
2. c.
3. a.

UNIT 4 • CHAPTER 3

page 142
A.
1. e.
2. d.
3. a.
4. f.
5. b.
6. c.

B. [word search with FORMULA, AREA, RECTANGLE, PERIMETER, WIDTH, LENGTH]

C.
1. rectangle
2. width
3. length
4. perimeter
5. area
6. formula

page 143
A.
1. a.
2. b.
3. a.

page 144
A.
1. data
2. a label
3. a label
4. data
5. a label

B.
1. width
2. 5 feet
3. length
4. 6 feet
5. Ana's science project

page 145
A.
1. b.
2. c.
3. a.

B.
1. 1 ft.
2. 3 yd.
3. 300 ft.
4. 33 in.

C.
1. The living room is 5 yd. wide by 8 yd. long.
2. Lok's poster is 24 in. wide by 36 in. long.
3. Rosa's living room window is 3 ft. wide by 4 ft. long.
4. Pat's piece of cloth is 5 yd. long.
5. The picture frame is 1 ft. long.

page 146
Answers will vary.

page 147
A. Answers will vary.

B.
1. b.
2. c.
3. a.

UNIT 5 • CHAPTER 1

page 148
A.
1. Answers will vary but should refer to *exit* sign.
2. Answers will vary but should refer to *bus stop* sign.
3. Answers will vary but should refer to *walk/don't walk* sign.
4. Answers will vary but should refer to *hospital* sign.
5. Answers will vary but should refer to *no parking* sign.

B.
1. in front of
2. next to
3. between

C.
1. a.
2. b.
3. a.

page 149
A.
1. are doing
2. am reading
3. are swimming
4. is writing
5. are running

B.
1. Are Maria and Tam walking to the subway?
2. Am I going to Benito's house?
3. Are we running between the post office and Elm Street?
4. Is Mara working at the mall after school?

page 150
A.
1. I am playing. I am not playing.
2. Pablo is reading. Pablo is not reading.
3. She is writing. She is not writing.
4. You are exercising. You are not exercising.
5. Frank and Jen are shopping. Frank and Jen are not shopping.

B.
1. They are not taking the bus.
2. Linda is not going to her dance class.
3. I am not meeting my friends. Or: We are not meeting our friends.
4. We are not swimming in the pool.
5. The bus is not stopping here.

page 151
1. Don't turn right at North Street.
2. Don't take the subway to the library.
3. Don't walk to the movie theater on the next street.
4. Don't drive past the fire station and turn left.
5. Don't take that bus to go to the community center.
6. Don't cross the street now.
7. Don't exercise after school.
8. Don't eat at the restaurant next to the hospital.
9. Don't park under the No Parking sign.
10. Don't take the bus to Center Street.

page 152
A.
1. ch; b.
2. sh; a.
3. ph; c.
4. ng; d.
5. wh; e.
6. th; f.

B.
1. ng
2. ph
3. th
4. sh
5. ch
6. Wh

page 153
Come to our new shop at 224 Cedar Street. It is near Palm Road in Tampa, Florida.
A. Jorge's is the biggest and best hair shop east of the Rocky Mountains and south of New York City. Look at Baker Lake while your hair is cut!

page 154
Answers will vary. Narrative should correctly use present continuous and prepositions of place.

page 155
A.
Answers will vary. Narrative should correctly use present continuous and prepositions of place.

B.
1. b.
2. a.
3. c.
4. c.

page 156
A.
In the *ite* column (any order): bite, excite, handwrite, invite, polite
In the *ight* column (any order): daylight, flashlight, fright, slight, tight

B. A big storm will come through East City (tonite / **tonight**). The snow will turn everything (**white** / whight). We (mite / **might**) even get some hail. The storm will be here by (midnite / **midnight**). This will be (**quite** / quight) a storm!

page 157
A.
1. Opinion
2. Fact
3. Fact
4. Opinion
5. Fact

B.
I live on East Lane. (Fact) Our street has no streetlights. (Fact) In my opinion, East Lane is too dark. (Opinion) I don't think it's safe. (Opinion) There are 23 children living on my block. (Fact) Children ride their bikes and play outside in the dark. (Fact) I don't think this city wants these children to be hurt. (Opinion) I believe streetlights will save lives here. (Opinion)

page 158
1. Dr. Lionel Jones
2. collecting books for children at the hospital
3. because there are no books for children. Or: The children are bored.
4. in the hospital, in schools, in the East City Community Center
5. June 10
6. They can put books in the boxes.

page 159
A.
1. was
2. were
3. Why
4. Who
5. What
6. said
7. says
8. Were
9. was
10. said

B.
1. Answers will vary but should include *who*.
2. Answers will vary but should include *what*.
3. Answers will vary but should include *why*.
4. Answers will vary but should include *was*.
5. Answers will vary but should include *were*.
6. Answers will vary but should include *says*.
7. Answers will vary but should include *said*.

page 160
Answers will vary.

page 161
A. Answers will vary.

B.
1. a.
2. c.
3. b.

page 162
A.
1. c.
2. e.
3. a.
4. d.
5. b.

B.
1. agriculture
2. raw materials
3. Manufacturing
4. natural resources
5. agriculture

page 163
Answers will vary. Possible answers:
1. There are many forests in the north. Giant redwood trees grow in the north.
2. California is the third largest state. It is smaller than Alaska and Texas.
3. The farmland in California is good. The weather in California is mild.
4. Lettuce, grapes, cotton, almonds, and grapefruit are important crops.
5. California has many businesses that make computers and electronics.

page 164
A.
1. Natural Resources
2. Agriculture
3. Manufacturing
4. Agriculture
5. Natural Resources

B.
Natural Resources: (in any order) How much coal does Illinois have? Are there many forests in Illinois?
Agriculture: (in any order) Is the soil in Illinois good for farming? Does Illinois grow a lot of soybeans?
Manufacturing: (in any order) What kinds of products are made in Illinois? Are many cars made in Illinois?

page 165
A.
1. a. 3. c. 5. a.
2. b. 4. b.

B.
The following should be circled: farmer's daily journal; keep corn popping; corny jokes for farmers; the complete book of corn; the weekly times
Farmer's Daily Journal (should be underlined by student)
"Keep Corn Popping."
Corny Jokes for Farmers (should be underlined by student)
The Complete Book of Corn (should be underlined by student)
The Weekly Times (should be underlined by student)

page 166
Answers will vary.

page 167
A. Answers will vary but should include information that answers *who, what, where, when, why,* and *how*.

B.
1. b. 2. b. 3. c.

UNIT 6 • CHAPTER 1

page 168
A.
Fruit (any order): apple, grapes, banana
Dairy (any order): ice cream, milk, cheese
Vegetables (any order): corn, carrot, onion
Meat, Fish, Poultry (any order): chicken, fish, turkey

B.
1. c. 3. b. 5. d.
2. e. 4. a

page 169
A.
Circled: dinner, friends, onion (two times), tomatoes (two times), bowls, glasses
Underlined: pasta (two times), butter, cheese, lemonade

B.
1. oranges 4. juice
2. strawberries 5. potatoes
3. peaches

C.
1. Joe ate an apple.
2. She put butter on the bread.
3. I made two sandwiches with cheese.
4. Did Mai drink juice or milk?
5. Do you want rice or pasta?

page 170
A.
1. b. 3. a. 5. b.
2. b. 4. a.

B.
1. c. 3. d. 5. b.
2. a. 4. e.

page 171
Answers may vary; possible answers shown here.
1. Lorenzo shouldn't eat strawberry ice cream.
2. Sim should bake bread.
3. Ana should eat fruit and cheese.
4. Ben and Tim shouldn't eat steak.
5. You should eat sliced carrots and tomatoes.
6. Vi should make burritos.
7. You shouldn't drink milk with pizza.
8. Vita shouldn't slice onions.
9. Loc should eat bananas.
10. Amparo and Joe should cook pasta.

page 172
A.
1.–4. (in any order): bread, cheese, egg, salt
5.–8. (in any order): chicken, oatmeal, onion, sandwich

B.
1. piz / za 5. pep / per
2. but / ter 6. pas / ta
3. sal / ad 7. car / rots
4. let / tuce 8. or / ange

page 173
A.
1. exclamation point
2. exclamation point
3. period
4. period
5. exclamation point
6. exclamation point
7. period
8. period

B.
1. Carlo ate rice for lunch.
2. The fried potatoes are very tasty!
3. Leave some pasta for me.
4. The soup is too hot!
5. I don't like pizza.
6. This cheese is yummy! Or: This is yummy cheese!
7. I think boiled onions are terrible!
8. Jin-Hee and So-ra would like some juice. Or: So-ra and Jin-Hee would like some juice.

page 174
A.
1. a. 2. b. 3. c. 4. b.

B.
1. The scrambled eggs are greasy.
2.–6. Answers will vary.

page 175
Answers will vary.

page 176
Down
1. fork
4. plate
5. spoon
7. glass

Across
2. bowl
3. napkin
6. cup
8. tablecloth
9. knife
10. set

page 177
A.
1. Answers may vary. Possible answer: I see tasty green vegetables.
2. Answers may vary. Possible answer: I see fresh, yellow bananas.
3. Answers may vary. Possible answer: I see a red strawberry.

B.
1. b. 3. b. 5. a.
2. a. 4. b.

page 178
1. tablecloth and snow
2. plates and moons
3. napkins and wings
4. eyes and stars
5. water and glass
6. bread and rock
7. spoon and mirror
8. smile and sun
9. hair and midnight
10. words and music

page 179
A.
1. short a 5. short u
2. short e 6. long a
3. long o 7. short i
4. long i 8. long e

B.
1. plate 5. glass
2. cup 6. egg
3. pea 7. dish
4. bowl

page 180
Answers will vary.

page 181
A. Answers will vary.

B.
1. c. 2. b. 3. a.

UNIT 6 • CHAPTER 3

page 182
A.
1. healthy 4. carbohydrates
2. Iron 5. unhealthy
3. nutrition

B.
1. b. 4. c.
2. d. 5. e.
3. a.

C.
Word search with CARBOHYDRATES, NUTRITION, HEALTH (circled).

page 183
A.
1. effect 4. effect 7. effect
2. cause 5. cause 8. effect
3. cause 6. cause 9. effect

B.
1. c. 2. b. 3. a. 4. b.

page 184
1. because; a.
2. since; c.
3. as a result of; a.
4. therefore; b.
5. because; b.
6. so that; c.
7. because; a.
8. since; a.

page 185
1. Incorrect; My teacher likes oranges.
2. Correct
3. Incorrect; How many servings of vegetables should you eat?
4. Correct
5. Correct
6. Incorrect; We need two or three servings of dairy food.
7. Incorrect; What foods are at the top of the food pyramid?
8. Correct
9. Correct
10. Incorrect; What fruit do you like?
11. Incorrect; Be careful! The soup is hot!
12. Correct

page 186
Answers will vary.

page 187
A.
Answers will vary.

B.
1. b. 2. c. 3. b. 4. a.

UNIT 7 • CHAPTER 1

page 188
A.
1. cheaper
2. better
3. more expensive
4. worse

B.
1. taller
2. nicest
3. more interesting
4. cheaper
5. best

page 189
A.
1. Sara will go to school. Sara will not go to school
2.–4. Answers will vary.

B.
1. They'll be on sale next week.
2. Tomorrow the stores won't open until noon.
3. I'll need some money.
4. Bo won't shop at that store.
5. She'll shop tomorrow.

page 190
A.
1. We are going to look for a better price.
2. Ali is going to help Tom.
3. I am not going to go with you.
4. He is not going to pay too much.
5. Vina is going to use her credit card.

B. 1–5: Answers will vary.

page 191
A.
1. We're going to eat cereal for breakfast.
2. They're going to live in California.
3. I'm going to go to school.
4. You're going to study math.
5. They're going to pay with a credit card.

B.
1. They're going to shop in the store.
2.–3. Answers will vary.

page 192
Across
2. unequal
6. rewrite
7. disobey
8. unhealthy
9. dislike
10. pretest

Down
1. rework
3. unimportant
4. reopen
5. replay
7. disagree

page 193
A.
1. queen
2. quarter
3. quiet
4. question
5. quick

B.
1. quarters
2. quick
3. quiet
4. equals
5. queen
6. question

page 194
Answers for Check 1128:
NAME AND ADDRESS: Answers will vary.
DATE: May 4, 2007
PAY TO THE ORDER OF: Artful Hats
AMOUNT IN NUMBERS: $27.98
AMOUNT IN WORDS: Twenty-seven and 98/100
MEMO: hat for class play
SIGNATURE: Answers will vary.

Answers for Check 1129:
NAME AND ADDRESS: Answers will vary.
DATE: May 8, 2007
PAY TO THE ORDER OF: Diane's Designs
AMOUNT IN NUMBERS: $39.99
AMOUNT IN WORDS: Thirty-nine and 99/100
MEMO: dress for party
SIGNATURE: Answers will vary.

page 195
Answers will vary, but check should be made out to *Main Street Clothes*.

page 196
A. Signpost words in story: *first, then, next, but, finally, however, from now on, also*

B. Sequence of Events: first, then, next, finally
Details to be Added: from now on, also
To Show Change or Contrast: but, however

page 197
Answers will vary.

page 198
A.
1. motivation
2. trait
3. motivation
4. motivation
5. trait
6. motivation
7. motivation
8. trait

B. 1.–2. Answers will vary.

page 199
1. Bill will buy food for Thanksgiving Day.
2. Are you going to the Spring Dance with Lok?
3. Is today Flag Day?
4. Graduation Day will be here soon!
5. Manuel has a Fourth of July party every year.
6. The Fall Feast will be on October eleventh.
7. Is the school closed on Martin Luther King Jr. Day?
8. Alma needs cash for the Desert County Festival.
9. The mall will be open on Labor Day.
10. The Winter Concert happens every year on December twenty-first.

page 200
Answers will vary.

page 201
A. Answers will vary.

B.
1. b. 2. a. 3. c. 4. b.

UNIT 7 • CHAPTER 3

page 202
A.
1. allowance
2. goal
3. budget
4. debt

(word search with INTEREST, GOAL, DEBT, BUDGET, ALLOWANCE circled)

page 203
1. c. 2. b. 3. a. 4. c.

page 204
1. food
2. going out with friends
3. clothes
4. more
5. 5% more
6. 15%

page 205
A.
1. ir; thirty
2. ir; bird
3. ar; dollar
4. ar; calendar
5. ir; circle

B.
1. af/ter/noon
2. cheap/er
3. curl/y
4. home/work
5. sur/prise

page 206
Answers will vary.

page 207
A. Answers will vary.

B.
1. b. 2. a. 3. b.

UNIT 8 • CHAPTER 1

page 208
A.
1. hairstylist
2. chef
3. child-care worker
4. cashier
5. doctor
6. firefighter

B.
1. reliable
2. enthusiastic
3. friendly
4. creative
5. energetic

page 209
A.
1. can
2. can
3. can
4. can
5. can't
6. could
7. could not
8. could
9. can
10. can

B.
1. a. 2. c. 3. b.

page 210
A.
1. us
2. it
3. me
4. him
5. them
6. you

B.
1. Ms. Gomez will hire him.
2. She told me to watch the children.
3. We helped them fix the computer.
4. Angela will give the notebook to her.
5. I will talk to Mr. Han about it.

page 211
A.
1. it
2. them
3. him
4. me
5. him
6. you
7. her
8. you
9. it

B. Answers may vary. Possible answers:
1. I will work with him.
2. That pizza is for them. Or: That pizza is not for them.
3. I need it. Or: I do not need it.
4. Joe wants it. Or: Joe does not want it.
5. I can help her. Or: I can't help her.

page 212
1. She erased the board completely.
2. I want to learn about our government.
3. Be careful with the hot pan.
4. Carlos drove slowly on the busy street.
5. Speak quietly in the library.
6. Hal cleaned the kitchen and the bathroom. He is very helpful.
7. These scissors are Beth's equipment.
8. She set the table very quickly.
9. I lost my library card. I need a replacement card.
10. Maria sent me a nice letter. She is so thoughtful.

page 213
A.
1. Incorrect
2. Correct
3. Correct

B.
1. : 2. : 3. , 4. , 5. :

page 214
A.
1. c. 2. d. 3. d. 4. a.

B.
1. 4, 2, 1, 5, 3
2. 3, 5, 2, 1, 4

page 215
1. Hana Cho
   123 Green Street
   Riverton, CA 09617
2. March 26, 2006
3. Mr. Gil Alvarez
   City Computer Company
   509 Main St.
   Riverton, CA 09617
4. Dear Mr. Alvarez:
5. I am writing to ask if I could visit your company.
6. I am very interested in computers.
7. Thank you for your time.
8. Sincerely,
9. Hana Cho

UNIT 8 • CHAPTER 2

page 216
A.
1. f. 3. e. 5. g. 7. b.
2. c. 4. d. 6. a.

B.
1. engineer
2. radioactive
3. an astronaut
4. recessive
5. dominant
6. an astronaut
7. radioactive
8. an engineer

page 217
A.
1. Answers will vary.
2. d.

B.
1. Answers will vary.
2. b.

page 218
1. a. 2. b. 3. c. 4. b.

page 219
A.
1. <u>or</u>; editor
2. <u>ist</u>; biologist
3. <u>ist</u>; guitarist
4. <u>er</u>; teacher
5. <u>or</u>; actor
6. <u>er</u>; writer
7. <u>ist</u>; pianist
8. <u>ist</u>; scientist
9. <u>er</u>; worker
10. <u>ist</u>; geologist

B.

```
B I O L O G I S T R
A R O S W I M M E R
D R I V E R S I S T
D I B A N K N R D C
E S B S W I P T O Q
D B A C U L C F Q U P
I P K L Y I B T N R I
T O E R S T A N K E A
O R R I L L P S T R A I S
R P S C I E N T I S T
```

page 220
Answers will vary.

page 221
A.
Answers will vary.

B.
1. c. 2. a. 3. b. 4. c.

UNIT 8 • CHAPTER 3

page 222
1. b.   6. a.
2. b.   7. b.
3. b.   8. a.
4. a.   9. a.
5. b.   10. a.

page 223
1. c. 2. a. 3. c. 4. a.

page 224
A.
1. encyclopedia   4. encyclopedia
2. Web site   5. Web site
3. encyclopedia

B.
1. b.   3. c.   5. b.
2. a.   4. c.

page 225
A.
1. a.   3. b.   5. c.
2. c.   4. a

B.
1. Incorrect; She took lots of science classes (like biology and chemistry) in school.
2. Correct
3. Correct
4. Incorrect; I used many adjectives (like efficient and friendly) in my business letter.

page 226
Answers will vary.

page 227
A.
Answers will vary.

B.
1. c.   2. a.   3. b.   4. a.